Advance Praise for *Revolution's End*

"*Revolution's End* is a stunning and chilling expose of one of the most bizarre political chapters in my lifetime—the rise of the Symbionese Liberation Army and the kidnapping of bad-girl heiress Patty Hearst. Brad Schreiber presents a compelling new case that the SLA was a creation of the police state to infiltrate, subvert, and destroy the growing radical movements of the period."

—David Talbot, bestselling author of *Season of the Witch*
and *The Devil's Chessboard: Allen Dulles,*
the CIA and the Rise of America's Secret Government

"*Revolution's End* is a gripping read—a persuasive, well-researched and detailed interpretation of what is known about the SLA kidnapping of Patty Hearst."
—Peter Dale Scott, author of *The American Deep State:*
Wall Street, Big Oil, and the Attack on U.S. Democracy

"This book careens to its bloody ending with all of the inevitability of a train wreck. Schreiber won't let us take our eyes off it. He ignites the past in chilling detail and at the same time shines an uncanny and unsettling light on who we are today."
—T. Jefferson Parker, three-time winner
of the Mystery Writers of America's Edgar Award

"'The Symbionese Liberation Army' was a counter-revolutionary front, carefully created . . . to infiltrate and discredit the *authentic* leftist movements then alive and well in California. Such is the unhappy, fascinating truth Brad Schreiber tells in *Revolution's End*—a careful book, and one as necessary as it is disturbing, not just for all it teaches us about what really happened with the SLA in

California, over forty years ago, but also—and especially—for what it teaches us about America today, and all the world, post-9/11."
—Mark Crispin Miller, Professor of Media Studies, New York University and author of *Loser Take All: Election Fraud and the Subversion of Democracy, 2000–2008*

REVOLUTION'S END

REVOLUTION'S END

THE PATTY HEARST KIDNAPPING, MIND CONTROL, *AND THE* SECRET HISTORY OF DONALD DEFREEZE AND THE SLA

BRAD SCHREIBER

Skyhorse Publishing

Skyhorse Publishing books may be purchased in bulk at special discounts for sales promotion, corporate gifts, fund-raising, or educational purposes. Special editions can also be created to specifications. For details, contact the Special Sales Department, Skyhorse Publishing, 307 West 36th Street, 11th Floor, New York, NY 10018 or info@skyhorsepublishing.com.

Skyhorse® and Skyhorse Publishing® are registered trademarks of Skyhorse Publishing, Inc.®, a Delaware corporation.

Visit our website at www.skyhorsepublishing.com.

10 9 8 7 6 5 4 3 2 1

Library of Congress Cataloging-in-Publication Data is available on file.

Cover design by Rain Saukas
Cover photos from the Federal Bureau of Investigation

Print ISBN: 978-1-5107-1425-0
Ebook ISBN: 978-1-5107-1427-4

Printed in the United States of America

Contents

Acknowledgments   ix

Introduction   xi

Chapter 1 ✦ A Collision Course with Infamy   1

Chapter 2 ✦ Paint It Black   12

Chapter 3 ✦ Behavior Modification, a.k.a., Mind Control   32

Chapter 4 ✦ Double Agents, False Identities, Secret Affairs   48

Chapter 5 ✦ The Other Symbionese Liberation Army   70

Chapter 6 ✦ The Illusion of Freedom   82

Chapter 7 ✦ A Tragic, Self-Defeating Mission   95

Chapter 8 ✦ People in Need   117

Chapter 9 ✦ Two Very Different Revolutionaries   132

Chapter 10 ✦ Ignoring the Evidence   153

Chapter 11 ✦ Broadcasting Terror Live   169

Chapter 12 ✦ No Peace, Even in Death   183

Epilogue ✦ Revolution's End   199

Appendix   214

Bibliography   219

Index   225

ACKNOWLEDGMENTS

I THANK THE FOLLOWING PEOPLE for their aid in research and support of my writing *Revolution's End*. The list is alphabetical, but you are all equally appreciated. Carrie Adamowski, Philadelphia field office, FBI; Angela Bell, FBI, Washington, DC; Linda Chester and Laurie Fox, Linda Chester Literary Agency; Judge Elliot Daum, Sonoma County Superior Court; Ken Deifik; Vanessa Dunstan, *The Nation*; Terence Hallinan; Rachael Hanel; John Hayes; Bonnie Kouneva; Tony Lyons and Joseph Craig at Skyhorse Publishing; Stephen Maitland-Lewis; Justin Manask; Jonathan Menchin; David Newman; Anna Nicholas; Jim Parish; Dr. Colin Ross, Colin A. Ross Institute for Psychological Trauma; Laurie Scheer; Brian Schindele; John Spencer; Roger Steffens; Douglas Valentine; Vesla Weaver, Center for the Study of Inequality, Yale University; Amy Wong, UCLA Library Dept of Special Collections.

In memory of the brilliant Robert Litz, the nicest writer who ever lived.

This book is dedicated to Dick Russell, who provided me the Rosetta Stone of research on the Symbionese Liberation Army and its prison origins, a forty-year-old file I thank God he still had, of unredacted, rare interviews, letters, notes, press releases, articles, affidavits, and court papers that shed so much light on one of the enduring mysteries of US history.

INTRODUCTION

WE FIND OURSELVES IN AN increasingly, even sickeningly undemocratic country. In 2014, tanks and military-grade weapons appeared in Ferguson, Missouri, when demonstrations erupted after a white police officer killed Michael Brown, an unarmed black youth. Law-abiding citizens and the press were attacked when they protested the callous response from local law enforcement to this deadly incident.

The militarization of our police, so clearly displayed on the streets of Ferguson, is due in major part to the Department of Defense's 1033 Program, which has transferred more than $5 billion in Army military hardware to local law enforcement since 1997.

At the same time, despite its clear and present danger to our freedom, our government spies on us, more frequently and more effectively than ever before in history. Whistleblower and National Security Agency infrastructure expert Edward Snowden, who left the United States, perhaps never to return, released staggering classified documents in 2013 to the media. He proved that Internet service providers and phone companies are allowing the NSA to illegally monitor all Americans, regardless of any connection to national security issues.

Police militarization and the diminishment of our rights of privacy and public protest have become the norm in an era of highly sophisticated electronic social control. The Occupy and

Black Lives Matter movements recall the burst of undiluted fury at this government that arose out of 1970s political unrest. Its epicenter in California, driven by the black prisoner reform movement and anti–Vietnam War activists, was the San Francisco Bay Area.

Without a doubt, the case that is still shrouded in the greatest mystery, despite its long-standing hold on the public's imagination, is the kidnapping of heiress Patricia Hearst by a previously unknown political group, the Symbionese Liberation Army (SLA). This story outstrips the historic Lindbergh baby kidnapping in sensationalism. It was America's first political kidnapping. The SLA saga was the only US case of a kidnap victim who participated in a bank robbery. And it resulted in six SLA members dying, after hundreds of police and SWAT team members surrounded the revolutionaries and fired a fusillade of more than five thousand bullets at them.

The yellow stucco bungalow in South Central Los Angeles, the last refuge of those six SLA members, caught fire due to the intentional use of riot control grenades thrown into the structure. The shoot-out and incineration were shockingly carried live, for two hours, on national television. It was the TV networks' first use of "minicam" technology to broadcast news live across the country, and those horrific images seared into American consciousness the ultimate power of the state.

The full story of Patricia Hearst, the supposed revolutionary group that kidnapped her, and its black leader, who was secretly a government informant, is a complex, bizarre, salacious, surreal, terrifying, immoral, and tragic tale. It illustrates how early 1970s Bay Area political activism led to one of the most audacious cases of government duplicity in American history.

The avowed head of the Symbionese Liberation Army, Donald David DeFreeze, also known as General Field Marshal Cinque (a.k.a., Cinque Mtume, Swahili for "fifth prophet") was arguably the most contradictory, puzzling, ill-fated, and psychologically complex character in the history of American radical politics.

By the time the American public became familiar with DeFreeze, he was perceived as a madman, using the *nom de guerre* Cinque, advocating a revolution against the most powerful nation in the world as the leader of the Symbionese Liberation Army. His army numbered no more than ten white and generally middle-class young people.

Had DeFreeze included his actual biography, rather than using quasi-military terms and titles in the SLA communiqués, he would have reached the hearts and imaginations of considerably more people. The hidden details of his life explain the complex relationship he had with Patty Hearst, elucidating the reason why she of all people was kidnapped and the shifting nature of her identity as a victim who was forced to break the law and become a revolutionary. Her unparalleled trial challenged the US system of justice in regard to the legal concept of coercive persuasion.

That alone makes DeFreeze's life story remarkable. But a full examination also reveals the twisted psychology of a desperate man who, unable to support his family, resorted to crime, became a police informant, and was then subjected to behavior modification in prison during a particularly violent phase of American history. DeFreeze made a Faustian bargain with the government. In exchange for his freedom, which proved to be short-lived, he agreed to run a violent and purposely irresponsible false revolutionary group.

The Symbionese Liberation Army exceeded the expectations of its creators, the Central Intelligence Agency and the California Department of Corrections. For it not only infiltrated remnants of the New Left but also destroyed the credibility of a legitimate progressive movement that protested racism, sexism, the Vietnam War and any form of societal inequality.

I ◆ A Collision Course with Infamy

Donald DeFreeze was born in Cleveland, Ohio, on November 15, 1943. His mother, Mary, worked in a convalescent home as a nurse. Any nurturing she provided her son, the eldest of eight, was obliterated by his father, a tool maker whose blind rages at his son included attacks on the boy with a baseball bat and a hammer. DeFreeze once told a prison therapist that his father broke his arm on three occasions, twice when he was ten and another time when he was twelve.

By the age of fourteen, DeFreeze's internal rage reached its first boiling point. He finished the ninth grade in Cleveland, but his animosity toward his father was so great that Mary DeFreeze, to avoid any more domestic violence, arranged for young Donald to live with a cousin in Buffalo, New York. After a brief stay, the sullen DeFreeze was then bounced to the home of a fundamentalist black preacher, the Reverend William L. Foster, and his family.

This was the chance for DeFreeze to follow a path of normalcy and acceptance. He studied the Bible with the commitment of someone yearning for a lifeline. Foster described him as a "get up and go kid" who made spare money by collecting and selling junk and scrap metal.

But the neighborhood took hold of DeFreeze in a way religion could not.

"He had a heart as big as a house," Reverend Foster said. "But some of the boys he used to hang out with I didn't care for. You just knew," he insisted, paraphrasing an old Ivory Snow soap advertisement, "they were 99 and 44/100 percent bad."

The boy who would be on the FBI's Most Wanted List began his criminal career with a gang called the Crooked Skulls. In August 1960, he was arrested attempting to break open a parking meter. A mere nine days later, when he attempted to steal a car and pistol, DeFreeze was again arrested. This time, stripped of the warm embrace of the Foster household, he was sent to a boys' reformatory in Elmira, New York. In a fourteen-page, 1970 letter to Superior Court Judge William Ritzi, detailing much of his past and asking for leniency in a bank robbery sentencing, DeFreeze referred to the Elmira reformatory as the beginning of his political consciousness.

"Life in the prison, as we called it, was nothing but fear and hate, day in and day out." He was denigrated by all the boys at Elmira because "I would not be a part of any of the gangs, black or white. . . . I didn't hate anyone, black or white, and they hated me for it."

In another genuine attempt to settle down and find a way to fit into society, he returned to the Fosters after two years, at the age of eighteen. In love with their daughter, Harriet, he asked her parents for her hand in marriage. She was fourteen years old. They refused, and he left Buffalo, bitter, rootless, and brokenhearted.

He drifted to Newark, New Jersey, where he met Gloria Thomas, who was twenty-three and already had three children. The father was nowhere in sight. "She was nice and lovely," he wrote in the 1970 letter. "I fell in love with her, I think. I believe I was just glad and happy that anyone would have me the way I was."

DeFreeze was legally obliged to get his parents' permission for the nuptials. They consented but told him he was a fool. In 1963, Donald and Gloria were married. He was nineteen years old, a high school dropout, and suddenly a father of three with no marketable skills.

The Reverend James A. Scott, who presided over the ceremony in Newark, observed the woman as being "very talkative while DeFreeze was quiet, passive, reserved."

"Things were lovely all the way up to a few months," DeFreeze stated in his fourteen-page autobiographical sketch sent to the aforementioned judge, but after a fight, Gloria yelled "she didn't love me at all, but that she needed a husband and father for her kids."

He hoped their first biological child would mend the rift in their marriage, "but as soon as the baby was born, it was the same thing, I had begun to drink very deeply but I was trying to put up with her and hope she would change. But as the years went by [she] never did."

Less than one year after the marriage, DeFreeze was ordered to appear in court for desertion.

DeFreeze and his wife eventually added a total of three children to the family, but his struggles to find steady work led Gloria to berate him and, according to DeFreeze, after a mere seven months, to be unfaithful.

"I came home sooner than I do most of the time from work and she and an old boyfriend had just had relationships." In disgust, DeFreeze claimed he told Thomas to go live with the boyfriend, who refused. He fought with her. He forgave her. But then he learned "that none of my wife's kids had the same father and that she had never been married," contrary to what he had been told.

"I was a little afraid but I said I would give her a good chance. . . . I really put faith in her but somehow, little stories kept coming to me. One was that my boss had come to my home looking from [sic] me and that my wife had come to the door in the nude."

DeFreeze abandoned his family once for a two-month trip to Canada, but when he returned, he learned that Gloria was pregnant. He obtained two jobs to try and pay for the overdue bills.

He heard rumors about Gloria being promiscuous during his Canadian trip. Concluding that the child she had just given birth to was not his, DeFreeze separated from Gloria, and for four months she lived with another man. Unable to bear it, she returned and begged DeFreeze to forgive her. DeFreeze took her back, even if he did not fully forgive her.

The pressure of half a dozen young children, sporadic employ-ment alternating with welfare, and a contentious marriage led the twenty-two-year-old DeFreeze to a fantasy refuge, handling guns and explosive materials.

"I started playing around with guns and fireworks and dogs and cars. Just anything to get away from life and how unhappy I was. I finely [sic] got into trouble with the police for shoting [sic] off a rifle in my basement and for a bomb I had made out of about 30 fireworks from fourth of July. After I went to court and got Probation, I was really ashamed of myself. I had not been in trouble with the police for years and now I had even lost that pride."

DeFreeze's 1970 autobiographical statement convincingly laid blame upon his father, his wife, and the crushing poverty he had to withstand. But nowhere did he detail his own inability to talk with others, to discuss the difficulties he encountered and thus, perhaps, amend them.

In fact, DeFreeze hid details of his life from friends and cowork-ers. He worked intermittently for an Orange, New Jersey, painting contractor who never even knew DeFreeze and his wife had any children. He perceived DeFreeze as unusually quiet except when the subject of guns came up, and then the young man waxed rhapsodic about caliber, firepower, and the like.

While in New Jersey, DeFreeze worked for a few different paint-ing contractors and then decided he wanted to be his own boss. He started his own business, House of DeFreeze, but overextended his credit and had to endure yet another failure.

In desperation to change something in his life, DeFreeze left his family behind in March 1965. But his obsession with guns and explosives continued unabated. While hitchhiking on Interstate 10, the San Bernardino Freeway, near West Covina, an act itself illegal, DeFreeze was stopped by police. The hitchhiking was the least of their concerns. As DeFreeze reached for his identification, the cops spotted a sharpened butter knife and a tear gas canister tucked into in his waistband. With probable cause, they asked to look inside his suitcase. It contained a sawed-off shotgun.

It was sixty-four days in the state prison at Chino before DeFreeze had his day in court for possession of the shotgun and tear gas bomb. A psychiatrist, hired by the state of California to evaluate DeFreeze's propensity for handling guns and small explosives, learned of his horrific childhood.

"DeFreeze states Father tried to kill him three times," the psychiatrist noted in truncated sentences. "Used to inflict human punishment—hit him with hammers, baseball bats, etc. He shows areas on his head where he was struck and had to receive sutures. Every time he went to the hospital, his Father told them he just got hurt. The time he was picked up with the gun [at age fourteen in Cleveland], he had planned to shoot Father who had been mistreating him."

DeFreeze was released after time served in jail.

Two weeks later, DeFreeze was back in New Jersey, standing in front of another judge for the bomb and gun charges in the basement of his home. The judge continued the case for a year, and in June 1966, DeFreeze received two years probation.

"All my friends and family knew of my wife's ways," DeFreeze wrote of this period of his life. "I moved all over New Jersey but everywhere I went someone knew me or my life or about my kids. I just couldn't take it anymore. I was slowly becoming a nothing."

Again, he planned to leave his family behind for California, but Gloria begged him to bring the large, poverty-stricken clan with him and DeFreeze relented. In Los Angeles, in 1967, their sixth child and last child, doomed like the others to be neglected, was born. Relocating to the Golden State did not better their lives in the least.

In the spring of 1967, DeFreeze was laid off from a car wash job. Because he was not a resident of California, he was refused welfare payments from the state. An employment training program for which he applied turned him away because of his extensive police record.

DeFreeze continued to possess illegal weapons without using them for any criminal purpose. And he also put himself in the position to be discovered with them. It was as if having guns and explosives on his person gave him a sense of power, of purpose.

Somewhat incongruously, DeFreeze was stopped on June 9, 1967, for the relatively minor infraction of running a red light on a bicycle at the intersection of Vermont and 60th Street in the inner city. He gave a fictitious name to the arresting officers and they quickly discovered his falsehood. The ensuing search revealed a homemade bomb in his pocket and another in a bag in the basket of the bike, along with a .22 caliber pistol.

DeFreeze claimed he had found these weapons and was going to sell them to support his family. His reason for not doing so was highly ironic: "I thought about the nut that would buy them and what no good he would probably have in mind and of the possibably [sic] of him killing someone with the gun, it give [sic] me a very funny feeling, a bad feeling of death in my mouth."

DeFreeze further explained that his car was repossessed and, as a result, he had lost his last job. The case was sent to Superior Court Judge Bernard Lawler, in the South Bay city of Torrance. DeFreeze brought testimonials from the Community Skill Center, where a Head Start Project worker had written that the petty criminal was "very energetic" and able to communicate well with young people.

Arnold Kaye, the probation officer assigned to DeFreeze after these charges, interviewed him and was convinced that he was not a hardened criminal but a wounded and confused man. Recommending probation rather than jail time, Kaye wrote in part, "The difficulties which the defendant has encountered in his life are real and serious. He feels his responsibilities deeply and is overcome when he cannot meet them. He appears to have a warm relationship with his wife and children.

"The type of behavior encountered in the present offense appears to be the defendant's way of compensating for feelings of inadequacy and powerlessness."

Kaye went on to conclude in his probation report that he was concerned about DeFreeze's mental stability and that it might be best to commit him, short-term, for psychiatric evaluation. He mentioned how ironic it was that only after the bicycle arrest did California's welfare department provide financial aid to the DeFreeze family and only after DeFreeze was out on bail did the job-training program make his case a priority.

To support this contention, Kaye quoted DeFreeze, who maintained, with unintentionally comedic effect, "If I had known that we could have got help by me going to jail, I could have did a lot of lesser things like broke a few windows or something." And then DeFreeze reverted to his default defense, "It would have been worth it to help my wife and kids."

Judge Lawler showed compassion. After DeFreeze pleaded guilty, the judge gave the wayward young man three more years' probation and stated, "You do have a bad record but I think you're entitled to a break in this particular instance, and I hope you will take advantage of it."

Donald DeFreeze became adept at convincing people like probation officer Kaye that he wanted to do right by his wife and children. That, coupled with no actual use of the explosives and weapons, kept him from a long sentence in jail.

But less than three months after the arrest at Vermont and 60th, DeFreeze came up with another criminal scheme. This time it involved engaging in infidelity, likely a response to being cuckolded by Gloria. In fact, the prostitute DeFreeze met shared his wife's first name. On December 2 at 3:30 in the morning, Gloria Yvonne Sanders went to a South Central Los Angeles motel with DeFreeze, where he paid her the going rate for that place and time, ten dollars, and they had sex.

Apparently less than content with Sanders's services, DeFreeze pulled out a small Derringer-style pistol, thrust it against her head, and demanded not only his ten dollars back but all the money she had made that day. Sanders stated that DeFreeze ordered her to have sex with him again, but this time, as she described it, they "performed unnatural acts."

Afterward, Sanders insisted she was cold and got DeFreeze's permission to get up and retrieve her coat. Seeing a fleeting chance to escape, she ran out the door and down the street.

DeFreeze did not flee the premises himself. He promptly fell asleep, his gun under the pillow.

He awoke to the reappearance of Sanders and to his surprise, two Los Angeles police officers. Sanders had called them on a pay phone, probably omitting the fact of what she did for a living. DeFreeze was arrested for robbery and obliterating the serial number of his stolen gun.

These charges were eventually dismissed. But DeFreeze made a crucial error in judgment as he was led away from the motel in handcuffs.

He asked Officer L. J. Henricks not to leave DeFreeze's own car at the motel for fear of it being stolen. The police obliged by impounding the vehicle. Naturally, they searched it, only to find in the trunk twelve stolen handguns in a blue canvas bag. The month before, the Western Surplus Store, 8505 S. Western Avenue in Torrance, had been robbed of about two hundred rifles and pistols. A major LAPD investigation of the weapons burglary was ongoing when they stumbled upon Donald DeFreeze and some of the two hundred firearms.

Two days later, on December 4, DeFreeze, looking at serious jail time but confident in his ability to gain probation, made an agreement with the LAPD. He promised to lead them to the man who sold DeFreeze the stolen guns in exchange for a recommendation of leniency in his sentence. The deal was accepted, and DeFreeze was escorted by officers to his home on New Hampshire Avenue, where he promised Gloria would lead them to the gun runner DeFreeze knew only as "Ron." But Gloria and the children were not at home.

DeFreeze suddenly broke and ran from his police escort. He hurled himself out of a screened window in the second floor apartment, landing in a roll on a garage roof. The stunned officers saw DeFreeze scramble off the garage roof, leap to the ground, and run. They pursued on foot, but he was gone.

The LAPD, now furious with DeFreeze, brought their wrath upon Gloria, who was in no position to resist, especially with six children to protect and raise. She suggested DeFreeze could be found at the apartment of a nearby acquaintance, a place where he often took sanctuary from his home life.

He was apprehended two days later, on December 4, 1967. In his arrest record, two officers are listed by last name, Toles and Farwell.

As will soon be seen in greater detail, DeFreeze's interaction with LAPD officer Ronald G. Farwell after the two-hundred–gun case at the Western Surplus Store drastically altered his life. Farwell entrapped DeFreeze in the life of an informant. It set DeFreeze on an inexorable path of living in constant fear of detection while trying to mentally compartmentalize the lives he ruined and the enemies he made. It was also his unendurable level of suspiciousness and intolerance for personal conflicts that eventually led him to kidnap the heiress Patty Hearst, whose secret liaison with DeFreeze ended with her abrupt rejection of him.

DeFreeze promised to lead the LAPD to his partner who ran guns. His full name, DeFreeze now remembered, was Ronald Coleman. It bought DeFreeze his freedom in the short run.

With policemen standing alongside him, DeFreeze called up Coleman and asked if he still had the two guns DeFreeze had sold him. When Coleman answered in the affirmative, DeFreeze said he would come over to talk to him about an unspecified subject. Hanging up, DeFreeze told the three detectives, who were watching him very carefully, "Ron is at his apartment." And then, as if he was already one of them, he added, "Let's hit him."

It didn't take long. Coleman lived in the same apartment building. Coleman casually opened the door to DeFreeze and his police entourage. DeFreeze led them through the apartment, to the anger and shock of Coleman. DeFreeze pointed out hiding places Coleman used for several dozen stolen guns and, for good measure, revealed a stash of marijuana. Despite the importance of the case and the size of the cache of guns, neither man was charged with that offense. This was the beginning of DeFreeze's peculiar relationship with the LAPD. DeFreeze pleaded guilty and, despite his burgeoning police record, he was given an additional five years of probation for receiving stolen property. Coleman got three years of probation for marijuana possession.

Donald DeFreeze blamed both himself and his wife for his life's path in his court-mandated, short autobiography of his family's time in Southern California. "More and more, I was unhappy with everything. I started back [sic] playing with guns, drinking, pills, but this time more than I had ever before did [sic]. . . . I really don't understand what I was doing. She wanted nice things and I was working and I was buying and selling guns and the next thing I know I had become a thief."

The core truth to DeFreeze's complex role in the radical politics of California is found in his contention that he initially bought guns to support his family. Clearly, he had an obsession with weapons. He derived a sense of power and some limited income from handling and dealing guns, but the biggest weapons deal he was involved with was in a sense the end of DeFreeze's dwindling freedom of choice in life.

When the two hundred guns from the 1967 Torrance robbery became part of DeFreeze's criminal record, he was already a thief. But when he wrote in his biographical sketch "the next thing I know I had become a thief," he was, in code, referring to the first time in his life he turned in another person to lessen his own potential sentence. DeFreeze showed no external concern when he turned in Ronald Coleman. DeFreeze never expressed any thoughts verbally or in writing about Coleman also being African American, Coleman's proximity in the same apartment building, or the possibility that Coleman might seek retribution for the betrayal.

Morgan W. Morten, the attorney who represented DeFreeze in the 1967 case, confirmed that it was "indicated that he had been cooperating with the police." The exact details of DeFreeze's collaboration efforts were not made known to the court.

It was both DeFreeze's willingness to secretly cooperate with law enforcement and the roiling political landscape of the time that combined to make him a police agent who turned his back on the left in general and his own race, especially the Black Panther Party, in particular.

2 ✦ Paint It Black

THERE CAN BE NO FULL understanding of the behavior of Donald DeFreeze or the creation of the Symbionese Liberation Army without, at the very least, an acknowledgment of the volatility of political life in the America of the late 1960s and early 1970s.

In 1976, the Final Report of the Senate Committee on Intelligence Activities and the Rights of Americans made it plain and irreducible: the Federal Bureau of Investigation, from 1956 to 1971, ran a counterintelligence program (COINTELPRO) of illegal covert actions against Americans. This was due to the Bureau's frustration with the Supreme Court's protection of the rights of political dissidents.

The techniques employed by the Bureau in COINTELPRO included burglary, vandalism, forged documents, telling spouses of false infidelities, accusing radicals of being informants when they were not, using tax investigations to harass radicals, prejudicing superiors of college professors or clergy sympathetic to radical politics, prevention of public speeches, and even pressure via grand juries when jury trials failed to convict suspects. Two of the five groups targeted, according to the Senate report, were the "New Left" program (1968–1971) and the "Black Nationalist-Hate Group" program (1967–1971). However, groups that had primarily black members but were nonviolent in nature, including the Southern Christian Leadership Conference, also were included in the Black Nationalist-Hate Group program.

The same FBI, willing to send messages to Martin Luther King Jr., encouraging him to commit suicide, was, not surprisingly, even more dedicated to the destruction of the Black Panther Party for Self-Defense, and used police agents like Donald DeFreeze for the purpose of setting up arrests or inciting violence to accomplish the goal.

Founded in East Oakland in 1966 by Huey Newton and Bobby Seale, the Panthers, in their ten-point party platform and program, made reasonable demands including an end to police brutality, against which they armed themselves; and decent housing and education; and full employment. Among their more controversial points were demands for financial reparations for slavery, still discussed today, and solely black juries for black defendants, an issue particular to that era.

The Panthers became the predominant focus of the FBI's Black Nationalist-Hate Group program. In citing revelations from the Senate's findings, the *New York Times* detailed, "The report portrays a campaign in which the bureau used a legion of informers, sometimes as provocateurs, and close cooperation with local police antiradical squads to sow confusion, fear, and dissension among Panthers."

When DeFreeze was caught in 1967 and turned in Ronald Coleman, he became, in street parlance, a "snitch." Arresting officer Ronald G. Farwell recruited DeFreeze to become an informant for the LAPD. The use of black police agents escalated in the aftermath of the 1965 Watts riots. Tension built in that suburb between 1962 and 1964, as sixty-five people were killed by the LAPD, including twenty-seven who were shot in the back. One single police case was found to be murder.

After six days of the racially charged insurrection, thirty-one civilians, two policemen, and a fireman were dead, and the LAPD was criticized for its brutality and its lack of preparedness. Numerous major American cities suffered the same violent fate in 1967. The growing presence of the Black Panthers in Southern California also was a factor in the eventual creation of the Criminal Conspiracy Section (CCS) of the Los Angeles Police Department, dedicated to infiltration, provocation, and arrest of Panthers and other radicals in the most dangerous areas of Los Angeles County.

Ronald Farwell saw in DeFreeze a man who was more fascinated with owning and selling guns than using them in the commission of crimes. Farwell knew the best way to infiltrate the Panthers was to sell them guns via police agents and then arrest them. He was not unsympathetic to the plight of DeFreeze. Farwell, a black officer trying to survive in a predominantly white police force, had seven children of his own. The combination of probation and some money to help pay bills lured DeFreeze into the fold as an informant, and when Farwell became assigned to the newly formed CCS in 1969, he continued to use DeFreeze. The following year, the CCS was put under the control of the newly created Public Disorder Intelligence Division. Farwell's authority increased during these changes.

Farwell ran other police agents in his network, and two proved to be notorious. Louis Tackwood, a black informant who eventually authored a book on his LAPD exploits, *The Glass House Tapes*, gave a clearer view of the structure of police intelligence operations in Los Angeles at the time.

Tackwood began cooperating with police in 1962, after a car theft arrest, and despite his personal history of drug sales and armed robbery, he told Steven V. Roberts at the *New York Times* that he received between $7,000 and $9,000 in payments from the LAPD as an informant and was given a "free hand" in pursuing his own crimes.

In a press conference covered by the *Los Angeles Free Press*, Tackwood said he was recruited in 1965 by Farwell. Tackwood stated that there were, as a maximum, about fifteen to twenty officers controlling approximately two hundred informant contacts throughout the state of California. The LAPD budget for the Criminal Conspiracy Section was secret, and informants were paid only in cash.

So Tackwood, like DeFreeze, was paid but not enough to serve as his sole source of income. LAPD informants found it very difficult to leave the criminal life behind. The police continued to use them and arranged one probationary sentence after another for crimes that would have sent the average perpetrator to jail.

Tackwood was not a model of reliability as an *agent provocateur* himself. But Leroy Aarons of the *Washington Post,* Carl Flemming of *Newsweek,* and Jerry Cohen of the *Los Angeles Times* supervised his polygraph examination, administered by Chris Gugas, a former FBI agent and then president of the American Polygraph Association. The three journalists reported that Tackwood "did answer all of the critical questions truthfully on the examination." The names of his police contacts were also later confirmed.

A third notable informant for Farwell and the CCS was Ron Everett, who changed his name to Maulana Ron Karenga. After the 1965 Watts riots, Karenga helped establish the Black Congress in order to restore that devastated community. In opposition to the Maoist politics of the Panthers, his Black Nationalist organization, United Slaves (US), also believed in cultural and racial separatism. US promoted the building of independent schools, African-American studies departments, and black student unions.

But like the Panthers, United Slaves was a target of the FBI's COINTELPRO. However, because he shared the FBI's antipathy toward the Black Panthers, a national rather than a regional movement, Karenga and his followers were clearly favored by law enforcement. Tackwood asserted in *The Glass House Tapes* that he was the liaison between the police and Karenga, providing money, weapons, and support.

January 17, 1969, was an infamous day in the history of the internecine battle between the Black Panther Party in Los Angeles and the United Slaves, also referred to as the US Organization. Panthers Alprentice "Bunchy" Carter and John Huggins were shot dead during an altercation in the lunchroom of Campbell Hall at the University of California, Los Angeles. Indicted were three members of US, although Karenga was not one of them.

Tackwood stated he gave money to Karenga to "take care of" Black Panthers in the Watts area, where Karenga was located. Karenga was certainly an atypical, anti-white Black Nationalist. The *Wall Street Journal* reported that he "maintained close ties to the eastern Rockefeller family." Furthermore, the paper reported, "a few weeks after the assassination of Martin Luther King . . . Mr. Karenga slipped into Sacramento for a private chat with Governor Ronald Reagan, at the governor's request." He met around the same time clandestinely with LA Police Chief Thomas Reddin, prompting speculation that of all police agents to serve the LAPD then, Karenga had the highest connections to the white power structure.

Any doubt that the FBI encouraged violent engagement between the Panthers and US was officially obliterated with a May 26, 1970, memo from the Los Angeles field office to Washington. By this time, four Panthers had been killed by US members, and others, on both sides, had been beaten and wounded by gunfire.

The memo summarized the Bureau's satisfaction with this violence:

> The Los Angeles Division is aware of the mutually hostile feelings harbored between the organizations and the first opportunity to capitalize on the situation will be maximized. It is intended that US, Inc. will be appropriately and discreetly advised of the time and location of BPP activities in order that the two organizations might be brought together and thus grant nature the opportunity to take her due course.

The beginning of the end of the cohesiveness of the Black Panthers came on March 9, 1971, when Robert Webb, a member of the Eldridge Cleaver faction, was shot dead while selling the *Black Panther* newspaper on 125th Street in Harlem. The perpetrators were loyal to Huey Newton's Oakland chapter.

As retaliation, on April 17, barely six weeks later, Samuel Lee Napier, circulation manager of the paper controlled by Newton's faction, was gunned down in Queens. COINTELPRO disinformation had created resentment between the East and West Coast Panthers. FBI informants permeated both camps. Legal problems nullified the efforts of many influential members, and confusion increased among supporters as to the future direction of the party. No single organizational head helped the Panthers cohere. Crime began to undercut legitimate militancy. All these were factors in the East-West ideological war and waning political influence of the Black Panthers.

But COINTELPRO was also doomed, as a group of radicals broke into the FBI's satellite office in Media, Pennsylvania, on March 8 of that year. In a 1970s equivalent of a data dump on the Wikileaks website, one thousand files were disseminated, including information on the illegal extent of COINTELPRO operations, and the FBI's domestic surveillance powers were curtailed.

As for Karenga, he remains a fascinating by-product of anti-Panther police intelligence. Karenga invented the Pan-African holiday Kwanzaa in 1966. Even more curious, the seven principles of Kwanzaa—*Umoja* (Unity), *Kujichagulia* (Self-Determination), *Ujima* (Collective Work and Responsibility), *Ujamaa* (Cooperative Production), *Nia* (Purpose), *Kuumba* (Creativity), and *Imani* (Faith)—wound up being used by another CCS alumnus, Donald DeFreeze, when the SLA designed a seven-headed cobra with those same Swahili principles.

Patty Hearst, even if she was not cognizant of all the machinations of DeFreeze, knew something of this Kwanzaa-SLA connection. She stated, "I had to memorize what each head of the seven-headed cobra meant. Of course, later on I learned that he had lifted that from the Kwanzaa celebration."

DONALD DEFREEZE WAS neither as calculating nor as politically savvy as Louis Tackwood or Ron Karenga. They welcomed the challenge of working undercover. They avoided arrest while serving the LAPD and FBI. DeFreeze was caught more often than not. And everywhere he traveled, he seemed to find trouble or it found him.

The greatest source of information about Donald DeFreeze and the hidden history of the Symbionese Liberation Army came from an organization called the Citizens Research and Investigation Committee. A screenwriter, author, playwright and journalist, Donald Freed, had already written about the assassinations of John F. Kennedy, Robert Kennedy, and Martin Luther King Jr. His white support group, Friends of the Panthers, also prompted FBI harassment of him. He hired investigators Rusty Rhodes and Lake Headley II to pursue the facts regarding the Black Panthers and police intelligence in Southern California. Of course, by association, it included the full story of DeFreeze, Hearst, and the SLA.

Headley was a former Las Vegas police intelligence officer who left his position because of the corruption he witnessed in what was then the Clark County Sheriff's Department. In a 1975 presentation, Headley wrote, "I know of unlawful arrests because I took part in them. I know of covert activities because I took part in them. . . . I know of intelligence activities leading to unnecessary death because I participated in just such an act prior to my resignation as deputy sheriff in Las Vegas, Nevada." With a thick beard and oversized eyeglasses, Headley looked more like a chemistry professor than, as Charles Manson prosecutor Vincent Bugliosi dubbed him, "the best private investigator on Earth."

According to the testimony of convict Fred Braswell to Headley, DeFreeze met Braswell in 1968, not in South Central Los Angeles, DeFreeze's usual base of operations, but at the Boston Hotel on Turk Street in one of San Francisco's seediest sections, the Tenderloin.

Braswell was at the time the largest dealer of methedrine in Northern California. But he was not content with that title alone, for he was also a cocaine dealer and apropos of DeFreeze's work, a major gun dealer for the Bay Area radical group, the Venceremos Organization.

Headley's research revealed that DeFreeze was working not only for Farwell at the Criminal Conspiracy Section but also for the California state equivalent of the FBI, the Criminal Investigation and Identification unit (CII). The Los Angeles area arrest record of DeFreeze lists him as CII case number 2771103. His affiliation with the CII explains DeFreeze's extracurricular activities in the San Francisco Bay Area and, soon thereafter, the state of New Jersey.

On April 10, 1968, DeFreeze was involved with yet another failed criminal endeavor. The owner of the Gun Corral on Prairie Avenue in Inglewood heard noises on his roof that night. Selecting one of many guns to choose from, the proprietor found Donald DeFreeze in an alley behind the store with a cache of tools, including crow bar, tin snips, and hammer. DeFreeze was once again humiliated, held at gunpoint by the owner of a gun store until the police arrived. After two days in jail, he was released. The charges were dismissed.

August 16, 1968 resulted in a brand new charge for DeFreeze in Los Angeles: 487.3 PC (Grand Larceny). Donald DeFreeze failed in his attempt to steal a motorcycle.

Nine days later, Gloria DeFreeze wrote to the trial judge, reminding him of her husband's sporadic work for the county and state and the protections that were to be extended to him. As her appeal euphemistically put it, DeFreeze "helped recover weapons for the police and they promised to help him in return." Yet again, probation was granted.

DeFreeze's continuous attempts to get guns resulted in an arrest barely a month later, on September 25, 1968, with his possession of approximately ninety firearms stolen from another Inglewood gun shop.

He was sent to the Chino Institute for Men for psychiatric evaluation. At Chino, psychiatrist Dr. Frederick J. Hacker, in his report, concluded that DeFreeze was an

> emotionally confused and conflicted young man with deep-rooted feelings of inadequacy. . . . His disorganization and impaired social

adjustment seem to suggest a schizophrenic potential. He seems to be a passive aggressive individual. He appears to have a fascination with regard to firearms and explosives. . . . It is felt he is in need of a structured twenty-four-hour program of treatment. . . . His fascination with firearms and explosives make him dangerous.

Doctor Hacker recommended imprisonment for DeFreeze. In a double irony, Hacker would be present just prior to the shoot-out and fire that involved the SLA in South Central Los Angeles.

Superior Court Judge Newell Barrett, after months of delays, presumably due to LAPD communication with the courts, considered a heartfelt letter DeFreeze wrote in November 1968. In it, DeFreeze rued his miserable life and extolled his newly rediscovered faith in God, echoing his life with Reverend Foster and family in Buffalo.

The last three paragraphs of DeFreeze's letter to Judge Barrett showed a man filled with self-loathing, and no matter how much of it was intended as manipulation, DeFreeze's shame about his inability to go straight came through strongly:

Sir, I have six kids and I don't want them to ever see [*sic*] like this again, nor do I want them to see their father a jailbird. I must give my kids something to follow, not a father who is forever behind bars. I must give them something to be proud of and also myself. I am 25 years old next Saturday and I have made that day to mark a sort of new life and new beginning in my family's future. Sir, I want you to know that I am not trying to fool you or myself. . . . I want you to look at my record and know that you are really my last chance. I want you to let me put to work all that I have found and let me show you all, the people at Chino and here, that all their help and prayers and time were not in vain.

Sir, I want you to answer my kids [*sic*] prayers that they have been praying all these many months: 'Dear Lord, please send our daddy home for Christmas. We don't want toys or trees or any-thing. We just want our daddy so we can be happy like we used to be. That's all we want for Christmas.' Sir, let 1968 be my last year behind bars. The future of myself and my family are in your hands. I am asking you to let me take both myself and my kids' future and prove myself and make them a better life. I believe in my Lord's hands, for his will is mine and my faith. I know he will never make me ashamed of that faith for he will give his judgment through you, and I will not fear for he is with me.

Merry Christmas and a Happy New Year to you, sir.

Yours,
Donald DeFreeze

Once again, DeFreeze amazingly received probation, despite his accumulated crimes. Barrett gave DeFreeze a five-year probation, including monthly psychotherapy sessions and an absolute ban on handling firearms of any kind.

Unlike the harsh assessment of Chino, the probation depart-ment serving Barrett's court defended their recommendation of intense supervision instead of prison based on DeFreeze's "warm and meaningful family relationship," the religiosity he professed, and "the lack of assaultive or violent behavior" in his record, despite the omnipresence of guns and bombs.

The legal system accommodated him over and over, providing numerous chances to shift his behavior. But Donald DeFreeze's life circumstances only worsened after ninety days at Chino and his release around Christmas of 1968. Court reports noted that two of his children had chronic asthma. Another child required a hernia operation and Gloria was hospitalized for a time as well. DeFreeze didn't find work, and even if he had, he couldn't afford to pay a housekeeper and babysitter.

Showing a lack of appreciation for Judge Barrett's tolerance, DeFreeze wrote another letter to him after the verdict, suggesting that DeFreeze's marriage was a sham. "I started to tell you to send me to jail and that I didn't want to go home . . . but you should never have sent me back to her."

DeFreeze declared that Gloria and he did not love each other any more. He even criticized himself as "too weak" to leave. DeFreeze had suggested divorce to her in the past. But Gloria angrily warned him that he would still have to pay alimony for her and six children, no matter where he went.

Gloria asked him to take them all back to New Jersey, where she had friends and family to help support her, emotionally, if not financially. DeFreeze's probation officer refused the idea.

In January 1969, DeFreeze's father, Louis, died in Cleveland. In a letter he wrote to Judge William Ritzi, DeFreeze insisted that he had dreamed the night before that a telegram would arrive announcing his father's death. Hours later, that telegram arrived. DeFreeze, unable to let go of the memories of brutality visited upon him, did not attend the funeral.

As it was out of the jurisdiction of the LAPD, when DeFreeze visited Fred Braswell at his home in the Bay Area in March 1969, DeFreeze was presumably working on behalf of the CII. Later that year, when DeFreeze and Braswell were arrested together for possession of methedrine, they were kept in separate cells and interrogated individually. DeFreeze, in typical fashion, due to his status as an informant, walked away.

Braswell remained in jail until his lawyer beat the charge on a technicality. But, oddly, Braswell was then repeatedly approached by a San Francisco police officer named Sullivan who suggested he become a drug informant. Braswell, like many criminals, envisioned how dangerous life would be as a snitch and he refused. Then the head of the San Mateo County Sheriff's Department Narcotics Division, Michael Dow, who had never met Braswell, approached him to be a drug informant for Dow. Braswell again refused, unaware that his friend Donald DeFreeze was the reason they attempted to recruit Braswell.

Braswell witnessed the early formation of the Symbionese Liberation Army, to be discussed later, as he and DeFreeze became reacquainted and grew to be confidants within prison walls.

DeFreeze continued to pursue the sale of guns to pay his bills, and his streak of arrests grew. On April 20, 1969, during a routine traffic stop, police found an M-68 nine-millimeter semiautomatic rifle, generally used only by the military or the police. It was not in the trunk of DeFreeze's car. It was not in a case or hidden in any way. It sat on the backseat in plain view, with two boxes of ammunition. In the police report, the rifle was described as fully loaded with a thirty-two-shot clip.

The rifle was registered in his own name and with the police. DeFreeze, always at the ready with a story, told the officers involved that he was on his way to sell the rifle to an Inglewood gun store owner to help pay to send his wife and children to New Jersey. And again, after police investigated his past history with the department, DeFreeze had the charges dismissed.

On May 9, 1969, DeFreeze was involved in the most convoluted of his crimes up to that point. Because DeFreeze had lived in New Jersey, whether by Attorney General Evelle Younger directly or by a member of the Criminal Investigation and Identification unit in Sacramento, he was assigned to attempt to set up for arrest Ralph Cobb, an influential Black Panther in the Jersey City chapter. DeFreeze's wife and children accompanied him on the trip.

In Newark, Alfred Whiters, thirty-two, custodian of the Temple B'nai Abraham, told local police that two black men, later identified as DeFreeze and Cobb, twenty, of Jersey City, abducted him on a rainy morning and drove Whiters around in his own car for an hour with a shotgun held to his head. Whiters said they demanded the phone number of Joachim Prinz, the temple's nationally renowned rabbi, in order to extort from him $5,000 to then be used to free a Black Panther "brother" in jail, referred to only as "the Enforcer."

Whiters gave DeFreeze and Cobb the number to the temple's answering service, and they left him. No one could explain why his abductors did not directly confront the rabbi, who was listed in the area phone book and lived in Orange, New Jersey.

A week after Cobb was arrested, the temple was seriously damaged by fire. Rabbi Prinz publicly stated that he assumed the Black Panthers were responsible, although no one ever claimed credit for the arson.

On May 28, Whiters was again questioned by the police, and under pressure, Whiters identified Cobb's accomplice via mug shot as Donald DeFreeze. Both Cobb and DeFreeze were investigated for assault, extortion, and the kidnapping of Whiters. But Cobb was released without an indictment.

DeFreeze, unsuccessful in his mission to undermine the Jersey City Black Panthers, took his family to Cleveland. He took on two jobs while they all crowded into the home of his mother, Mary DeFreeze.

If DeFreeze was paid in advance by either the CII or the Criminal Conspiracy Section of the LAPD for his police agent work in New Jersey, it was not enough to support his family for long. His next attempt at criminal compensation came on October 11, 1969. Police responded to a report that a man was on the roof of the Cleveland Trust Bank, just blocks away from Mary DeFreeze's house on St. Clair Avenue. DeFreeze was caught by responding officers while he was running from the building.

DeFreeze possessed an eight-inch dagger, a .38 revolver and a .25 caliber pistol. After he was apprehended, police recovered nearby a tool kit and a hand grenade. Possession of a grenade alone was a federal offense. He identified himself as Steven Robinson, a Cleveland man who had only a traffic citation on his record. DeFreeze's mother went through the humiliation of posting bond on $5,000 bail. Before the police or FBI discovered the real identity of Steven Robinson, DeFreeze skipped town and once again returned to Los Angeles with his family.

It was November 15, 1969, when DeFreeze hatched his next crime, which was partially fueled, he later admitted, by pills he had taken. Sitting in her car in downtown Los Angeles, a young Filipino woman, Mrs. Milagros Bacalbos, visiting from Hawaii, had her trip ruined when DeFreeze walked up to her, took her purse, shoved her to the floor of her automobile, and clubbed her with his pistol.

Two days later, DeFreeze entered a Los Angeles branch of Bank of America and tried to cash a check for $1,000 made out to Milagros Bacalbos. Unable to account convincingly for the woman's name on the check, DeFreeze aroused suspicion, and when a teller called the police, DeFreeze fled.

The security guard in the branch was joined by police in pursuit of DeFreeze outside. They collectively opened fire on DeFreeze, who emptied his .32 caliber Beretta, missing everyone with his seven shots. He was hit in the left hand and left foot by gunfire and arrested yet again, another episode in an unceasing parade of failed crimes.

But showing his ability to adapt under dire circumstances, DeFreeze actually surprised everyone, including his own wife. He fired his public defender and decided to handle his own defense. He was ruled competent by the judge and began studying law books, filling yellow legal-sized pages with notes.

DeFreeze was a quick study, using proper legal terminology and motions in his self-defense. But his actual explanation was not convincing. He claimed he had found the stolen purse, denied assaulting Mrs. Bacalbos, and, while he admitted he tried to cash her check, he told the court that he suddenly remembered his car was illegally parked and went outside to move it.

It was at that point, DeFreeze maintained, that a "gun-happy" security guard fired upon him, prompting DeFreeze to run to his car, where he allegedly got out his own pistol and returned the fire of the guard and the police in "self defense."

As if there was not enough jeopardy in his life, while on trial for the assault and robbery at the Bank of America, DeFreeze was indicted in January 1970 along with Ralph Cobb on the Whiters kidnapping in Newark.

According to a story in *New York* magazine, Essex County prosecutor Hugh Francis expressed strong questions about the relationships between DeFreeze, Cobb, and Whiters.

Francis told New York attorney Milton Friedman, who defended Cobb and the New Jersey Black Panther Party, that the case should never have come to the court. There was a plethora of inconsistencies and unanswered questions that Francis noted to *New York*.

To begin with, Whiters's grand jury testimony was confusing. He also contradicted his own statements at times and suspiciously refused to take a lie detector test. Francis and Friedman recognized that kidnapping a caretaker to demand the phone number of a wealthy rabbi listed in the phone book in order to make a ransom demand made little sense. And the charge of kidnapping carried a sentence of thirty years to life, all to free a Black Panther they refused to cite by name.

While DeFreeze was in jail for the November assault and robbery attempt in Los Angeles, in New Jersey, Temple B'nai Abraham was still receiving threatening phone calls about the incident.

One anonymous caller chillingly stated, "Your caretaker [Whiters] identified the wrong man in court. And we want $10,000 or we'll blow up the temple." No bombing took place. It appeared to be a clumsy attempt to implicate the Jersey City Black Panthers and create the context for a reprisal by law enforcement.

DeFreeze, for the first time, faced the distinct possibility of a long jail sentence. In an effort to help her husband remain free from incarceration, Gloria DeFreeze wrote again to the court, emphasizing how hard DeFreeze had worked to provide for the family. She cited several jobs, including one as a delivery man for a takeout chicken restaurant, where he had been dubbed "Speedy" for his prompt deliveries and was eventually promoted to cook.

Gloria DeFreeze also mentioned in the letter that her husband had done construction work, although she admitted the foreman on that job prophetically referred to DeFreeze as "the Jinx." It was an all-too-appropriate nickname.

The CCS, after the failed armed robbery at the Bank of America, was done arranging probation for DeFreeze. One of the main reasons was the .32 Beretta he used in that incident. DeFreeze fired upon the security guard and police with one of the guns acquired among the two hundred in the Coleman case. For his cooperation, DeFreeze was allowed to keep some of them, for resale and, likely, to set up Panthers in future police agent activity. But now with a gun potentially traceable to the LAPD, recovered after a bust, DeFreeze was jeopardizing the department.

It wasn't a case of the LAPD no longer needing DeFreeze's services. In June 1970, the *Los Angeles Times* noted that Black Panthers announced their intention to make the South Central area a "liberated territory," armed to prevent the presence of any law enforcement. In addition, a $10 million lawsuit on behalf of the Los Angeles chapter of the Panthers was filed against the LAPD. It alleged, among numerous charges, fourteen police assaults, ten beatings, fifty-six false arrests, and nine incidents of destroying or taking personal property. The Criminal Conspiracy Section had grown substantially by that time. At the CCS in Parker Center, the police headquarters, intelligence was received by informants who worked not only for the LAPD but for the FBI and CIA as well. But Donald DeFreeze was no longer one of those informants.

Lake Headley actually had a phone conversation with DeFreeze's CCS contact, Sergeant Farwell, who carefully acknowledged DeFreeze's previous association with the LAPD but gave a different explanation of why they severed their contact with him:

> *Headley:* Did you ever read the letter to [Judge William] Ritzi? He wrote a fourteen-page letter from the joint [Vacaville] to Ritzi in 1970 that is really interesting. It goes into all this heavy Christ stuff.
>
> *Farwell:* Well, that is why I cut him loose. He was getting into that and I knew that he was [unstable], as far as psychological things are concerned.

DeFreeze knew that the LAPD was finished interceding on his behalf. As he sat in the downtown jail, awaiting trial, he hit upon a desperate plot to lighten his sentence in the only way he knew how: by being an informant. DeFreeze had overheard a conversation in the next cell between a prisoner and a visitor regarding a planned crime.

The plot was the robbery of the Supply Sergeant surplus store on Hollywood Boulevard. The prisoner next door to DeFreeze was named Charles Manson. DeFreeze called a contact in the Hollywood Division of the police department, asked for leniency in sentencing, and informed him as to the plans of the Manson Family.

The police provided a presence around the Supply Sergeant. There was no attempted break-in of the store. DeFreeze was out of options. With the highly controversial, indeterminate sentencing of the time, he could receive a few years ranging up to a life sentence.

And then the worst possible news befell Donald DeFreeze at, for him, the worst possible time. Back in New Jersey, Essex County prosecutor Hugh Francis and defense attorney Milton Friedman, representing Ralph Cobb and the New Jersey Black Panther Party, arranged to visit DeFreeze to ask him pointed questions about the Alfred Whiters case. They came closer than any legal official or law enforcement officer to discovering the Faustian bargain DeFreeze had made with the LAPD.

Francis, like Friedman, was highly skeptical about the case and its ultimate motivation. Cobb was a respected leader at the Jersey City chapter of the Black Panthers. In addition, the idea of kidnapping Rabbi Prinz to get ransom for a Panther whose name was never mentioned also sounded highly suspicious.

"It occurred to me," Francis told *New York* magazine, "that the FBI had engineered the whole thing."

If Francis and Friedman, when they interrogated DeFreeze in Los Angeles County Jail, had known that he was an informant for the LAPD and the Criminal Investigation and Identification unit in Sacramento, it would have embarrassed the city of Los Angeles,

California Attorney General Younger, and Governor Reagan, and it would have further infuriated the Black Panther Party.

As a result of his precarious position, DeFreeze was extremely nervous and hostile when Francis and Friedman appeared before him in an interrogation room at the Hall of Justice in downtown Los Angeles. At first, he foolishly claimed he did not even know Ralph Cobb and had nothing to do with the case. Asked about his reason for being in Newark, DeFreeze panicked and insisted he was dealing with his house painting company, House of DeFreeze, in East Orange. Of course, it was not true. The business had, by that time, failed.

Friedman recalled DeFreeze as angry, suspicious, and unwilling to say much about the case. "He was just a cheap, young hood," Friedman remarked critically. "Paranoid. He thought we were somehow trying to set him up."

When pushed on the subject of leaving Newark for Cleveland, DeFreeze concocted an even more outlandish excuse, saying his wife told him that when he last left New Jersey, no less than one hundred armed policemen ransacked his apartment. What was the charge for such a major assault on a single individual? "Parole violation," declared DeFreeze weakly.

As his interlocutors pressed him harder, asking about his possible connections to the Black Panther Party, DeFreeze's scattershot replies indicated he had not planned a way to circumvent their questions. He admitted to being asked by others if he was a member of the Black Panthers or Black Muslims and swore he was only a member of a church.

As for the threats he and Cobb made against Whiters, DeFreeze, in jail for assault and robbery, declared, "I don't walk around slapping people in the face and talking about sticking them up. This ain't my bag. I'm too nervous to be slapping people because they might slap back."

After two hours of their relentless questions and his unconvincing answers, DeFreeze could not take the pressure any longer.

He psychologically snapped. He grabbed the stenographer's notes, jumped up suddenly, and ran furiously down the hall, with correctional officers, Francis, and Friedman in bleakly comedic pursuit. DeFreeze tried to flush the notes down a toilet. He was restrained, and the notes were scooped out of the water and dried, for later use.

"In all my dealings," Francis later assessed, "I get some impression of which individuals have the capacity to lead. This fellow didn't have any of that."

Francis and Friedman left DeFreeze and headed back to New Jersey, convinced he was hiding something. They relinquished their investigation, since he was about to be tried on the Bank of America case charges. Cobb was eventually acquitted on April 28, 1970. The prosecution, in desperation, cited the Black Panthers Party's ten-point program as actual evidence of the crime. Friedman successfully convinced the jury that if Cobb had not been a Panther, the case would not have gone to trial.

When DeFreeze returned to the court in Los Angeles, he again decided to legally represent himself. He began to voraciously read law books, studiously looking for a legal angle that would, if not exonerate him, at least lessen his sentence.

The prosecutor and others who observed him in court found DeFreeze to be well mannered and professional. He presented a solid case, using legal terminology correctly.

But tellingly, Donald DeFreeze could neither hold his life nor his own defense together. In his final summation, undoing his impressive legal work up to that point, he read from the Bible, sang hymns, and then, dramatically unburdening himself, broke down and cried.

According to trial transcripts, prosecutor Daniel Johnson wrote in his final report on DeFreeze, ". . . This person is a high-risk danger to society and . . . as soon as he is released from prison, he will return to his same violent career. It is my opinion, further, that this defendant will eventually kill someone."

DeFreeze attempted to have Attorney General Evelle Younger appear in the court, to testify as to DeFreeze's "cooperation" for the

State of California. It was a hopeless measure and was predictably met with no response.

DeFreeze, trying to offset the emotional meltdown he exhibited during his summary, told Superior Court Judge William Ritzi, "The court, my wife, the doctors for the last fifteen years, have spent the doggone time telling me I have a problem. I'm sick. I'm this or that but they never tell me why, what it is, what's wrong with me."

The jury deliberated for five hours and found him guilty on all charges.

Judge Ritzi, appointed by Ronald Reagan earlier in 1969, had spent twenty-three years as a prosecutor in the Los Angeles District Attorney's office. DeFreeze, a.k.a., The Jinx, had drawn one of the least lenient judges possible.

DeFreeze was found guilty of two counts of Assault to Murder, plus 211 PC (First Degree Robbery) and 475 (a) PC (Possession of a Fraudulent Completed Check).

Ritzi, at the sentencing hearing, recommended psychiatric treatment for DeFreeze. "As I have stated," Ritzi summarized, "I do not now declare a present doubt as to his sanity, but I do feel he needs help and needs a lot of it."

So Donald DeFreeze, on December 3, 1970, prior to his incarceration in a penitentiary, was sent to the California Medical Facility, Vacaville, for psychiatric evaluation. His sentence was five years to life in prison. With California's indeterminate sentencing, instead of a judge, the Adult Authority in the penal system would determine if DeFreeze would ever see the world outside of a prison again.

3 • Behavior Modification, a.k.a., Mind Control

DeFreeze was remanded to the custody of the California Medical Facility at Vacaville, forty-one miles from the overt radical activism of Berkeley, during a horrifying confluence of events in America. Because of his collusion with the LAPD and the Criminal Investigation and Identification unit, authorities inside the California Department of Corrections (CDC) deemed DeFreeze as a potential prison informant. And it was DeFreeze's sad destiny to be incarcerated at a time when President Richard Nixon's CIA and FBI, alongside Governor Reagan and CDC director Raymond Procunier, were willing to take extreme, even illegal, measures to counter what they judged as threats to law and order.

The epicenter of revolutionary activity was the San Francisco Bay Area, and the political discourse was fueled to a significant degree by the Black Panther Party. And it went hand-in-hand with what was termed the "black prisoner reform movement."

And Northern California prisons especially, as DeFreeze and other inmates there knew, were a kind of ground zero for the black prisoner reform movement in the early 1970s. In August 1970, Jonathan Jackson, the younger brother of black prisoner, revolutionary icon, and *Soledad Brother* author George Jackson, led an attempted jailbreak at the Marin County Courthouse, north of San Francisco. The younger Jackson, two other prisoners, and Judge Harold Haley were killed in the resulting gunfire in an outside parking lot. George Jackson's death during an attempted jailbreak at San Quentin the following August made him a martyr, revered by many in the black prisoner movement and other radical circles. Black prisoners in the Bay Area began to gain more political clout in the radical politics of 1970s California.

Further, the voluntary manslaughter conviction and jailing of Black Panther Party cofounder Huey Newton after a shoot-out in Oakland that left a police officer dead also drove the agenda that placed black prisoners in the vanguard of political radicalism.

Newton was freed two years and two trials later on appeal. The rallying cry of "Free Huey" was also joined by an addition to the left's political lexicon. All black prisoners, regardless of their past histories or crimes, were referred to as "political prisoners." White radicals bent on changing the country concurred that the leaders of black prisoner reform were inspiration for mass action outside the prisons.

The radicalization of inmates in California exploded into numerous factions and politically motivated violence against each other, at times encouraged by correctional officers. Between 1970 and 1976, more than two hundred inmates were killed and four hundred more were injured due to stabbings inside California prisons.

Raymond Procunier, whose strong-arm tactics were generally the first response during the most confrontational period in the history of California prisons, bluntly admitted in 1973, "We've lost control. We've become so used to it, we hardly even pay attention to a fatal stabbing anymore."

Procunier and the wardens were the overall power, but direct control over prisoners was administered by correctional officers and the heads of prison units. Donald DeFreeze was imprisoned at Vacaville during a dark era when it was not unusual for guards to funnel street drugs to certain inmate dealers, taking 70 percent of the profits to augment their CDC salaries.

In fact, CDC corruption was so out of control that inmates were put in isolation if they did not do favors like dealing or snitching.

There were even occasions, documented by Headley and Rhodes, when guards offered to compensate prisoners willing to kill other prisoners deemed troublesome or uncooperative.

Stuart Hanlon, the San Francisco attorney who defended SLA members Bill and Emily Harris, as well as Russell Little and Joseph Remiro, framed the context of 70s activism. "This was happening when the whole left was falling apart. They saw the leadership of the country as racist."

Black inmates as leaders of a revolution might today seem like a counterintuitive choice. At the most basic level, they were severely limited in communications with the outside world. The left, as Hanlon described, was desperate to find an effective route for change. The nonviolence of Dr. Martin Luther King Jr., the race riots of the 1960s, and the anti–Vietnam War marches failed to bring significant opportunities to racial minorities in America or to end the war in Southeast Asia. The eloquence of Eldridge Cleaver's *Soul on Ice* and, later, Jackson's *Soledad Brother*, coupled with the cruelty of indeterminate sentencing and horrific treatment of prisoners, disproportionately black and Hispanic, led to the conceptual rise of the political prisoner. It prompted efforts by the administrations of Governor Reagan and President Nixon to crush that movement's proponents.

THE 1975 ROCKEFELLER Report, prompted by Seymour Hersh's *New York Times* investigation into CIA domestic spying, revealed, among other illegalities, a program called Operation CHAOS. CHAOS ran from 1967 to 1972, tightly compartmentalized, unnoticed by any congressional review of the agency. Later research revealed that CHAOS entered into at least forty-four different operations with state, local, and county police forces, far exceeding the number cited in the Rockefeller Report.

The complex of CIA programs that used state and local facilities for behavior modification on American citizens is staggering. Best known is the CIA's notorious MKULTRA, which originated in the

mid-1950s and included the use of witting and unwitting test subjects who were given a wide variety of drugs and then psychologically studied.

Vacaville already had CIA funding for psychological research
before DeFreeze arrived in 1970. It was called Subproject 3 of a
program known as MKSEARCH (which replaced MKULTRA
Subproject 140). This was confirmed in a letter to Representative
Leo J. Ryan (D-San Mateo) from Deputy Director of the CIA Frank
Carlucci, October 18, 1978.

Ryan was a true maverick as a politician. After the 1965 Watts
riots, as a California assemblyman, he spent a few days there as a
substitute teacher. In 1970, he used a pseudonym, arranged for his
own arrest, and observed the pressures, for ten days, inside Folsom
Prison. Ryan often showed up unannounced at the CIA headquarters in Langley, Virginia, to posit tough questions. As one of the
most ardent advocates of congressional oversight of the CIA, he
learned about the treatment of Donald DeFreeze, as well as a convict named Clifford Jefferson, who was incarcerated with DeFreeze
at the same time.

Jefferson, known as "Death Row Jeff" for his numerous appeals
regarding his death sentence for murder, was at Vacaville in 1971
and 1972 with DeFreeze. Syndicated columnist Jack Anderson
reported that Jefferson's affidavit for Patty Hearst's initial lawyer,
Terence Hallinan, specified drug experimentation on both DeFreeze
and himself:

"In the early part of 1971," Jefferson wrote, "DeFreeze stated to
me that the CIA was conducting tests to try out certain drugs on
inmates. These tests were on the third floor of the facility in B3. I
went there and met two CIA men who were giving these tests. They
gave me drugs, including mescaline, Quaalude, and Artane. These
drugs made me terribly frightened. Then other drugs were given to
calm me down.

"DeFreeze stated that he had gone through the same tests and
also knew of stress tests that were given to prisoners, in which they

were kept in solitary, harassed and annoyed until they would do anything that was asked of them to get out. Then they were given these drugs and would become like robots."

Jefferson added that DeFreeze gave him a preview of his intent to kidnap and murder, although targets were not named. "He said that when he got out, he would get a revolutionary group to kidnap some rich person. They would hold that person tied up in a dark place, keep him frightened and in fear for his life, then give him some mescaline and other drugs, and the person would become a robot and do anything he was asked to do—including killing others."

Carlucci's letter to Leo Ryan acknowledged voluntary testing on prisoners at Vacaville with a drug called magnesium pemoline and claimed it had concluded in 1968. The letter, however, did not address other drugs or techniques that had been or were still used at the facility.

Carlucci's carefully worded reply to Ryan merely stated that neither DeFreeze nor Jefferson had been involved in the pemoline experiments: "Insofar as our reports reflect the names of the participants, there is nothing to indicate that either was in any way involved in the project."

While we cannot know exactly all the drugs DeFreeze was subjected to at Vacaville, there is no doubt that he underwent coercive treatments. DeFreeze was injected with Prolixin himself, according to research by investigator Rusty Rhodes and attorney William Nestel. No less of an authority than Vacaville Superintendent T. Lawrence Clanon went on record with columnist Jack Anderson, saying DeFreeze volunteered for "medical research" in July 1970.

In the context of Vacaville Medical Facility, "volunteering" meant the inmate signed paperwork agreeing to treatment rather than being punished. But DeFreeze, while mentally troubled, was not the kind of prisoner to organize, to protest his treatment, or to cause concern on the part of the administration. His jail letters to Judge Ritzi, which continued for about eighteen months, did not condemn or even mention his treatment inside the prison walls. Instead, DeFreeze used self-pity about his personal life and an emphasis on his religious beliefs to try and convince Ritzi to shorten his five-to-life sentence.

How, then, did DeFreeze become a prisoner who allegedly planned to break out of the institution, kidnap someone, and use the selfsame behavior modification techniques on the victim that Vacaville used on him? And if he was induced to commit violence, as Patty Hearst was when she helped rob banks and fired at others who attempted to arrest two SLA allies, it prompts the question of how responsible he was for his actions.

THE HISTORY OF using prisoners in behavior modification experiments is long and harsh. In California, Vacaville, a supposed way station for aggressive or mentally unbalanced inmates, and the Atascadero State Hospital for the Criminally Insane had terrifying, government-sponsored projects ranging from aversion therapy to psychosurgery.

In *The Atlantic*, Jessica Mitford, author of *The American Way of Death*, an exposé of unscrupulous business practices in the funeral industry, also noted that there was another beneficiary of the drug experimentation at Vacaville:

> Over the past ten years, a brisk traffic in human subjects for drug company experimentation has grown up in the California Medical Facility at Vacaville, a prison specifically designated for men deemed by the authorities to be in need of psychiatric treatment. Vacaville has a population of some 1500 of whom 300 to more than 1000 may be in the volunteer medical research program at any time. . . . The giant pharmaceutical firms give their money to University of California medical schools and physicians who conduct experiments at Vacaville.

The CIA, in the late 1960s and early 1970s, funded prisoner experiments at Vacaville during a time when Governor Reagan and his cabinet were cracking down on student protesters, prisoners, and the mentally ill. It was Reagan who, during his reign in Sacramento, abolished the Department of Mental Health and began closing state mental hospitals. It was an early policy of a conservative movement that advocated less reliance on government programs, and it resulted in a dramatic increase in the state's homelessness.

Dr. Earl Brian, Reagan's Secretary of Health, felt that behavior modification, a.k.a., mind control, was important in the prevention of crime. The law-and-order doctrine of Reagan and Brian was concentrated on the volatility of the Black Panthers and leftist political activism in general, especially at UC Berkeley and throughout the Bay Area.

Later in the 1970s, Dr. Brian and Reagan's counterintelligence advisor, William Herrmann, worked together on the Center for the Study and Reduction of Violence, a project that intended to explore social control of those prone toward violence, even children. It failed when increased media scrutiny revealed the California Department of Corrections, rather than the medical establishment, would have control.

Eventually, both Brian and Herrmann worked with Reagan when he became president. In a highly complex and internecine case, Brian was accused by former Attorney General Elliot Richardson of stealing software from a company called Inslaw. Brian was also an alleged accomplice in the Reagan attempt to undercut President Jimmy Carter's negotiations to free Americans kidnapped by Iran. Brian was never indicted on either charge. Herrmann, who was later affiliated with the CIA and FBI, also participated in the aforementioned Iran arms-for-hostages deal, the "October Surprise," on behalf of Reagan.

Herrmann was a counterintelligence expert for System Development Corporation, which designed, integrated, and tested complex computer systems for military applications. Herrmann also worked with the Stanford Research Institute, the Rand Corporation, and the Hoover Center on Violence.

Herrmann's background fit in well with Reagan's animosity toward social protest. It was during the early part of DeFreeze's incarceration, in 1970, that Reagan infamously summed up his attitude about using force against college demonstrations: "If it takes a bloodbath, let's get it over with. No more appeasement."

Herrmann himself told the *Los Angeles Times* that a good computer intelligence system "would separate out the activist bent on destroying the system" and then develop a master plan "to win the hearts and minds of the people."

The *Napa Sentinel* series "Mind Control," as well as journalism by other researchers, confirmed that Herrmann worked in a Psychological Operations unit (psy-ops) in both Vietnam and Cambodia. Clearly, Herrmann crossed paths with the man who was instrumental in the creation of the Symbionese Liberation Army, Colston Westbrook.

Colston Richard Westbrook became Donald DeFreeze's early Vacaville confidant, sponsor, and supporter. Eventually, he would be DeFreeze's mortal enemy and receive a public death threat from DeFreeze and the Symbionese Liberation Army, announced to the world via a communiqué.

Westbrook was an acerbic character who could only have existed in that time and place. He was black, pot-bellied, and wore dashikis and other African garb. And while he spoke seven languages, including Swahili, he preferred to use black street language, especially what we now call "the *N* word," whenever possible.

Westbrook was born in Chambersburg, Pennsylvania. His father, Edward, an Army sergeant, fought and died in Germany during World War II. Colston followed his father's military path, serving at Travis Air Force Base in Northern California, just miles from the town of Vacaville.

Westbrook's facility with languages enabled him to travel all over the world in his military career. Political researcher Mae Brussell, a former Beverly Hills housewife, with the urging of her friend, novelist Henry Miller, spent seventeen years broadcasting her findings on small, listener-sponsored radio stations in California. She helped disseminate Westbrook's clandestine work, along with Donald Freed and his Citizens Research Investigation Committee, while the SLA–Patty Hearst case was unfolding. Westbrook was an advisor to the KCIA, the South Korean equivalent of the CIA. He also claimed to have had a direct line of communication, in a past assignment, to Cambodian Prime Minister Lon Nol, who replaced Prince Norodom Sihanouk in a coup orchestrated by the CIA.

Between 1967 and 1969, Westbrook was an advisor to the South Vietnamese Police Special Branch, under the cover of working as an employee of Pacific Architects and Engineers (PA&E). Westbrook was in South Vietnam during the CIA's Phoenix Program, during which twenty thousand to forty thousand citizens—alleged Viet Cong sympathizers—were murdered over a two-year period.

Professor Peter Dale Scott wrote in the essay "The Assassinations of the 1960s as Deep Events" that Westbrook, after the destruction of the SLA, applied for a teaching job in Scott's English Department at UC Berkeley. "The chairman asked me to peruse Westbrook's *curriculum vitae;* and I immediately noticed that while in Vietnam, Westbrook had worked as a civilian employee of Pacific Architects & Engineers. PA&E was a well-known cover for the CIA in Saigon, and I so notified the Chairman. Westbrook did not get the job."

Westbrook, questioned by the press about his past, defended his work at Pacific Architects and Engineers and his extensive travel by insisting the company simply had the best employee vacation benefits imaginable. "It's a civilian company, and I took paid vacations to Cambodia, Thailand, India, Japan, Hong Kong, the Philippines, Okinawa, and Russia."

Among others who confirmed PA&E was a proprietary of the CIA was Bart Osborn (also spelled "Osborne" in the media) of the Fifth Estate, a Washington, DC, research group made up of former intelligence community members who changed their minds about the validity of the Vietnam War. Osborn himself was in charge of teams of men involved in the notorious Phoenix Program.

Pacific Architects and Engineers contracted the building of the interrogation-torture centers known as Province Interrogation Centers (PICs) in every one of South Vietnam's forty-four provinces. These compounds were surrounded by high walls and gun towers and could communicate instantly with CIA headquarters in Saigon. The interrogation centers were staffed by South Vietnam's plainclothes secret police, the Special Branch, working in conjunction with South Vietnamese military intelligence officers and advised by undercover CIA "liaison" officers, like Colston Westbrook, who used the cover of PA&E.

The CIA's Phoenix Program (*Phung Hoang*) targeted only civilians, known as Viet Cong Infrastructure (VCI), presumed to be sympathetic to the Viet Cong. VCI prisoners, like their American and South Vietnamese counterparts, experienced torture and deprivation. But these noncombatants had no form of redress and were not protected by the Geneva Conventions. Once accused, they were swept up and imprisoned, without confirmation or any form of due process.

Bart Osborn testified before Congress that all of the VCI suspects he dealt with in Vietnam died due to their mistreatment. When a VCI gave what was deemed actionable intelligence, a Provincial Reconnaissance Unit (PRU) was assigned to hunt down and kill the target. PRUs were a mixture of South Vietnamese and American military, mostly Navy SEAL teams, under the command of the CIA.

Four years after the Phoenix Program was initiated, the *New York Times* on July 15, 1971, revealed that 26,843 nonmilitary Vietcong insurgents and sympathizers had been "neutralized" in the previous fourteen-month period. The exact total of civilian injuries and deaths due to Phoenix will never be known. When questioned in front of Congress, CIA Director William Colby stated directly that assassinations were not part of the Phoenix Program.

According to Douglas Valentine, author of *The Phoenix Program*, Colston Westbrook might have been employed in one of two ways under cover of PA&E during Phoenix. He could have had an office job, running networks of agents in pursuit of targeted VCI. However, similar to the Iraq War, Vietnam had military contractors, and thus Westbrook "may not have been a fully integrated and backstopped CIA officer. . . . The CIA hired lots of big city detectives and sheriffs as contractors to run the PICs and work with Special Branch, because of their background."

After Westbrook returned to the United States from Vietnam, William Herrmann, advising Governor Ronald Reagan on counterintelligence measures to combat leftist militancy, enlisted Westbrook to create and run the Black Cultural Association (BCA) at Vacaville Medical Facility. The BCA was ostensibly an education program designed to instill black pride in Vacaville inmates. In reality, it became a cover for an experimental project to explore the extent to which unstable or susceptible prisoners could be controlled for the purpose of infiltration of Bay Area radical groups.

Westbrook was euphemistically named an "outside guest coordinator" while in control of the BCA. His cover was as a teaching assistant at UC Berkeley's Afro-American Studies department, specializing in black linguistics. His master's thesis was entitled "The Dual Linguistic Heritage of Afro-Americans," and he lived up to the title, a psychological warfare expert who used "the N word" with such regularity that he was quoted in the *San Francisco Chronicle* using that term, clearly during a time of different linguistic norms. His encouragement of black prisoners to talk about their experiences and identities, coupled with his outsized personality, helped him initially gain the trust of many inmates at Vacaville.

Westbrook chose to befriend Donald DeFreeze, the former LAPD informant, in a prison where coercive treatment of prisoners was the norm. As Dr. Colin Ross noted in *The CIA Doctors,* there was a process by which DeFreeze later treated Patricia Hearst as kidnap victim. It utilized isolation, psychological threats, physical abuse, and alleged dosing of Hearst with hallucinogenic drugs. All in all, it was a methodology that DeFreeze learned from his experience in Vacaville.

"Where did a street hood and unsuccessful robber like Donald DeFreeze," Dr. Ross wrote, "learn such sophisticated programming techniques? . . . My conclusion is that DeFreeze was a controlled controller, created in part by Phoenix Program veteran Colston Westbrook."

THE SAN FRANCISCO Chronicle did a series in 1971 on California prisons, including the California Medical Facility at Vacaville. In the first full year of Donald DeFreeze's stay, about 4,200 men were processed through its doors before being assigned, usually after six weeks but generally no more than ninety days, to one of a dozen prisons in the state, housing approximately twenty-four thousand felons in total. At the time, the top two countries in terms of total incarcerated people were China and the Soviet Union. The state of California was third.

S-Wing was the designation for the area that contained the most damaged inmates, some of whom seemed lobotomized and had no ability to communicate. Psychosurgery had been performed in Vacaville since 1968, according to United Press International (UPI). The other wings each housed 150 men, in three tiers of fifty cells.

One of the prisoners who met DeFreeze after his arrival at Vacaville noted how quiet and studious he was, not at all an organizer or a firebrand. Inmate Ron Eagles saw a man who seemed too philosophical and introspective to lead a violent, radical organization. "DeFreeze spent a majority of his time in the joint reading. Every time I'd catch him, I'd catch him with a book. . . . He was always concerned about black people's position in [the] struggle, black people's position in society, on his particular position as a black man in relation to society, especially [as] a black convict."

DeFreeze was at first a participant in the mildest form of control at Vacaville, group therapy sessions. But it was routine to use electroconvulsive therapy (electroshock) on prisoners. And two years before DeFreeze arrived, Vacaville was already experimenting with drugs that would have qualified as torture if used by the American military today.

Anectine (succinylcholine chloride) was used with regularity in Vacaville. It paralyzed the prisoner's fingers, toes, and eyes within thirty to forty seconds after injection. Then, the diaphragm and intercostal muscles (between the ribs) stopped functioning. It caused the sensation of drowning for up to two minutes. In essence, Anectine created the same basic reaction as an Iraqi prisoner being "waterboarded" at the Abu Ghraib prison in Baghdad during the American occupation of Iraq.

It was not necessary to cover the face of the prisoner with a cloth and pour water into his open mouth. Anectine, like waterboarding, gave the inmate the sensation he was literally dying. In addition to this biological effect, the attending physician told the gasping prisoner that he would feel the sensation again if he didn't cooperate in the way that was requested.

UPI reported in October 1970 that Anectine was used at Vacaville on sixty-eight prisoners. Arthur Nugent, a staff psychiatrist, admitted that "even some of the toughest inmates hate and fear" the use of it.

Prolixin was another drug utilized on prisoners at Vacaville. Its effects could be felt for up to two weeks. In addition to generating intense, ongoing nausea, Prolixin delivered a deep pain that ground one down and blurred the vision so that the recipient could not even read. It created restlessness, necessitating pacing, followed by exhaustion. The constant alternation of these two extremes drove the prisoner to the brink of madness.

Those who were given Prolixin described it as "sheer torture" as well as "being a zombie" and "liquid shock treatment." Bernard Weiner, writing in *The Nation*, revealed that Prolixin was injected into Vacaville prisoners a staggering 1,093 times in 1970. Electroshock was administered five hundred times in 1971.

DeFreeze, like any other prisoner at Vacaville, saw the effects of these drugs on those around him. Furthermore, prisoners described to newly arrived inmates the sensations caused by the various "treatments" in the medical facility. In this way, DeFreeze and other prisoners had fear instilled in them by the descriptions of these procedures as well as the actual treatments.

Friends and relatives who knew DeFreeze in his earlier years in Ohio, New Jersey, and California saw him as volatile, animated, even violent at times. But Symbionese Liberation Army member Russ Little's summation of DeFreeze when they first met at the BCA in Vacaville was quite telling. For a supposed radical who eventually committed kidnapping and murder, not only was he outwardly calm, but also he did not have a strong sense of political ideology.

"He didn't use contemporary Marxist-Leninist language," Little remembered, "but he studied all that shit, man. . . . He understood it intellectually and he could run it down that way if he wanted to, but he wasn't about to do that. He didn't think that was going to get him anywhere, doing that."

SLA member Joe Remiro recalled that DeFreeze was cautious in speech and action while in jail at Vacaville. "He studied the whole situation carefully before he acted. He didn't get involved in any public political activities until the BCA thing, and then he saw what a shuck it was and he got out of it right away."

The impression DeFreeze gave to Little and Remiro as well as fellow inmates was completely negated by Westbrook. Journalist-author Dick Russell, who utilized much of the Freed, Headley, and Rhodes data in an *Argosy* magazine story on the creation of the SLA, also did his own homework. In a phone conversation, Russell was told by Westbrook that DeFreeze "could sit down and talk to me a lot easier than a lot of other people, especially whites. He's a racist, hates white people with a passion."

If that was the case, it raised the question why DeFreeze agreed to not only attend but eventually speak to others at the BCA, a group that encouraged communication between black inmates and outside, primarily white, radicals. Westbrook's assertion that DeFreeze was a racist didn't explain why the entire composition of the Symbionese Liberation Army, except for DeFreeze, was white. Ostensibly, the BCA existed to allow black prisoners to air their frustrations with sympathetic, young whites. It enabled Westbrook to befriend some of those white leftists with the secret intention of manipulating them for infiltration purposes with the aid of a cooperative black BCA member.

According to Russell's phone transcript, Westbrook admitted he had strong organizational control over the white activists allowed in, many of them Maoists and former members of the radical Venceremos Organization. "I was able to organize, consolidate, and submit lists for BCA people, various lists from Sacramento, Oakland, Berkeley. My role was to centralize, because many people were turned down. They [Vacaville] had many organizations to worry about."

Russell asked Westbrook point blank about the BCA as a cover for clandestine work with prisoners. "If it's a behavior modification program," Westbrook asked, "who organized it? Prison authorities did not organize it. Black inmates did."

Of all the "outside guest coordinators" that could have been chosen for the Black Cultural Association, such as people with experience in social work, criminal justice, or organizations advocating prisoner rights, Vacaville wound up with Colston Westbrook, undercover liaison for the CIA during the Phoenix Program. And he was handpicked by former psy-ops officer William Herrmann, then advising Governor Ronald Reagan on counterintelligence. And it happened at the height of the black prisoner reform movement, right after the CIA's Operation CHAOS provided funds to Vacaville, which was an ongoing MKULTRA and MKSEARCH site for experimentation on prisoners.

And of all the black prisoners who attended BCA meetings, Westbrook chose to particularly befriend Donald DeFreeze. The handsome, shy, wide-eyed convict was quiet, compliant, had no political ideology, had no regular visitors at first, and, most importantly, had been a police agent for the LAPD. He could be manipulated, and if he resisted, Vacaville could threaten to expose him as a former snitch, a status that would endanger his life among certain prisoners.

Colston Westbrook encouraged DeFreeze to participate more fully in the BCA. He gave him the Africanized name "Cinque." But even that was a ruse. Convict Ruchell Magee, who sustained a bullet wound during the George Jackson escape attempt and shooting, had already been given the name Cinque. It was mispronounced as "sin-cue."

There was a vicious and truthful irony in that name, for Joseph Cinqué (pronounced "sin-kay") was the Americanized name of the Mende chief who in 1839 organized a slave revolt on the Spanish ship *La Amistad*. On the surface, Magee's use of the name seemed heroic and noble. But, historically, after a trial in New Haven that freed the captives, Joseph Cinqué returned to Africa and enslaved and traded members of his own race.

As the second prisoner named Cinque, DeFreeze adapted to a bizarre and treacherous dream world. A fellow prisoner at Vacaville, Damyon Tomita, confirmed DeFreeze was given the privilege of dealing marijuana for one of the officers, with the typical split: thirty percent to the prisoner, seventy percent to the corrections officer.

Tomita explained that DeFreeze's motives were seen as highly suspicious by some other prisoners. "Don DeFreeze struck me as a very intelligent, sensitive person, who was also very self-assured. Even though we became very close, I sensed that there was something behind his personality that he was concealing, although I could never put my finger on it. I realized he was involved in selling narcotics to the inmates for the guards."

Donald DeFreeze did not fully understand why Westbrook and other officials were clearly favoring him over other inmates who had been in Vacaville longer. By the time he realized the reason, it would be too late to alter his destiny.

4 · Double Agents, False Identities, Secret Affairs

The nickname was "Willie the Wolfe," used by prisoners at Vacaville. But Willie Wolfe was anything but intimidating. At nineteen years old, a lanky six-foot-one, easygoing, and quick with a warm smile, Wolfe began visiting the Black Cultural Association at the California Medical Facility at Vacaville in March 1972.

At the time, Wolfe was living with Dave Gunnell and his Chinese-American girlfriend Jean Wah Chan at what was dubbed Peking House or Peking Man House, at 5939 Chabot Road in North Berkeley. The house received that name because Gunnell and Chan ran a mobile food stand near the UC Berkeley campus called Peking Man. It was a reference as well to the political discussions around the rough-hewn living room coffee table, incorporating Maoist revolutionary ideas that included armed struggle.

Wolfe was inspired to visit the BCA by an Afro-American Studies class at Berkeley. "He had to do a term paper project," Gunnell remembered. "From someone, he got the idea of going in as a visitor to the BCA and doing his project on them. Willie went up to Vacaville and came back and told me about it. He was excited about the BCA. He was going to go back, and then I started going with him."

Wolfe was a highly unlikely candidate for violent radicalism. His father, Dr. L. S. Wolfe, was an anesthesiologist in Emmaus, Pennsylvania, and had sent his older sons to excellent prep schools and then on to Yale. But Willie's strong idealism and social consciousness made him bypass New Haven to live in Harlem with Michael Carreras, a foster brother from the Fresh Air Fund. Carreras, with Spanish, Puerto Rican, and African blood, spent summers in the liberal Wolfe household.

"He was looking for a life of a little deprivation," Carreras commented. "When you've had it easy, maybe you feel guilty because you haven't been able to experience life in the raw."

Wolfe was a finalist for the National Merit Scholarships and showed remarkable aptitude during an archaeological dig in Wyoming. Despite his overwhelming compassion for the underclass, he exhibited no early taste for weaponry or violent radicalism.

"My son was a pussycat," Dr. Wolfe said after the shoot-out and fire that killed six SLA members. "A gentle kid who even convinced me to give up my hunting rifles."

Willie went to Berkeley in April 1971 to study archaeology and astronomy. But he was judged harshly, albeit privately, by the people who lived in or frequented Peking Man House. Chris Thompson, a former Black Panther who briefly lived at the North Berkeley house and bedded some of the female members of the SLA, was outright cruel in his description of Willie.

"Hell, no, Willie was no leader," Thompson told journalist Marilyn Baker. "Nobody would go anywhere with Willie. People wouldn't follow Willie Wolfe to the bathroom. He was a loser. He was just a rich white kid playing at politics. No one respected him, not even in Peking Man House."

Like Thompson, Amanda de Normanville was an SLA fringe dweller. She became an attendee of the BCA as well, due to Wolfe's influence. But her assessment of Wolfe was also effete and caustic. She felt he was merely a follower of Dave Gunnell. "David I would listen to. Jean Wah (Chan) I would listen to. I felt more on the same wavelength. But Willie seemed so young. I would sort of think, 'Ah, Willie. There's Willie, all talk and no action.'"

What both Thompson and de Normanville failed to see was that the good-natured Wolfe, in rejecting his affluent, liberal background, did not want to pick up a gun as much as he wanted to address the black prisoner reform movement and social inequality in general. By condemning Wolfe for not being a wild-eyed revolutionary, Thompson and de Normanville missed the essential fact that Willie Wolfe was an unwitting conduit. Through the supercilious urging of Colston Westbrook, who commended him, Wolfe brought together the parties in the SLA.

THE SYMBIONESE LIBERATION Army, the one that assembled outside the walls of California prisons, began with Wolfe meeting Westbrook at the Black Cultural Association. Those twice-weekly meetings in the library brought together in discussion black prisoners and primarily white radicals who felt the inmates were "political prisoners."

The BCA functions at Vacaville drew about one hundred inmates during peak attendance in late 1972 and early 1973, according to Captain Stanley Feaster, who oversaw the program. Westbrook contradicted this, saying there were never more than forty prisoners and visitors combined per session.

Westbrook saw in Wolfe an ideal "connector," someone new to the political landscape, not suspicious or embittered, a person who yearned to be cooperative but did not have any idea how to do so. But Westbrook did. He introduced Wolfe to a soft-spoken, black prisoner named Donald DeFreeze.

Wolfe's altruistic recruitment of other radicals to participate in the lectures and discussions at the BCA took an exponentially important step when he befriended eventual SLA member Russell Little.

Russ Little was no privileged, middle-class kid. He grew up in a duplex in a government project and then in a working-class subdivision near Pensacola, Florida. His father was a mechanic and Little planned to study electrical engineering when he attended the University of Florida, Gainesville. But in the fall of 1969, he took a philosophy course taught by a charismatic Marxist graduate student. As a result, Little's feelings evolved about his obligations to better society.

Little's participation in protests against the Vietnam War, the arrests of members of the Black Student Union at Gainesville, plus the killings at Kent State in Ohio and Jackson State in Mississippi fueled his decision to travel with girlfriend Robyn Steiner to Berkeley for a short trip. In the wake of the shooting of George Jackson at San Quentin Prison, they expected to see street demonstrations in Berkeley. There were none, and Little and Steiner, crestfallen, left for Florida again. But they eventually returned to Berkeley, where they happened to find a home at Peking House in August 1972.

One pivotal social gathering brought many of the ten core SLA members together in one place. Wolfe and Little attended a weekly, free film screening, followed by political discussion, at San Francisco's influential and progressive Glide Memorial Church. One of the organizers was soon-to-be SLA member Joseph Remiro, a San Francisco native and Vietnam veteran who came back from the war deeply shaken by the atrocities he saw.

The beginning of Remiro's Vietnam tour was as part of so-called Long Range Reconnaissance Patrols (LRRP), during which small, six-man platoons were flown by helicopter into enemy zones, where they killed anyone they encountered, even civilian suspects.

The second part of Remiro's tour was no better. Between May and December 1968, Remiro and his 1st Brigade, 101st Airborne Division fellow soldiers conducted numerous "search and destroy" missions in Quang Ngai province. It was the same area where the My Lai massacre, the killing of more than five hundred unarmed men, women, and children, occurred. Remiro and his men were witnesses to and participants in torture and mutilation of prisoners, killing of unarmed civilians, calling in artillery strikes for sport and other horrors that psychologically followed Remiro back home to San Francisco.

"My Lai wasn't no isolated incident," he told author John Bryan. "I saw a lot of that kind of thing."

Remiro's military record indicated that he was charged by the Army with smuggling marijuana, but there is no trace of the case's disposition. After his two-year tour, Remiro became active in the Venceremos Organization, a high-profile Maoist radical group in the Bay Area. It was founded in 1970 by Stanford professor Bruce Franklin, who eventually lost his job due to his activism. The group, a splinter of Students for a Democratic Society, derived its name from the rallying cry of Fidel Castro's Cuban revolution, "*Patria o muerte, venceremos!*" ("Nation or death, we shall triumph!") The phrase was later used by kidnapped heiress-turned-revolutionary Patricia Hearst. The wiry, hyperactive Remiro also helped found the East Bay chapter of the Vietnam Veterans Against the War/Winter Soldiers Organization.

Married SLA members Bill and Emily Harris came to the Bay Area in 1972 from Indiana. Bill, as a Marine in Vietnam, tore a ligament in Da Nang playing touch football. After surgery, he was sent to Okinawa for a desk job, where he witnessed racial hatred toward blacks by both Japanese citizens and white soldiers. Like Joe Remiro, Bill Harris experienced a 180-degree turn in his worldview after the military. After his father, a building materials salesman, died unexpectedly in 1966, Harris marched on the Pentagon in 1967, and in 1968 he was in the streets of Chicago, as police savagely bludgeoned protesters on live television outside the Democratic National Convention.

Emily Montague Schwartz was the daughter of a consulting engineer in Clarendon Hills, outside of Chicago. Despite being raised in a well-to-do family who lived on the edge of a golf course, Emily's political consciousness developed in high school, where she collected money for the poor. At Indiana University, the Harrises befriended and followed Angela Atwood, another of the core ten SLA participants, out to the West Coast.

Angela De Angelis Atwood was called "Angel" and was a prom queen in high school in North Haledon, New Jersey. Elegant, popular, and excelling in theatre, she fell for her husband-to-be, Gary Atwood, at Indiana University. But Gary, a conscientious objector to the Vietnam War, brought in no income. He also objected to the discussions of violent revolution that Angela, Bill, and Emily had at the Atwood apartment on Delaware Street in Berkeley.

Angela, later referred to as General Gelina in the SLA, held an unlikely job for a revolutionary. She was, for a brief time, a waitress at the Great Electric Underground, a restaurant-bar on a subfloor of the world headquarters of the Bank of America, in San Francisco's financial district. Atwood's revulsion regarding her revealing attire and the sexism of male patrons resulted in her trying to organize waitresses in the city's topless clubs, but the women she approached met her with derisive laughter. Her marriage was punctuated by many fights, some physical, and Gary returned to Indiana, alone. Angela eventually moved in with the Harrises.

Bill and Emily met Joseph Remiro at an Oakland Safeway supermarket in 1972. Bill was registering voters for the upcoming election. Remiro, who noticed his Venceremos button, was handing out leaflets supporting Cesar Chavez and the United Farm Workers. He invited the couple and they came to the same film screening and meeting at Glide Memorial Church that drew Wolfe and Little.

THE SLA WAS considerably different from other radical Bay Area groups because it was composed of as many women as men. Unlike radical groups in the 1960s, which often relegated women to menial roles, with little ideological or logistical influence, the SLA embraced its women and allowed them to write and record communiqués and participate in militant actions.

As Cinque, Donald DeFreeze, who was the lover of three SLA women, was open-minded about the sexual mores of the group. Two female members became lovers. Patricia Soltysik was the daughter of a pharmacist in Goleta, near Santa Barbara, who at times inflicted physical punishment upon his children. Soltysik's mother had escaped the Nazis in Belgium during World War II. Pat was an honors student in high school, treasurer of the student senate, and president of the Usherettes, a benevolent service organization. In 1971, despite winning three scholastic prizes, she dropped out of

UC Berkeley and became involved in the United Prisoners Union. Despite her attraction to black radical men, in May of that year, Soltysik began a love affair with Camilla Hall, who she met in a hallway of their apartment complex on Channing Way in Berkeley.

Hall was the most reticent of the original SLA members and arguably the most tragic figure of them all. Her father was a Lutheran minister, and both parents, as missionaries, took her as a child to what is now Tanzania in Africa. They witnessed her younger brother Terry die at seven of a heart condition; brother Peter, at eight, succumb to kidney disease; and Nan, her sister, die also of kidney failure at seven. Hall, nicknamed "Candy" for her kind demeanor, was known as a class clown at Washburn High School in Minneapolis. Her sense of humor helped protect her against cruel boys who called her "fatso" because she was then fifty pounds overweight.

While very gentle, Hall was not without a sense of outrage about social injustice. Her father, Reverend George Hall, remembered that in high school Candy was impacted deeply by *Judgment at Nuremberg*, a film dealing with the German citizenry's failure to protest Nazism. "The message was you have to object if your government is doing something wrong. This is a message she got very, very vividly."

Hall gave Soltysik her SLA *nom de guerre*, Mizmoon, as an expression of fondness. One love poem Hall wrote for her read, in part, "I will cradle you in my woman hips/Kiss you with my woman lips/Fold you to my heart and sing/sister woman/you are a joy to me." Soltysik was the first lover, male or female, that Hall ever had.

But Soltysik's bisexuality made Hall miserable. She wanted their relationship to be exclusive. Hall broke up with Soltysik in October 1972 and nursed her despondency for three months in Europe. When Hall returned, in desperation, she reunited with Soltysik, who was then sexually involved with Chris Thompson. Hall, in order to be near the woman she loved, accepted the limitations Soltysik demanded. Sweet, open-hearted Camilla Hall, a gardener, artist, and poet, with no other option, joined the organization that was taking up so much of Soltysik's time, the Symbionese Liberation Army.

Nancy Ling Perry, along with Donald DeFreeze, was the most psychologically complex and contradictory member of the SLA. Perry, who was in charge of drafting their early communiqués, was a Barry Goldwater supporter during the 1964 presidential campaign. The daughter of Hal Ling, an ultraconservative Santa Rosa, California, furniture store owner, Perry was a cheerleader in junior high school and maintained an A average in high school. According to the FBI's HEARNAP files on the SLA, there were few hints at Montgomery High School of her rebelliousness. She did grow angry with the parents of her friends when those adults were rude to the only black student at the school. Perry told one Montgomery High friend that she had two very disparate dreams: she wanted to go to Hollywood and get discovered or travel to the Soviet Union, become a maid for Nikita Kruschev, and then assassinate him.

The diminutive Perry, less than five feet tall and one hundred pounds, left Whittier College, Richard Nixon's alma mater, for UC Berkeley, got a BA in English, pursued chemistry, but dropped out. In 1967, at the age of 19, she married black composer-keyboardist Gilbert Perry. Their tumultuous marriage was an on-and-off affair. Nancy was, for a while, a topless blackjack dealer in a sleazy tourist trap in San Francisco's North Beach. In her chaotic lifestyle, she turned tricks, shoplifted, sold marijuana and hash oil, and lived in San Francisco's Western Addition–Fillmore district because, as she once said, "It provides quicker access to crime."

But her smoking up to ten joints a day, often dipped in liquid opium for a greater high, was indicative of a deeper malaise for Perry. She told a friend that her separation from her husband led to "incredible self-hatred, that sometimes her mind was completely obliterated by her venom toward herself."

The beautiful and brilliant Nancy Ling Perry, exhausted by her own dissipation, fought her way back to stasis. She gave away her remaining stock of marijuana and got a job working at a juice stand with an orange and green awning, Fruity Rudy's, in Berkeley, where the end of bustling Telegraph Avenue met the university's Sproul Plaza. Ironically, Perry had claustrophobia and did not like being inside the cart all day. But she grew close to her boss, Rudy Henderson, an older black man with whom she had a brief fling but an enduring friendship. Perry quit smoking and taking psychedelics and nurtured both her physical health and her political activism. By 1972, she was writing to and sending most of her wages to black prisoners in Bay Area penitentiaries.

ONCE AGAIN, WILLIE Wolfe's sunny disposition led to the interconnectivity of the white radicals. He met Perry on Telegraph Avenue and was hanging out at Fruity Rudy's when he introduced her to Soltysik. Perry, the eventual rhetorician for the SLA, soon after had an affair with Joe Remiro and, after him, Russell Little, who eventually joined Perry on trips to Vacaville Medical Facility.

When Wolfe first met Westbrook and DeFreeze at the Black Cultural Association at Vacaville, he was immediately taken in by them both. Westbrook was almost comical in his overly expressive face, his strident use of black slang, his sardonic, bitter way of talking. And DeFreeze was otherworldly, a man who, despite a limited vocabulary, spoke with calm, almost unnerving certainty.

The greatest irony of Willie Wolfe's manipulation by Westbrook, the CIA, and the California Department of Corrections was that Wolfe was in a position to realize their plot to infiltrate and undermine Bay Area radicals. He knew that the Maximum Psychiatric Diagnostic Unit at Vacaville, set up in February 1972, was doing illegal experimentation on prisoners.

Wolfe wrote to his mother after his first Vacaville visit in March 1972. In part, he stated, "Last night, I went to the Vacaville Medical Treatment Center of California's Department of Corrections. This place is known for its lobotomies and terrifying drug treatments (which I've had described to me, second-hand) which are used to vegetable-ize those who are troublesome in their political fervor. I sure wish you would step out of wonderland to see what the real world is like."

A letter sent to Dr. Wolfe by Willie urged him to lobby against tranquilizer drugs administered to prisoners against their will. If Donald DeFreeze told the younger Wolfe about his own treatment at Vacaville, it is certain DeFreeze left out pertinent details, including his preferential treatment by guards and his background as an informant.

Wolfe's passion was much keener than his intuition about the bleaker aspects of the Maximum Psychiatric Diagnostic Unit. A black Vacaville information officer, Thomas Charleston, remembered Wolfe as "a friendly kid with good manners who came walking in here one night with his flyaway hair in a pigtail."

Mike Carreras lived across the country from his foster brother, but from what Willie Wolfe told him about the BCA and Vacaville, Carreras felt great concern and gave him prescient advice. "They were using Willie," said Carreras, "pulling him down to their level in every way they knew how, so that he would stay involved." Eventually, Carreras warned Wolfe that the convicts "will try and get you to commit an act of violence."

But at least for the first half of 1972, Wolfe engaged a stream of white radicals who sympathized with the black prisoner movement. Those activists attended BCA meetings with the approval of Colston Westbrook. And Westbrook, with Wolfe's enthusiastic help, made sure they all got to meet and know Donald DeFreeze.

The DeFreeze those white radicals knew was a noble survivor of one of "America's concentration camps," a highly provocative slang term the left used for the prison system. None of the outsiders who visited DeFreeze knew he was a snitch who provided to Westbrook and CDC officials valuable information for maintaining order and collecting intelligence on inmates who challenged the status quo.

To further secure his cooperation, prison officials gave DeFreeze access to the conjugal trailers at Vacaville, which were otherwise used only by married prisoners; inmates who cooperated in every way were rewarded with occasional sex with their visiting wives.

Two white radical women Willie Wolfe encouraged to attend BCA meetings became lovers with DeFreeze. Both Nancy Ling Perry and Patricia Soltysik, who preferred black men, were allowed to have private sexual liaisons with DeFreeze in the Vacaville trailers.

When Colston Westbrook was interviewed on the subject of sexual relations between female radicals and DeFreeze during the BCA days, in a peculiar and highly sexist way, he skated around the issue, pretending black rather than white women attended and that they were allowed there merely to entice inmates and increase overall prisoner attendance. "They accused me of taking sexy-looking black women wearing high miniskirts into the prison. Sure, I took some foxes—some of my prime stock—in there. Because if you want to dangle a carrot in front of the inmates to get them to learn and come to some meetings, you don't dangle communism. You dangle fine-looking chicks. The SLA women say I tortured the inmates by taking in chicks they couldn't do anything to. That's why those lesbians were mad at me."

A third white woman also became enamored of Donald DeFreeze. But their relationship led to a bizarre, secretive, and unparalleled situation, a political kidnapping that resulted in the victim, under physical and emotional duress, joining her captors in their activities, including robbery.

PATTY HEARST WAS an art history major at UC Berkeley. The slim, auburn-haired Hearst lived a seemingly sedate life with her fiancé Steven Weed. But Hearst had a wild streak in her. Her mother, Catherine, with whom she had a difficult relationship, had insisted she attend a Catholic school. Hearst, who was close to her father, convinced him to transfer her to an elite school near their home. When she met Weed, an instructor at the Crystal Springs School for Girls in her upscale hometown of Hillsborough, Hearst instantly knew, despite the female competition, that she would seduce him.

Asking for private help on math homework, Hearst visited his cottage on the grounds and sultrily announced that she was taking birth control pills. Their affair began when she was sixteen.

Hearst's involvement with Weed intensified an already fragile relationship with her highly conservative mother. Catherine Hearst, a member of the Board of Regents for the University of California for twenty years, backed Governor Ronald Reagan on his hard line against protesters on and off UC campuses.

A friend of the Hearst family told Sara Davidson in the *New York Times Magazine* that Patty and Steven living together made family dynamics even worse. At dinner parties, "there were subjects everyone tacitly agreed not to bring up. Sooner or later, Mrs. Hearst would voice some absurd opinion like, 'We've got to stop nudity.' She had seen a nude ballet and was terribly upset. Among the young people, it got to be a game: Who in the room would flinch or be first to change the subject?"

Despite Catherine Hearst's objections, Patty and Weed moved into a respectable $250 a month apartment at 2603 Benvenue Avenue #4, on a tree-lined side street five blocks off of the Berkeley campus. Despite the signposts of her family's wealth and power—Hearst Amphitheatre, Hearst Gym, even Hearst Avenue—Patty Hearst lived a middle-class and quiet existence, not at all demanding her family's largesse. Weed was a teaching assistant in the Philosophy Department. He derived distinct enjoyment discussing logic with undergraduates, but he was completely blind to what was going on secretly in his girlfriend's life, including the fact that she found him "a little boring."

When Hearst met Patricia Soltysik in Berkeley and was invited to attend a women's rights meeting, her path toward meeting Donald DeFreeze at Vacaville was set.

Lake Headley's research revealed that eighteen-year-old heiress Patricia Hearst, daughter of Randolph Hearst, the publishing magnate, not only visited DeFreeze in 1972 at Vacaville, but also had sex with him in those conjugal trailers.

One of Headley's affidavits, based on investigator Rusty Rhodes's interviews with numerous inmates, read in part:

(1) PATRICIA CAMPBELL HEARST became involved with first the Black Cultural Association (BCA) and then the "Unisight" Project sometime during 1972, at Vacaville, California.

(2) PATRICIA CAMPBELL HEARST visited these prison projects under an assumed identity . . .

(3) PATRICIA CAMPBELL HEARST developed a personal and political relationship at Vacaville Prison with DONALD DAVID DEFREEZE ("Cinque") while DEFREEZE was the head of the "Unisight" Project, but still a prisoner.

Hearst's fascination with radical politics in general and the black prisoner reform movement specifically was shared by a fellow UC Berkeley student, Mary Alice Siems (also spelled Siem in the media). Hearst, in an effort to avoid bringing infamy to her renowned family name, borrowed Siems's student identification card to visit DeFreeze at Vacaville.

This was accomplished because Hearst and Siems were very similar in appearance, facially, in height, and in their slim physiques. Sharing Hearst's political views, Siems was committed to the Movement, serving as a worker at a medical clinic for Venceremos in Redwood City, San Mateo County. She was also beneficiary of a $250,000 trust fund, based on her family's holdings in the Northern California company Coggins Lumber.

Hearst's secret relationship with DeFreeze is absolutely essential to understanding why she was kidnapped. Recovered from the SLA safe house in Clayton, near Concord, and the Harris's apartment in Oakland were a score of figures the SLA wanted to kidnap. Those marked as enemies ranged from the predictable (banking executives and corporate honchos) to the absurd (a man identified as Tyrone T., a twenty-eight-year-old San Francisco bar owner and pimp). The media never questioned why Patricia

Hearst's name appeared on that list rather than the more obvious choice, Randolph Hearst.

Inmate Damyon Tomita, later clandestinely invited by California Department of Corrections officials to join DeFreeze on the outside, claimed he was not the only convict who knew about the sexual relationship between DeFreeze and Hearst at Vacaville. "DeFreeze would talk to me about his visits with radicals and left-wing people from the outside. One celebrity mentioned from time to time was Patty Hearst. She was spoken of at Vacaville as one who was into a left-wing bag. . . . It was also well known through the prison grapevine that Patty visited DeFreeze at Soledad [Prison, later] and Vacaville several times."

Tom Smith, protégé of Westbrook and cofounder of the Black Cultural Association, insisted that Hearst was a regular visitor at Vacaville, stating, "There is no question. She came in several times."

The only public discussion about this long-obscured Hearst-DeFreeze connection came on June 8, 1974. Colston Westbrook, never afraid of the spotlight, despite his numerous contradictory statements, was a guest on KGO-AM radio in San Francisco. On the "Carlo Prescott Show," political researcher David Hastings challenged Westbrook on the identities of DeFreeze's visitors while in prison. When Hastings cited a visit to DeFreeze by Patricia Hearst and Willie Wolfe in 1973, the program inexplicably ended mid-show. In 1993, Lake Headley detailed in his book *Vegas P.I.* many of his discoveries about DeFreeze and the SLA.

MARY ALICE SIEMS, in addition to lending Hearst her UC Berkeley ID, was attracted to a black prisoner, a man linked to DeFreeze's secret mission, an inmate named Thero Wheeler.

Wheeler, a very dark-skinned black man with a penetrating stare, grew up around San Francisco's Western Addition district. He was arrested in Los Angeles for battery against a police officer and, with California's indeterminate sentencing, was given one year to life. Wheeler was shuttled between San Quentin, Soledad, and Chino, and he spent many hours seriously studying Marxism. He wrote an April 1972 letter to *Pamoja Venceremos*, the official publication of the Venceremos Organization, claiming to be a prisoner member.

When he befriended DeFreeze at Vacaville, Wheeler hoped for but received no favorable treatment because of their association. In fact, Wheeler had a peptic ulcer and it required surgery. But despite his numerous, desperate requests to prison officials, Wheeler was given nothing more than over-the-counter stomach medication and repeatedly denied the operation.

During this time, the normally quiet DeFreeze was preoccupied with his burgeoning position in Vacaville. He became increasingly more vocal at BCA meetings, with the encouragement of Westbrook. The bylaws of the BCA called for elections every six months. With the June election approaching, DeFreeze offered himself as a candidate.

Willie Wolfe, in a notebook, wrote down the names of candidates running for the leadership of the Black Cultural Association. He noted incorrectly the last name "DeFriese" and also underlined the name "Cecil Moody," another Vacaville con who was running for chairman.

But the presiding BCA chairman, inmate Robert Jackson, announced that DeFreeze was ineligible to run because he had not attended the minimum number of meetings required to do so. DeFreeze angrily approached the administration at Vacaville and complained that the ruling was unfair. He was already used to preferential treatment at Vacaville and assumed that with the help of Westbrook, who was in charge of the BCA, he would override the decision.

Robert Jackson, however, suspected DeFreeze was a snitch. In the volatile world of 1970s Bay Area prisons, one inmate did not dare accuse another outright of being an informant. True or false, it was the kind of declaration that could get the accuser thrown into solitary by guards or killed by another convict in a rival gang. Jackson spread the word among those he trusted in the BCA. The official line, when prisoners were asked about their objections to DeFreeze, was that he overly militant as a Black Nationalist.

The rules of the BCA, coupled with private inmate discussions about DeFreeze, blocked any chance of his being the head of the organization. When DeFreeze learned that there would be no reversal of Jackson's decision, he was not just upset—he was livid. Ignoring the Black Cultural Association constitution, he threatened to sue the BCA in the California state court system. Even if he had filed suit, the courts would never have heard the case. It would have been remanded back to the California Department of Corrections.

DeFreeze's sense of entitlement was so great that he created a legal writ to protest his elimination as a BCA candidate but it was never filed. Cecil Moody, part of the Black Nationalism bloc, won the chairmanship of the BCA.

During the BCA election maelstrom, a curious local story was published in the June 18 *Washington Post*, one that gradually grew in stature and ran parallel in time to the Symbionese Liberation Army's most notorious events.

The headline was "5 Held in Plot to Bug Democrats' Office Here." *Post* reporter Alfred Lewis noted the 2:30 a.m. arrest of five men inside the Democratic National Committee offices. One was connected to the Central Intelligence Agency. They were caught with listening devices, cameras, unexposed film, and even three pen-sized tear gas guns. Few in America had yet heard the names of *Post* reporters Bob Woodward and Carl Bernstein. And the article mentioned once, in passing, the location: the sixth floor "of the plush Watergate."

Also in June, back in the San Francisco Bay Area, a strange event, seemingly forgotten in the whirlwind of 1970s political protest, took place. Catherine Hearst was being driven to a University of California Board of Regents meeting in Los Angeles, when a bullet from an unknown assailant was fired at the car.

The bullet missed both her driver and Mrs. Hearst and lodged in the back seat of the car. It was symbolic of the resentment toward the strong-arm tactics of Reagan, Attorney General Evelle Younger, and the Board of Regents, in response to the activism of the Black Panthers and antiwar teach-ins and demonstrations on California college campuses. The attempted assassination eerily preceded the kidnapping of Catherine and Randolph Hearst's daughter by eighteen months. The perpetrator was never caught.

THE FALLOUT FROM the June 1972 BCA election was one of many topics Colston Westbrook answered with confidence when DeFreeze, as Cinque, was grabbing headlines with the SLA. Westbrook claimed numerous times that the BCA was overrun with white radicals whose Maoist politics shifted the intentions of the BCA's black inmate members.

No reporters followed up with Westbrook on how the California Department of Corrections could possibly lose control of a prisoner group within the walls of one of its prisons and be forced against its will to have white Maoists unduly influence the convicts. All visitors to the BCA were cleared by Westbrook. Their visiting privileges could have been revoked at any time.

Westbrook's warm and convivial relationship with Maoist revolutionary Willie Wolfe, who brought in other white radicals from Peking House, was not harmed during the BCA election crisis. In fact, Wolfe, Russ Little, Robyn Steiner, Dave Gunnell, and Amanda de Normanville were part of a dedicated Donald DeFreeze following that continued past June 1972.

The month of August began with a turning point in the otherwise overlooked story taking place in Washington. On August 1, the *Washington Post* reported that a $25,000 cashier's check, meant for Richard Nixon's reelection committee, had somehow found its way into the account of one of the Watergate burglars. It was the story that set Woodward and Bernstein on their historic course and led to the constitutional crisis that culminated in Nixon's downfall.

August was also the month that Little and Steiner moved into Peking House on Chabot Road, tightening the bonds of those who regularly drove up to Vacaville. Russ Little's respect for Donald DeFreeze was so great that on October 23, he wrote a letter to the Adult Authority of the CDC, an entity that controlled changes in sentencing. Little asked that DeFreeze be paroled. The request was ridiculous on the face of it: DeFreeze was in year three of a minimum five-year sentence that could have lasted for life. Nevertheless, the letter was filed, and, not surprisingly, nothing was done about parole.

Westbrook successfully used DeFreeze and Wolfe to assemble a group of white radical Maoists, connected to Venceremos, Vietnam Veterans Against the War, and other groups. It was the foundation of a unit that could, with DeFreeze's cooperation, provide the state of California with crucial intelligence on underground activities.

But the problem that haunted Westbrook, the CDC, and the formation of the Symbionese Liberation Army was that black inmates, who had to be suspicious of others to simply survive, had strong doubts about not only DeFreeze but Westbrook as well.

The suspicions spread like a cancerous growth when Westbrook interceded with the administration of Vacaville to let Donald DeFreeze have his own organization, Unisight, after DeFreeze was removed from the ballot for chairman of the Black Cultural Association.

The favoritism toward DeFreeze in Vacaville was clearer than ever to those around him. And as Vin McLellan and Paul Avery noted in *The Voices of Guns*, Unisight's stated aims had no correlation to its actual function.

The pamphlet that was passed around, introducing inmates to Unisight, opened with a description of its purpose as "a community-prison information service" with language that was so corporate-sounding, it seemed to have no clear meaning.

But the pamphlet also stated, albeit clumsily, "The Unisight Committee is also responsible for the BCA family re-organization and education classes, which purpose it is to reassimilate and re-educate the black male to the needs and responsibility of the black family and to give the black female an understanding of her past and the relationship between the black male and herself."

Unisight purported to tell black inmates and their families how to interact harmoniously, and yet Donald DeFreeze had a wife and six children and did not know where they were living.

DeFreeze now held an exalted position of authority on black family dynamics, despite the fact that he was secretly favored with sexual relations with white radicals Soltysik, Perry, and Hearst. No one in Vacaville's administration ever questioned his complete lack of competency in talking about the issues of black family unity.

And those who supported Robert Jackson and Cecil Moody at the BCA had reason to suspect the makeup of the Unisight Committee. Willie Wolfe and Russ Little were involved from the start. In comparison to the one hundred people the BCA drew as a maximum, Unisight was more of a personal favor than a functional organization. It had ten inmate participants and five outsiders, and two of those were Westbrook's wife and sister.

It was clear that DeFreeze was either being rewarded for coop- eration in the past or service he would perform in the future. And Westbrook irritated BCA members even more because he circum- vented their bylaws, supported DeFreeze, and was still in control of the BCA as outside coordinator.

But that was not going to last much longer. In December 1972, a sharp turn changed the lives and fortunes of both Donald DeFreeze and Colston Westbrook. Prisoners who attended the Black Cultural Association began discussing a rumor that Colston Westbrook was connected to the Central Intelligence Agency. Clifford Jefferson could well have been a source for this discussion, as he stated that Vacaville had CIA agents who administered drugs to him and DeFreeze.

It is also possible that one of the inmates had someone on the outside research Westbrook's previous employ at Pacific Architects and Engineers and learned it was a proprietary of the CIA.

When BCA members came to suspect Westbrook, they made their grievances known to the administrators. It had an instantaneous effect. Normally, a prisoner's objection to the behavior of a correctional officer achieved no change in prison policy. But when the rumors about Westbrook's intelligence background became official complaints, there was a quick capitulation on the part of the California Medical Facility at Vacaville.

The executive board of the BCA voted to demand Westbrook's resignation as outside guest coordinator and the prison quickly complied, as if a spy's cover had been blown and he had to be relocated for his own protection. Vacaville's administration put a public relations spin on the ouster and announced, in a rather vague manner, that Westbrook's resignation was due to his insistence on a more structured BCA agenda based on education.

But the outspoken, brazen Westbrook, not one to go quietly into that good night, replied with rancor and vulgarity to the press that his removal was due to "the CIA and all that shit." In the months that followed, Westbrook committed his energies to publicly denying his intelligence background and placing blame in a number of directions.

He was replaced by another black outside guest coordinator, a young Oakland man named James Mayfield, who later was instrumental in aiding DeFreeze in a highly suspicious escape from Soledad Prison.

THE PIVOTAL YEAR for the SLA, 1972, closed in dramatic fashion. On December 12, Ronald Beaty, a Venceremos member, was recaptured two months after he escaped from prison. Beaty, a thirty-five-year-old black man arrested for armed robbery, was freed October 6 in a violent ambush of a convoy, during which two unarmed guards were shot, one fatally. When Beaty was caught, he cooperated so fully with the FBI that he gave them names of people who both were and were not in Venceremos.

It was indicative of the brutal and omnipresent insecurity of the 1970s that Beaty made a suggestion that sounded reminiscent of the kinds of experiments that went on in the CIA's MKULTRA and similar behavior modification programs: Beaty offered the FBI the right to surgically insert a tiny radio transmitter under his skin, so that he might serve as a human "bug," able to record conversations with other radicals and set them up for arrest. While this was not done with Beaty, his snitching on some actual Venceremos members led to a dozen arrests, including founder Bruce Franklin.

Ultimately, the decimation of the influential Venceremos Organization in the Bay Area did not stop the plan to use a charismatic black prisoner to infiltrate any and all groups opposed to Ronald Reagan and Evelle Younger's repression of political dissent.

The day before Beaty's capture, December 11, Donald DeFreeze was transferred from Vacaville to Soledad Prison, without an official explanation. The California Medical Facility at Vacaville was meant for psychiatric evaluation of prisoners before transfer to mainline penitentiaries like Folsom, San Quentin, Soledad, and Chino. The prisoners were usually at Vacaville for ninety days. DeFreeze, who was never cited for causing trouble, was subjected to a three-year stay that changed him forever.

Colston Westbrook's connection to DeFreeze was not over. In fact, the rotund, jive-talking former coordinator for the BCA was soon to be named as an intelligence agent by the man he had controlled.

DeFreeze's sexual liaisons with Patty Hearst and Nancy Ling Perry continued, not only after Unisight was formed at Vacaville, but also after DeFreeze was shipped off to Soledad. Simultaneously, the California Department of Corrections searched for reliable black prisoners to work with DeFreeze as police agents. Shortly before DeFreeze left Vacaville, his fellow inmate and confidant Damyon Tomita was sent. DeFreeze's old San Francisco methedrine dealer contact from the late 1960s, Fred Braswell, was reintroduced to him at Soledad as well.

And for a short while, Thero Wheeler held the leadership of the Unisight Committee at Vacaville. All three men, Tomita, Braswell, and Wheeler, would soon be offered the chance, along with DeFreeze, to walk away from their incarceration and help set up a group to infiltrate Bay Area radicals, black, white, and Chicano (Latino). That group already existed as a prison gang, recruited by a very unlikely inmate, and was known as the Symbionese Liberation Army.

5 ✦ The Other Symbionese Liberation Army

After DeFreeze and the SLA kidnapped Patricia Hearst, his mother, Mary DeFreeze, was interviewed and admitted she had not seen her son in years. She recalled he had always been in trouble as a boy, without referring to the savage abuse at the hands of his father.

"I really think he's sick," she announced. "But I don't think he could hurt anybody." And then, without knowing how close she was to the obscured truth, Mary DeFreeze, when asked about the Symbionese Liberation Army, stated, "I don't believe he's running it. . . . Where do these organizations come from? Where do they pop up from?"

In point of fact, the SLA was not a genuine radical organization. It had its origins in the prison system of Northern California, and the first inmate to hear the name and to be offered the opportunity to run it was certainly not Donald DeFreeze.

Robert Hyde was a tall, thin, white-haired black man in his early fifties incarcerated in San Quentin, beginning in August 1969, serving a fifteen-to-life sentence. He was neither murderer nor rapist. According to the handwritten notes of investigator Rusty Rhodes, who interviewed numerous convicts regarding the SLA, Hyde was in a mainline penitentiary for at least fifteen years for possession, not use, of a deadly weapon and no other charges.

Hyde certainly did not fit the mold of a hardened criminal sent to a maximum security penitentiary. In fact, he claimed that his brother was Colonel John Francis Hyde, attached to the US Army at the Defense Intelligence Agency in Washington, DC. Committed to helping other convicts whose harsh sentences did not always fit the crimes they perpetrated, Hyde passed the California Bar and became a jailhouse lawyer.

In 1971, he formed a group called PROBE (Political Reform Organization for Better Education) inside San Quentin that offered legal aid to his fellow inmates.

"The California Department of Corrections approached me about a deal to recruit snitches," Hyde recalled. "They wanted me to enlarge my legal assistance efforts to include all races and organizations inside the prison, so I could bring them tips."

Certainly, the CDC wanted information on the gangs at San Quentin, but in addition, by secretly using Hyde, they could control prisoners inside from communicating anything negative to the outside world about the prison, as well as circumventing any legal actions taken by prisoners against San Quentin. The plan also provided a way to prevent prisoners from organizing within the walls for better conditions.

It was a highly effective concept. And it represented a new direction for the CDC, as Attorney General Evelle Younger decided to take control of all Department of Corrections programs, including the initiative that used Hyde and PROBE. Directives to Hyde were, he stated, communicated by Sam Brown, head of the Special Security Unit (SSU), on behalf of a CDC official who was involved in attempts to create a gang within prison walls called the Symbionese Liberation Army. His name was Lieutenant James D. "Red" Nelson, and he served the CDC in a department that sounded vaguely sinister, known as Special Services.

With increased violence in Northern California prisons and the influence of "political prisoners" within the walls of San Quentin, Younger calculated that CDC Director Procunier needed to take stronger action, even if it subverted the limited civil liberties of convicts.

However, what they did not count on was Hyde's refusal to cooperate. Unlike Donald DeFreeze, who was willing to take his chances as an informant for the LAPD, Hyde concluded that if it became known that he shared private information with the CDC, he would become a target for a stabbing. And stabbings in Northern California prisons had been occurring at an alarming, record rate since 1970.

"At first I refused," Hyde explained, "but their 'goon squad' beat me and threw me into isolation."

Hyde tried to remain strong for seven months in solitary confinement at San Quentin. But the alienation and deprivation, coupled with periodic beatings, caused him to relent. Finally, assuming he would never get out of solitary confinement alive unless he made a deal, Hyde agreed to cooperate, taking orders from Lieutenant Nelson.

Hyde provided legal advice via PROBE to all races of prisoners, attempting to ostensibly help them, whether they were guilty of mere possession of a firearm, like Hyde himself, or homicide, or anything in between the two.

The "unification of tips program," as Hyde termed it, began around the middle of 1971. Some of those who searched out help from the jailhouse lawyer belonged to the existing San Quentin gangs. Tom Thompson, city editor at the *Los Angeles Free Press*, noted in his piece "How the SLA Was Born" that the rival gangs at the time included the Black Guerrilla Family, Black Liberation Army, Nuestra Familia, the Mexican Mafia, the Aryan Brotherhood and the American Nazi Party.

In the handwritten notes of Rusty Rhodes and San Francisco attorney William Nestel was this quote from Hyde: "In late 1971, Nelson ordered me to begin recruiting inmates for a new organization called the Symbionese Liberation Army. I was very successful. I personally recruited one hundred or more SLA members."

But as Hyde's responsibility for the prison-based SLA grew, so too did his fears. There was more and more attention focused on him, which meant an even greater chance that his complicity with Nelson and the CDC might be revealed. It was an untenable position: if Hyde refused to serve the CDC, he feared being stabbed by a prisoner cooperating with officials. Thompson's *Los Angeles Free Press* article research revealed that between 1970 and 1974, California penitentiaries had over one hundred fatalities and four hundred injuries due to stabbings.

On the other hand, if Hyde were discovered by a San Quentin prisoner to be a snitch, his life would also be in grave danger. He was psychologically unprepared to lead the secret life he was thrust into and yet was immobilized, afraid to take action.

The intensity of Hyde's situation increased when on August 21, 1971, George Jackson was killed in a shoot-out at San Quentin. He had been holding a smuggled nine-millimeter handgun. Three other prisoners and two guards were also killed. Louis Tackwood, the informant who, like Donald DeFreeze, had served the LAPD, later claimed he was responsible for getting the gun to Jackson, via radical lawyer Stephen Bingham, to set up Jackson. Bingham countered that he had nothing to do with the transportation of the weapon and theorized that Jackson obtained the gun from within San Quentin.

The case today remains shrouded in mystery, but Jackson's martyrdom increased the tension inside and outside the prison system in California.

Reagan himself entered the ongoing legal battle for control of California's prisoners, also in 1971. He vetoed a law that passed in the state senate and assembly that would have established a prison ombudsman, an official who could directly take legal issues concerning prisoners to Sacramento.

Hyde knew he could not count on going to anyone in the California Department of Corrections to appeal for help. Ironically, he turned to the man who was central to the search for Patty Hearst and the SLA, after her kidnapping. Hyde wrote to Charles Bates, Special Agent in Charge, FBI, San Francisco. Hyde would have benefited more from contacting a major media outlet in the Bay Area, such as the *San Francisco Chronicle*, which noted in Bates's 1999 obituary that he had run agents in the area for COINTELPRO and proposed mailing fake letters, printing false documents, and filing fraudulent legal complaints to disrupt the Black Panthers and Students for a Democratic Society.

Hyde's coerced behavior at San Quentin shifted from sharing tips told in confidence by other prisoners to being in charge of a gang that at first had no unspecified purpose. Later, Lieutenant Nelson informed Hyde that the prison gang known as the Symbionese Liberation Army was going to provide agents to infiltrate political dissidents on the outside.

"When I became suspicious of all this recruitment," Hyde wrote, "I got word to Charles Bates, the head of the FBI in San Francisco. He didn't respond, but in early 1972 a Secret Service agent named Miller came in to see me and I gave him all the information I had."

Hyde was confused by the fact that rather than an agent of the FBI in San Francisco, he was visited by a member of an unrelated agency. Hyde's letter to Bates did not alleviate his problem. To the contrary, authorities now knew that Hyde was anxious to tell someone outside the prison system about the mysterious Symbionese Liberation Army. The man who identified himself as Miller gave Hyde no promise of a resolution, nor any way to directly stay in touch with him.

What had started as an altruistic dissemination of legal advice from Hyde spiraled out of control. By the time he wrote to Bates, Hyde was providing tips on SLA gang members, of all races and backgrounds, at San Quentin, Soledad, and Vacaville.

While Hyde was without redress, the medical mistreatment of prisoners in Northern California suddenly came under scrutiny. In January 1972, Vacaville Superintendent Lester Pope responded to an outcry from Bay Area psychiatrists, who objected to the reconstruction and expansion of a unit at Vacaville that used coercive methods on prisoners. Pope claimed the work would not be finished until the spring and that the actual program of treatments had not been formulated.

It was an outright lie. The very next month, in mid-February, the California Medical Facility at Vacaville opened the highly controversial Lister Unit, also known as the Maximum Psychiatric Diagnostic Unit (MPDU). It contained eighty-four concrete and steel bar cells for the most recalcitrant of prisoners, taken from the Adjustment Centers (maximum security wings) of other California penitentiaries. In essence, the area where Donald DeFreeze and Death Row Jeff had been experimented upon in Vacaville was now larger and able to accommodate more prisoners.

The construction of the MPDU was done by Brown & Root, based in Texas, and Morrison-Knudsen in Idaho. The two firms did reconstruction work on the infamous "tiger cages" at Con Son Island off the coast of South Vietnam during the war in Southeast Asia. The cells, which dated back to 1939 and the French colonization of Vietnam, were given that name because they were not tall enough to allow prisoners to stand upright in them. Based in the South China Sea, Con Son Prison, which held up to 9,600 people, was not unlike the US prison at Guantanamo Bay, Cuba, for terrorism suspects, in that it was highly inaccessible and there was no due process for prisoners. But without minimizing Guantanamo's torture or "enhanced interrogation techniques," as it became known during the George W. Bush administration, the conditions at Con Son were utterly abhorrent. A US delegation in 1970, headed by Senator Tom Harkin of Iowa, found prisoners there stricken with disease, horrible bruises, and even mutilations.

The structural engineering work at Con Son Prison and at Vacaville, done by the same firms, raises the question of whether Colston Westbrook, CIA liaison for interrogation of Viet Cong suspects, was consulted on the design or implementation of the Maximum Psychiatric Diagnostic Unit while he ran the BCA at Vacaville.

In March 1972, the Bay Area medical establishment immediately protested again. Dr. Richard Fine of the Bay Area Medical

Committee for Human Rights spoke passionately against it at a San Francisco press conference. Fine, a staff doctor at San Francisco General Hospital, recounted "six or so brothers at San Quentin, four to six at Folsom, and at least four at [Deuel Vocational Institute] Tracy" who as prisoners had refused to sign forms authorizing treatment at the MPDU.

Fine claimed that the unit was meant for black militants and "political prisoners." At that point, according to the CDC's L. M. Stutsman, there were twelve inmates and another twenty-four who had signed informed consent forms and were soon to arrive.

By April, the California State Assembly Select Committee on Prison Reform had heard testimony that, despite paying for the MPDU, Vacaville was woefully understaffed. Dr. Algin Groupe, a staff psychiatrist at Vacaville, said his colleagues and he "cannot possibly do an adequate job in treating roughly 1,400 inmates."

There was other testimony about the use of unsanitary bandages, a cockroach infestation, and poor equipment, including a respirator that failed. Groupe summarized that it was "probably true" that Vacaville was "manufacturing more hardened criminals than useful citizens." He was contradicted during the hearing by chief medical officer Dr. Eugene Prout, and there was no reference at all in the article to behavior modification at the prison, neither what was planned in the future nor what had been used on prisoners like Donald DeFreeze and Clifford Jefferson.

AFTER THE OPENING of the MPDU at Vacaville, a major rearrangement of prisoners who had ties to the Symbionese Liberation Army occurred during the last half of 1972.

Hyde contended that one of the inmates whom he recruited for the prison SLA was Thero Wheeler. The CDC sensed in Wheeler a respected and influential prisoner and told him that if he continued his association with Venceremos in any way, he would never be considered for an eventual parole. Desperate to get medical help on his bleeding ulcer, Wheeler promptly renounced his participation in Venceremos.

He was transferred from Folsom Prison to Vacaville in September 1972. Although he was not given the surgery he needed, Wheeler did eventually succeed DeFreeze at Unisight. Wheeler was very well read, spoke his political rhetoric with authority and fire, and had gotten along with DeFreeze. Furthermore, he had many contacts who were involved in the Venceremos Organization.

During this realignment of the SLA, the California Department of Corrections was doing battle not only with liberal-minded psychiatrists in the Bay Area but also with a judiciary that was by no means in lockstep with the policies of Ronald Reagan and Evelle Younger. Near the time of Wheeler's transfer to Vacaville, the California Supreme Court overturned CDC Director Procunier's April 1971 rule preventing prisoners from writing sealed letters to their attorneys. Younger defended Procunier's rule despite the fact that it was invalidated, and he accused radical attorneys of conducting "revolution by mail."

In this climate, there were many reasons why Donald DeFreeze was transferred to Soledad on December 13, 1972. The most obvious was the rumor of Westbrook as a CIA asset and DeFreeze as a snitch, based on the events at the BCA in Vacaville.

Additionally, the media attention on Bay Area psychiatrists' complaints earlier in 1972 about the opening of the Maximum Psychiatric Diagnostic Unit at Vacaville made it less than conducive to keep DeFreeze there.

DeFreeze himself showed a certain volatility in his behavior, which prompted Westbrook to create Unisight for him. Therefore, moving him eliminated possible confrontations between DeFreeze and BCA members.

Neither DeFreeze's transfer to Soledad nor that of his close companion, Damyon Tomita, had any official explanation by the California Department of Corrections. At Soledad, DeFreeze once again received preferential treatment. He was provided access to a "trustee visitation house," usually reserved for married, compliant prisoners. As described from the research of Freed, Headley, and Rhodes, DeFreeze renewed his relationship with Patty Hearst, as well as Nancy Ling Perry.

In the mind of DeFreeze, the transfer to Soledad was neither a retreat nor a punishment. It was a promotion, based on his cooperation with Westbrook and the CDC. Due to Robert Hyde's coerced expansion of PROBE, there were already SLA followers at Soledad, and the appearance of DeFreeze signified the arrival of an official leader.

The existing five gangs at Soledad were composed along ethnic lines: the Mexican Mafia, Nuestra Familia, Aryan Brotherhood, American Nazis, and Black Liberation Army. At first, the SLA puzzled the other prisoners at Soledad because it was racially mixed. It used a seven-headed cobra as its symbol, provided by Westbrook, and the seven principles derived from Ron Karenga. The word "Symbionese" was created by Westbrook, suggesting symbiosis, the long-term interaction of different species. Secretly, the symbiosis was the use of black, white, and Latino prisoners for prison intelligence purposes. And its new leader, who called himself Cinque, appeared to be nonviolent, very ethereal in speech, and high on drugs most of the time.

The best description of Donald DeFreeze's thoughts and beliefs while at Soledad Prison came from Fred Braswell, DeFreeze's old contact from the Boston Hotel in San Francisco.

Braswell wound up at Soledad for voluntary manslaughter and possession of narcotics, with a sentence of five years to life, according to Robert Hyde. Because he had known DeFreeze longer than anyone else jailed at Soledad, Braswell became his closest aide in the Soledad SLA, still unaware that the San Francisco policeman and San Mateo Sheriff's Department officer who asked him to be an informant were sent by DeFreeze.

"He talked crazy sometimes," Braswell wrote. "I looked in his locker one day and found a big bottle of Eferol. They use this drug on the inside for thought control. But Don was taking these pills of his own free will, like candy." (The drug Braswell referred to was not related to E-Ferol, an intravenous vitamin supplement for premature babies that was eventually pulled off the market for dangerous side effects.)

In addition to any drugs, electroshock, and/or psychological coercion DeFreeze underwent in prison, just the actuality of being locked away changed the nature of his personality, as it does for all convicts. Soledad chief psychiatrist Frank Rundle wrote an essay, "The Roots of Violence in Soledad." In it, he discussed how isolation, for the prisoner, alters the way the brain functions. "There was, simply stated, no opportunity to apply the reality checking logic which is imperative to the maintenance of a rational state of mind. Many inmates slipped in and out of an autistic world of fantasy as a consequence of this isolation."

DeFreeze, after his ruinous personal life and at least a dozen failed crimes, was starkly removed from any connection to normal society. And yet, despite his lack of freedom, he was ironically rewarded, with the help of Colston Westbrook. DeFreeze never lacked for drugs. In fact, Braswell's depiction of DeFreeze willingly and regularly taking a mind control drug suggested DeFreeze wanted to live in the fantasy world of prisoner king. He had the respect of outside visitors who were inspired by his thoughts, the power of a gang behind him at Soledad, and white radical women who physically desired him.

Damyon Tomita went on the record regarding DeFreeze's obsession with Hearst. "DeFreeze would talk to me about his visits with radicals and left-wing people from the outside. One celebrity mentioned from time to time was Patty Hearst. She was spoken of at Vacaville as one who was into a left-wing bag. In 1973, while at Soledad, Don DeFreeze mentioned her name on at least two occasions . . . describing her social status while mentioning her radical beliefs.

"I also heard through several sources," Tomita wrote in long hand, "at the prison grapevine [before the Hearst kidnapping] that

Patty visited Soledad and Vacaville several times during the last two years."

Fred Braswell confirmed to investigator Rusty Rhodes that DeFreeze was rewarded with sexual favors before he escaped from Soledad. "In early '73, Nancy Perry and Patty Hearst came down to see Don on numerous occasions. I couldn't believe it at first but he was having sexual intercourse with both of them here at the prison. I know of one occasion when he balled Nancy Perry right here in the visiting area. But he also had access to the trustees' visitation house, where he told me he had had relations with Patty Hearst. He had to keep tight, though, or he would lose his privileges. I was the only one [among the prisoners] that knew about the visitation house here at Soledad."

But there was a disruption to his penal fantasy world. Patty Hearst rejected him, and his fury was that of a man who was accustomed to always getting his way. Hearst's admiration for DeFreeze took a dramatic turn, when, at Soledad Prison, he brought up the subject of kidnapping for ransom.

As Headley's affidavit stated, "Discussions were held between Patricia Campbell Hearst and the Symbionese Liberation Army concerning a kidnapping."

DeFreeze knew that Hearst, the black sheep of her patrician family, did not have a warm relationship with her younger sisters, Vicki and Anne, and he suggested that they be kidnapped and brought to a remote Colorado location, after which Randolph Hearst would pay a significant amount for their safe release.

Patty forcefully rejected this idea immediately. When DeFreeze made a counteroffer to pretend to kidnap her and keep her hidden until a ransom was paid, Hearst suddenly realized that her exciting, secretive, political prisoner love affair was out of control. Her trips to Soledad Prison, posing as Mary Alice Siems, ended abruptly.

DeFreeze mentioned to Braswell, his most trusted Soledad confidant, his intention to get even with Hearst for her rejection. Their sexual relationship and her financial support of a group she had yet to see in action were replaced by DeFreeze's rage.

DeFreeze entrusted Braswell with his initial plan to gain revenge. "Don said he wanted to hit Hearst, for the recognition that would be involved," Braswell informed Rhodes. "He said he wanted to see her beaten and broken to the lowest thing on earth, lower than even himself."

As second in command to the head of the Soledad gang known as the Symbionese Liberation Army, Braswell was ready to try and break out alongside General Field Marshal Cinque. But he soon learned that the plan involved more people than just the two of them. Furthermore, the plot was created by someone other than the leader of the SLA, and its true purpose involved much more than mere revenge against Patricia Campbell Hearst.

6 · THE ILLUSION OF FREEDOM

DAMYON TOMITA FIRST MET DONALD DeFreeze when they were both incarcerated on the same tier at Vacaville. In the testimonial he provided Rusty Rhodes, Tomita claimed they were close friends, and yet, at the same time, Tomita suspected there was much DeFreeze was not telling him.

They were in different wings of Soledad Prison, but after the California winter warmed into the spring of 1973, Tomita and DeFreeze regularly met in the prison yard and talked. Tomita was by no means naïve about prison life. He was twenty-three at the time and had been in San Quentin, Vacaville, and Folsom Prisons prior to Soledad. His life behind bars, again significantly different from the current American penal system, began at the age of sixteen.

When DeFreeze offered a vague reference to getting away from Soledad, Tomita knew that convicts often made bold assertions and angry threats.

"Before leaving Soledad," Tomita noted, "DeFreeze told me he was going to leave soon, but because of our close relationship, he told me that very soon he would send friends who would 'help' me. . . . He told me he had a lot of friends 'outside' and in the prison authorities [*sic*]."

What appeared to be braggadocio on the part of DeFreeze was actually feeding Tomita information on an operational, need-to-know basis. It was Fred Braswell, who used the unintentionally amusing *nom de guerre* General Khan, who understood fully, or so he thought, the plans of Cinque.

"We discussed the [SLA's] complete plan of action early in 1973," wrote Braswell in an affidavit. "It was obvious Don was going to split Soledad, that he had a lot of help. He would set up 'safe houses' in Berkeley, and once that was done, I would get word and lead the 'second wave' out. There were eight of us who would escape and make our way to San Francisco, and we'd all meet Don at a flophouse next to the Greyhound bus station.

"Don and his group would snatch Patty. The second wave, my command, would grab the two younger Hearst girls. Both commands would then set up in the area, but I'd go to Colorado and find a place. I used to live in Colorado and would get a place outside Denver. I would notify the command units in two or three weeks, and they would hit the road with the three Hearst girls. This was the plan I expected to follow until I happened upon some new information."

Colorado, as it turned out, was confirmed as a potential site for hiding the Hearst girls for this theoretical group kidnapping. In a March 1975 *Newsweek* article, while Patty Hearst was on the run, there was a story about the arrest of her younger sister Anne and two companions in Niagara Falls, New York, crossing into Canada, for possession of amphetamine.

The article also claimed that law enforcement sources in Colorado told *Newsweek* that there were unconfirmed reports that Patty might have stayed in a lesbian commune in the tiny town of Nederland, a place bisexual SLA member Patricia Soltysik had previously visited. But what was most significant about the article was the parenthetical mention of another SLA-Colorado connection. In the previous month, San Francisco FBI agents had arrested former Vacaville BCA head Cecil Robert Moody in connection with a series of holdups.

Moody, who was elected to run the BCA when DeFreeze's candidacy was invalidated, served his time and was released from Vacaville one month before Patty was kidnapped. He lived up until January of 1975 in Colorado and was a frequent visitor to Nederland. Even more intriguing, the three girls who shared Moody's Denver apartment were interviewed by law enforcement and all insisted that Moody bragged he was a member of the SLA and that the newspapers "aren't telling the truth about Patty Hearst."

So SLA soldiers Braswell and Tomita, while having different levels of understanding, were left with the impression that DeFreeze was going to secretly break out of prison, set up the SLA on the outside, and help other prisoners to escape and join him.

The most specific testimony about DeFreeze being allowed to escape Soledad came from Fred Braswell. He made the discovery by accident. "I caught DeFreeze and Lieutenant James Nelson talking in the custody room, one day," Braswell wrote, "and that's when I was sure the CDC knew of our plans. They were discussing the SLA when Nelson saw me and ordered me into the recreation yard. DeFreeze told Nelson, 'No, let him stay. He knows everything. He's the second man.' So then, Nelson looked at me and told me I was going to escape. I didn't trust Nelson. I quietly started warning some of my people that the Department of Corrections knew our plans."

Braswell, unlike DeFreeze, feared the expendability of a prisoner who worked clandestinely with the prison. He refused to cooperate, assuming that once they had done their duty, black SLA soldiers on the outside would be hunted down and killed, rather than rearrested and allowed the chance to publicize their incriminating knowledge.

Robert Hyde confirmed that Soledad Associate Superintendent Paul J. Morris was involved with the secret operation. Hyde also named another SLA soldier, prisoner Daniel Reyes, as the person who later risked his life to share with Rusty Rhodes and Bill Nestel a "death list" of prisoners who had been killed, injured, or were targeted for attack in the California prison system.

Hyde's affidavit painted a horrifying picture of corruption in the prisons. It included CDC use of inmate drug dealers for everything from marijuana to heroin. There were also threats to prisoners who did not deal for the CDC or cooperate on other illicit actions. These punishments included isolation for months at a time or even CDC promises to have a rival gang member, in the parlance of the era, "book" or assassinate prisoners.

Early 1973 at Soledad grew stranger by the week. In addition to Braswell's discovery of the plot discussed by DeFreeze and Nelson, Hyde recalled DeFreeze twice referred to the new gang as the "Lebanese Liberation Army," suggesting that DeFreeze was incredibly high or that he did not remember the name of the organization he was told he was going to lead.

Adding to the mayhem was the arrival at Soledad of Timothy Leary, ex-Harvard professor, philosopher, LSD guru, short-term compatriot of Eldridge Cleaver of the Black Panthers, and jail escapee, who was initially arrested for less than half an ounce of marijuana. He became chairman for PROBE, communicating with Hyde while trying to find a way to lessen his decades-long prison sentence as, according to Richard Nixon, "the most dangerous man in America."

LAKE HEADLEY'S BOOK *Vegas P.I.* included his prison investigation into the behavior of DeFreeze and the foundation of the Symbionese Liberation Army. He learned that at Soledad, many prisoners who met DeFreeze had little to do with him because of his aloofness.

Headley spoke to a Soledad inmate who recounted he made an offer to help DeFreeze get a better work assignment. DeFreeze's reply was that in a few days, he was going to work in the boiler room of the South Facility.

This was peculiar. Those taken from Central Facility to South Facility tended to be trusted by the administration, because there were no guards or gun towers there. Prisoners did their work in South Facility and were escorted back to the mainline. DeFreeze was at Soledad less than three months and his contentious history with the Black Cultural Association at Vacaville did not make him an ideal candidate for an unsupervised job.

DeFreeze was asked by the same Soledad prisoner how he managed to get such an assignment when other convicts who had been at Soledad much longer had been turned down for it. He answered by merely giving a wide, enigmatic smile.

True to his prediction, Donald DeFreeze was given the midnight to 8 a.m. shift at the boiler room in South Facility on March 5, 1973. The area was going to be reconstructed as a training area for correctional officers. Headley reported that a number of prisoners claimed that the South Facility was used at the time as a holding area for informers. Fred Braswell said that prisoners understood South Facility was used by parolees.

After prison guard Jim Tucker accompanied DeFreeze, driving him in a pickup truck to South Facility, he left, returning the prisoner who had served the 4 p.m. to midnight shift. By the time Tucker returned, less than an hour later, DeFreeze was nowhere to be seen and could not be found.

According to *The Voices of Guns*, without encountering any other security, after scaling a six-foot tall fence outside the South Facility, DeFreeze walked until he received a ride from a Hispanic man who took him to his home in the nearby farming town of Gonzales. From there, DeFreeze hitchhiked to the Bay Area, was turned away from Venceremos contacts in Palo Alto, and eventually showed up unannounced at James Mayfield's home in Oakland. Mayfield, who replaced Colston Westbrook as outside guest coordinator for the BCA at Vacaville, was instrumental in hiding DeFreeze, initially.

A different version of DeFreeze's trip is found in *The Life and Death of the SLA* by Les Payne, Tim Findley, and Carolyn Craven. Their sources state DeFreeze called Mayfield from Gonzales and was picked up. In an April 13, 1976, interview with the FBI, Patty Hearst confirmed that Mayfield played a role in bringing DeFreeze to the Bay Area.

What should not be lost in the speculation about these logistics is the fact the few walkaways from Soledad Prison during the early 1970s were usually found within twenty-four hours. There was no pursuit of DeFreeze. Neither the CDC nor law enforcement of any kind made any contact with the white radicals DeFreeze knew from the Black Cultural Association in Vacaville, even though all their names were listed on visitation sheets and Westbrook knew many of them personally.

Due to the frequency that radical organizations were infiltrated, most leftist groups in the San Francisco Bay Area were highly concerned about undercover agents working for law enforcement. This explains why the first people DeFreeze approached in the Oakland-Berkeley area for safe haven refused him. Even if they believed DeFreeze was a true revolutionary, they might have suspected Mayfield or simply feared eventual discovery and prosecution.

The one place DeFreeze found refuge was at the Chabot Road home of Dave Gunnell, where other white members and associates of the SLA had lived. DeFreeze once described Gunnell as "kind of freaky," but he was in no position to be judgmental when he settled briefly in the North Berkeley commune. In one of the many absurdities connected with the SLA that existed outside of prison walls, Chris Thompson, a former Chabot Road resident, had sold Russ Little a .38 Rossi pistol for sixty-five dollars on March 3, two days before the DeFreeze exit from Soledad. This gun was later used in a high-profile murder, which necessitated Thompson explaining its origin to the FBI and a grand jury.

But for the moment, Thompson, a handsome black man who dressed nattily and liked wearing straw hats from Mozambique, was told by Little that he needed "a place that's cool for a friend."

"That's all he needed to say," Thompson, the former East Coast Black Panther, told Marilyn Baker in *Exclusive*. "I knew what it meant: an escaped convict. I sent the guy to Mizmoon. Funny, I did it because she wasn't a leader of anything. She wasn't even well enough known in the radical movement to be suspected of hiding an escaped con." Thompson led DeFreeze to the safety of Patricia Soltysik.

Soltysik's previous involvement with Camilla Hall was undone by Hall's need for exclusivity. Soltysik broke up with Chris Thompson, whom she found lacking in sensitivity. But beginning with her prison visits, she grew close instantly with the man who called himself Cinque.

DeFreeze lived with Soltysik in a quaint little yellow cottage she rented, recessed from view at 2135 Parker Street in Berkeley. It was the most idyllic two months of DeFreeze's life. It was the first time he was out of prison in over three years. Soltysik worked during the day as a janitor at a Berkeley library, trying to organize the workers into a union. DeFreeze, as far as she knew, was studying radical literature, cooking dinner, and cleaning the house—a domestic escaped convict.

Soltysik's neighborhood, just blocks from the bustle of Telegraph Avenue, was a slice of counterculture heaven and not far from where she met Hall on Channing Way. Marijuana was grown and smoked openly and local cops avoided the area, as previous arrests had drawn angry crowds. A giant, red papier-mâché fist had adorned the front of a building, the Red Fist Commune, until recently. A crowded community bulletin board alerted passersby to demonstrations, classes, and aid to the needy. Boxes of free books, records, and useful household possessions sat near the bulletin board. Soltysik and DeFreeze lived across from an old Victorian-style home that had a coffeehouse in the back, where community meetings and political organizing took place.

Fred Soltysik, the brother of Patricia, made some pointed observations about DeFreeze in the book *In Search of a Sister*. Fred's initial, generally positive impression of DeFreeze came in the spring of 1973 when he arrived at Parker Street for dinner. Fred's description of the man introduced to him as Cinque is testament to how cleverly DeFreeze used quiet sincerity and the occasional lie about his past to ingratiate himself with others.

At one point in the evening, Fred learned that DeFreeze had lived in New Jersey. Fred asked what he did there for a living.

In an effort to show a compassionate side that would impress both Soltysiks, DeFreeze created a complete fabrication. "I used to take four-year-olds to museums." There was nothing mentioned about his wife and six children, none of whom were contacted by him during this newly arranged freedom.

Because he was reliant upon Patricia Soltysik to hide him from authorities, DeFreeze also constructed a phony past for her as well. Fred Soltysik wrote how enamored his sister, now legally renamed Mizmoon, was of Cinque. "Confident without sounding brash, he awed Mizmoon with his apparent realm of experience. Mizmoon relished the fact that Cin had once been a pimp back east, that he'd seen firsthand the exploitation of women, which so upset her."

The closest DeFreeze had been to acting the role of a pimp was the incident during which he robbed and raped at gunpoint the prostitute Gloria Sanders in a South Central motel, before he fell asleep and was eventually arrested.

Fred Soltysik noticed that during the course of the evening on Parker Street, his sister's new boyfriend became comfortable enough to express his political viewpoint, using the term "corporate state" numerous times. But the language that governed many 1970s radicals, slang like "pigs" and "fascists," words also used in official SLA communications, was not used. It was as if DeFreeze played a role, not quite General Field Marshal Cinque, testing the boundaries of his acceptability to Fred Soltysik.

Months after the dinner on Parker Street, Fred Soltysik argued with his sister vehemently, after he noticed she was drafting a document called "Declaration of Revolutionary War."

"You are white, middle class, writing for poor people," he admonished her. "It's not going to be a lasting, enduring change. Enduring changes historically come from the people themselves."

As a schoolteacher, Fred Soltysik was very attuned to how people spoke, and he made a critical analysis of DeFreeze's less-than-commanding oratory. "He spoke slowly, reaching for polysyllabic words and accenting the syllables so evenly that I sensed his particular unfamiliarity with the vocabulary."

David Inua, one of the BCA founders who knew DeFreeze at Vacaville, challenged the notion that DeFreeze was a born leader who independently crafted his own political ideology. "Cinque is not a bright man. He has no ability as a teacher or a leader. Those were not his phrases on the SLA tapes. That's not the way he talks."

Even with his training to be a radical leader by Colston Westbrook, at the Black Cultural Association and Unisight, DeFreeze still did not fully inhabit the role. But Soltysik was ready to follow him.

In April, DeFreeze moved from Parker Street to a hideout in East Oakland, and finally, in June, he and Soltysik shared a place on East 17th Street, in the Oakland ghetto where the Black Panthers, a group he was employed to subvert, began.

BACK AT SOLEDAD, the CDC's plan for the second wave of black SLA prisoners to operate on the outside was being prepared. Braswell received a document dated April 18, from the Unit II Classification Committee. It was titled "Custody Reduction to Minimum," also referred to as "Reclass Chrono." Braswell was assigned as grounds-keeper for the boiler area in South Facility, from September 1972 to August 1973. Officer C. T. Coker put into motion a lowering of his classification and wrote about Braswell, "I feel that the subject's prognosis for future adjustment if his custody was reduced would be very good premised upon his extreme stability and actions which I have come into contact with."

Unlike Robert Hyde, Fred Braswell did not dare write to any authorities about the prison gang known as the Symbionese Liberation Army. He warned his closest prison allies about the conversation he witnessed between DeFreeze and Nelson, to avoid being labeled as a snitch, and hoped he would be left alone to simply serve his time. He wasn't.

"After Don split," Braswell remembered, "I got my cue in June, when I was ordered to minimum security at 'South' [Facility]. I refused this offer because I knew we would all die. Several weeks later, I was in the recreation yard and a guard motioned for me to walk towards him. He was standing next to the gate and I started walking towards him. The guard opened the gate and walked away. I then turned around and walked back to the recreation yard."

Because Braswell refused to be involved in the undercover, counterrevolutionary, black prisoner SLA, the California Department of Corrections moved to the next candidate, Damyon Tomita.

Like Thero Wheeler, whose peptic ulcer went untreated, Tomita suffered from medical neglect. For a year, Tomita was in chronic pain from a prostate infection that he could not get medically treated at Soledad. With no money and unable to endure the agony, Tomita arranged credit to buy marijuana in his cellblock, beginning in July 1972.

A year later, James Nelson called Tomita into his office, well aware of the money Tomita owed for the marijuana he smoked, more for pain control than pleasure. He forced Tomita to agree to sell marijuana in the prison with the usual split, 30 percent to the convict and 70 percent to the prison.

"During this year, I was called into his office several more times," Tomita wrote, "and Nelson tried to pressure me to sell 'harder' drugs, such as heroin, cocaine, and morphine. . . . However, since I had been in prison eight years, and additionally because my brother had become a narcotics addict at a young age, I continually refused these requests."

Incurring the wrath of Nelson led to Tomita's name being put on an "execution list," as he termed it. Fearing he would be "set up" in a false confrontation that would lead to either a guard or a cooperative prisoner killing him, Tomita procured a homemade knife for his protection.

"I lived under perpetual fear of danger until late August 1973, when I was approached by Nelson in my cell. To my astonishment, instead of threats or further pressure, he told me, 'Well, I have information that you are supposed to be leaving here soon.'"

Tomita indicated Nelson was no longer part of Special Services. He was head of the Prison Tactical Unit, otherwise referred to as the "goon squad." Nelson, a menacing presence in a number of

California prisons, with no limitations on his authority, caught Tomita off-guard with a surprising announcement.

"While I was still reacting to this first statement, he continued, 'Yes, DeFreeze tells me that you are supposed to be leaving soon.' DeFreeze had already 'escaped.' These statements stunned me for a moment and I asked him, 'What the hell is going on here?' But the lieutenant only replied, 'You'll be notified when you are supposed to leave. You are supposed to be a new recruit of DeFreeze's. Either accept this or suffer the consequences here.'"

Toward the end of the month, Tomita was approached by two guards, who informed him they were working with DeFreeze. Soon thereafter, one of the guards brought a dummy, which was placed as a decoy in Tomita's bunk. He was told to hide in a plumbing fixture in the prison yard, wait until dark, climb over the fence, and walk to the highway, where a car with two white men waited for him.

"They drove me to Berkeley, California," Tomita wrote, "where a room was waiting for me. I was told that I would be contacted soon and they left. The location of the room was a few blocks southwest of the university."

Tomita explained that his initial feeling of elation about being free of prison changed quickly to fear of what his future held. "However, with knowledge that DeFreeze had connections with the officials at the prison, I panicked and left the room twenty minutes later. I was picked up twenty minutes later and brought back to the 'hole' at Soledad."

The third man recruited for DeFreeze's team was Thero Wheeler. Despite his previous affiliation with Venceremos and his clearly Marxist philosophy, Wheeler was given a work assignment that, like Braswell, would allow him to flee without incident. At Vacaville, Wheeler's detail was to maintain a baseball field. On August 2, he "escaped," after which he and his girlfriend, Mary Alice Siems, Patty Hearst's lookalike friend from UC Berkeley who had been visiting Wheeler in prison, stayed together on the Bay Area peninsula.

As the only black prisoner the California Department of Corrections convinced to secretly work with DeFreeze, Wheeler proved to be a fascinating case. He deceived both the CDC and DeFreeze into thinking he was a loyal SLA soldier, when his motive was to get surgery on his ulcer and merge, undetected, back into society.

Wheeler knew that DeFreeze, like himself, had been allowed to escape. But Wheeler did not know what DeFreeze's orders were. The question of what Donald DeFreeze was tasked to do is a complex one, because the mission changed more than once, and DeFreeze inevitably began operating on his own. But his first assignment was one that no other revolutionary in the Bay Area would remotely consider.

While in preparation for that mission, DeFreeze lived in East Oakland with Nancy Ling Perry, who had quit her job at Fruity Rudy's, and Soltysik, who had left her job as janitor at the Berkeley public library. Without their income, more money for their survival became crucial. On September 30, 1973, Soltysik and Perry robbed Seifert's Floral Company on Piedmont Avenue in Oakland of between $400 and $600. Because they saw several onlookers writing down the license plate number of the van they used, it was abandoned. But DeFreeze had two lovers who were willing to be soldiers, even if he could not recruit others, *en masse.*

Tim Findley, who wrote often on the SLA for the *San Francisco Chronicle*, filed a story that quoted many Berkeley community activists who met DeFreeze after he had escaped from Soledad. Findley noted that a number of these radical organizers had their suspicions about DeFreeze and included a quote from one person who said DeFreeze "came on so heavy that he might be a provocateur." This section of the story was inexplicably deleted before it went to press.

The public television station in San Francisco, KQED, ran a news report after the kidnapping of Patty Hearst, stating that a few leftist groups in the Bay Area were approached by DeFreeze, shortly after he "escaped" from Soledad. DeFreeze startled them by offering his services as a "hit man" or contract killer. While late-night bombings of presumably unoccupied buildings which represented oppression had occurred with regularity years before, via the Weather Underground and others, the idea of a radical hit man seemed incomprehensible to the groups that were approached. The KQED report said these activists suspected DeFreeze of being a police agent.

The *San Francisco Chronicle* had even more detail about DeFreeze's outrageous offers to the radical left. It cited the fact that DeFreeze had reversed the process with some Bay Area activists. Instead of offering his services as a killer, he asked if any of the groups would agree to be paid for a contract killing. The target, as it turned out, was a man whose eventual murder at the hands of the SLA alienated them politically from left, right, and center and called into question not only the methods of the Symbionese Liberation Army but who, in fact, was running it and why.

7 · A Tragic, Self-Defeating Mission

Donald DeFreeze wouldn't have been manipulated into being the figurehead of the SLA if other black prisoners had been willing to play the role. But none were. Colston Westbrook knew no other member of the Black Cultural Association who had been a police agent. And other inmates would not risk their lives as the head of a false-front counterrevolutionary gang, in exchange for sexual privileges and a conditional freedom that could spell their doom.

But DeFreeze failed to assemble a significant movement under his leadership in the Bay Area. Westbrook and the CDC were very disappointed. With Hyde, Braswell, and Tomita unwilling to serve, the mission to kidnap Patty Hearst and her sisters could no longer be pursued. Thero Wheeler's arranged "escape" from Vacaville indicated that those in charge of DeFreeze's SLA did not believe DeFreeze could accomplish much on his own. Wheeler had many more radical contacts who might join the SLA and yield more information.

Concurrent with all this was the unraveling of the US presidency. On July 13, Alexander Butterfield, former appointments secretary to Richard Nixon, testified to the congressional Watergate hearings that since 1971, Nixon had a built-in system in his office for recording all phone calls and conversations. Ten days later, Nixon refused to turn over the recordings to either the special prosecutor or the Senate Watergate Committee, launching a yearlong constitutional crisis and legal battle.

Meanwhile, the conceptualizing and drafting of the structure and purpose of the Symbionese Liberation Army was being done. Bill Harris stated that Nancy Ling Perry, Patricia Soltysik, and DeFreeze together "developed the concept of the Symbionese Federation, autonomous combat units that would operate underground (Symbionese Liberation Army) and an above-ground, political support structure." Perry became known as the "chief theoretician" of the SLA, drafting much of the literature they disseminated based on her thoughts and those of the acknowledged leader, Cinque. It was Perry's handwriting on the documents that would soon be found at a safe house in an East Bay suburb.

Thero Wheeler once gave an interview from Harris County Jail in Houston to his hometown newspaper, the *San Francisco Chronicle*. It was the closest he ever came to stating the full story of how he and DeFreeze were coerced and used to subvert the left.

"I think he was being used by a lot of other people," Wheeler said of DeFreeze, "that felt certain things should be done but they didn't have the nerve to do, and because he was an escaped convict and was mad, you know, at the world and what was happening to him that they used him."

Wheeler walked a fine line. He expressed his disgust and yet he never fully stated what he knew about the SLA that operated inside the prisons. "I didn't know DeFreeze had anything to do with my escape until, you know, I saw him."

To protect himself, Wheeler vaguely referred to "well-connected" activists who he claimed helped him escape, but he never named them or their organizations. "When I got out, there was no SLA. Donald DeFreeze was in the Bay Area, trying to find members, trying to get them to join. But nobody was going for it."

Wheeler also used subtle language to express his sadness for what had been done to DeFreeze and how he was no longer the person he had been. "They were living out of books, man. They weren't living everyday existence. You can't readily equate what you read in books and reality. To the people out there, trying to survive takes priority over dreams. He [DeFreeze] wasn't in a real frame of mind. He didn't understand the people he said he wanted to help."

Mary Alice Siems, as a former member of Venceremos, which advocated the overthrow of the US government, was with Wheeler, romantically and ideologically. Neither of them believed a tiny vanguard movement bent on physical violence was the way to cause a revolution. But she supported Wheeler, who had no other choice but to pretend to be part of the SLA.

Siems claimed she and Wheeler visited with SLA members "about twenty times" between August and October of 1973. She said she was blindfolded, taken to a tiny apartment in Oakland where curtains darkened all of the windows, and DeFreeze lectured on the organization. It is highly doubtful that DeFreeze insisted on the blindfolding of the girlfriend of Wheeler, his second-in-command, at these sessions.

What does seem correct, based on others' observations of DeFreeze, was Siems's description of the leader of the SLA as an alcoholic who favored plum wine. The brand Akadama, imported from Japan, was his favorite. And he tolerated absolutely no criticism. Siems confirmed that Patricia Soltysik and Nancy Ling Perry were in attendance at these early meetings.

Eventually, Siems was represented by Charles Garry, renowned San Francisco radical lawyer who had handled cases for the Black Panther Party. Garry told the *San Francisco Examiner* two very unlikely facts, both of which served to protect Siems from prosecution. First, Garry declared that Siems did not know Soltysik and Perry were affiliated with the SLA. And even more irrational, Garry said Siems did not know Thero Wheeler had escaped from prison.

Garry was ready to protect Siems as accessory to an escaped convict. When he was asked if it were true that Siems met Wheeler after he escaped, Garry's calculatedly lackluster reply was a total evasion. "I presume so. I wouldn't let her go into any of those questions with the FBI."

Siems was not only terrified of the SLA, but also of any revelations about her sharing her ID with Patty Hearst. Siems, from her trust fund, gave Wheeler money to hand DeFreeze to keep the SLA afloat, usually three or four hundred dollars at a time. It was a way of buying time, keeping the dangerous DeFreeze from involving Wheeler in anything violent.

Wheeler left the Bay Area, hoping that he could get medical help and live somewhere with Siems out of the range of DeFreeze and his masters. Wheeler first traveled to New York to try and get help from "radical doctors." They provided him painkillers, but they were all afraid to operate on an escaped convict. After New York, he spent some days in August in a Chicago hotel room. Not only did he not find a helpful doctor, Wheeler was barely able to get out of bed due to the increasing pain of his ulcer.

Upon Wheeler's return to the Bay Area, the tension between him and DeFreeze seriously escalated, just after the drafting of the August 21 SLA document defining the "United Federated Forces."

Ed Montgomery, a journalist at the *San Francisco Examiner*, wrote an article about Wheeler on August 26, and incorrectly claimed Wheeler had broken out of Vacaville with the aid of connections in Venceremos. The group had by that time collapsed as a functioning organization.

Wheeler told *City* magazine in San Francisco that DeFreeze was enraged and drafted a furious letter to send to Montgomery and the *Examiner,* stating that Wheeler was under the protection of the SLA.

Wheeler strongly denounced the idea. "I told him if he sent it, I'd write another letter saying it was a lie. They weren't helping me. There was no way they could help me. The only way he could have done anything for me was if he was a surgeon."

DeFreeze resented Wheeler's reticence about being publicly affiliated with the SLA. Wheeler, for his part, was worried about being aligned with a group he thought was destined for a suicidal mission based on their militaristic rhetoric and attitudes. When he and

Siems met with the rest of the SLA, they all practiced karate and the use of weapons. DeFreeze, mesmerized by guns and explosives, impressed Wheeler only in this regard. "I never seen anyone who knew guns as well as he did. He'd be blindfolded and take them all apart and reassemble them in a minute."

Wheeler was stuck. He placated DeFreeze and claimed he would be part of a secondary support unit. It didn't help. In the mind of Donald DeFreeze, Wheeler's lack of cooperation endangered DeFreeze's status as police agent and, thus, his very life. And it was another betrayal, like Patty Hearst refusing to cooperate with his plans.

Some of Wheeler's quotes about DeFreeze's motivations went right up to the edge of full confession and then retreated. He either ended the thought or referred to anonymous radical participants. Wheeler, quoted in *The Voices of Guns,* stated categorically, "DeFreeze was being dictated to."

Wheeler also rejected DeFreeze as a planner and a theoretician. "Donald DeFreeze was locked up in jail, messed up like thousands of others that go in and out of there. He was bitter, he was uneducated, and he was trying to find a way out. It's easy, if you can find a person that's embittered, to convince him to do something."

Wheeler recalled that by the end of September, Willie Wolfe and Bill and Emily Harris had come by the Oakland apartment but were not yet official members. DeFreeze was about to expand the SLA, but Wheeler refused to help.

"He became awfully frustrated with me," Wheeler confessed, "because I wouldn't get the support for him that he wanted, that I had the potential to get. I wouldn't get people to deliver guns. I wouldn't get people to join the organization."

If he and Wheeler had been true revolutionaries at the time, free from the encumbrance of the CDC, DeFreeze would have dealt very simply with Wheeler's intransigence by dismissing him from the ranks of the SLA.

On October 23, Wheeler and Siems were confronted in their apartment by DeFreeze and Soltysik at gunpoint. DeFreeze said he was going to kill Wheeler, Siems, and her two-year-old baby from a previous lover.

"So they came by and asked me to clarify my position," Wheeler stated. "There was a .357 stuck at me by DeFreeze. He understood that I didn't give him the help that they felt they should have, as far as creating his unit."

Wheeler was told in no uncertain terms that he was to recruit actively. Media reports cite Siems being robbed by DeFreeze of either $300 or $600. Wheeler knew the source of DeFreeze's desperation. He could no longer sidestep DeFreeze's demands. Wheeler agreed on the spot to be in the combat unit and bring more of his circle into the SLA.

Wheeler reported that he left Siems and the apartment forever, right after the death threat. Siems disappeared from sight soon after with her baby. Wheeler went to Houston, with fake identification, using the name Bradley Bruce. He began to look for his father, John, whom he had never met, and tried to arrange the operation that he so desperately needed.

THE FIRST OPERATION of DeFreeze's SLA was not yet decided, even by early October. Police later discovered some undelivered communiqués, including "Communique No. 1," dated October 8. It was written to claim credit for an attack on Avis Rent-a-Car and the General Tire and Rubber Company. Both were accused of supporting "fascist governments" of Israel, Portugal, South Africa, Chile, and America's close ally, Great Britain.

An ominous and unexplained allusion to the criminal act the SLA was soon to commit was found in October. In the East Bay suburb of San Leandro, a pamphlet attributed to the American Nazi Party was handed out to passersby. Filled with anti-Semitic and anti-black hate speech, it read in part, "There might be shotgun blasts into the guts of mixmaster principals and superintendents."

It seemed to be a veiled threat against Marcus Foster, the first black superintendent of Oakland schools. But there was no confirmation by anyone affiliated with the American Nazi Party.

Meanwhile, during that same October, Sergeant Ronald Farwell of the Criminal Conspiracy Section of the Public Disorder Intelligence Division (PDID) of the LAPD became enmeshed in a plot to sway the result of the next Los Angeles mayoral election.

A PDID lieutenant, Justin Dyer, asked Farwell to investigate whether John Floyd, a black campaign aide for black mayoral challenger Tom Bradley, was a member of the Black Panthers. The white mayor of the city, Sam Yorty, was highly concerned about Bradley's popularity in the polls.

Farwell looked through the files at Parker Center and found that Floyd was once acquitted of the charge of loitering. There was also a reference to Floyd being a former member of the Black Panther political party. When Farwell relayed this information back to Dyer, Farwell didn't explain that the Panther political party was not connected to the militant Black Panther Party for Self-Defense in Oakland.

The next day, Farwell was shocked to read in his daily paper that in a press conference, Yorty cited Floyd's Panther connection as proof that City Councilman Tom Bradley was anti-police and supportive of black, racist militants.

Days later, during a local, televised debate, Yorty again brought up the same accusation. One of the questioners of the candidates pointed out that the aide was not affiliated with the Black Panthers created by Huey Newton.

Yorty mumbled, "Well, I don't know."

The manipulation of Farwell's research by the PDID did not harm Bradley, who became the next mayor of Los Angeles. But it did impact Farwell. It was discovered that Farwell's name appeared on a record sheet for signing out the documents regarding John Floyd. Farwell was ostracized by a number of black officers who had been his friends. For the rest of his career, they assumed Farwell

purposely attempted to destroy Tom Bradley's candidacy. As the
PDID began investigating nonviolent groups, such as the Southern
Christian Leadership Conference and Jesse Jackson's Operation
PUSH, Farwell began to lose respect for what his bosses were doing
and questioned why he became a police officer in the first place.

The ascendancy of Tom Bradley was tragically offset by a racially
motivated, high-profile murder that introduced the world to the
Symbionese Liberation Army.

On election night, November 6, 1973, Dr. Marcus Foster,
fifty, Oakland Unified School District Superintendent, and Robert
Blackburn, thirty-eight, his white deputy superintendent, left the
school district headquarters after another long day of work. The
two had grown very close. Foster, who worked for the Philadelphia
public school system with Blackburn, insisted he join Foster in
Oakland.

The SLA had secured an additional apartment at 1621 Seventh
Avenue in Oakland, a mere six-tenths of a mile from the school district building, as a staging area for their first mission.

It was 7:05 p.m. Blackburn walked slightly in front of Foster,
heading for his car. He noticed two figures huddled against the
building, thought it seemed odd but dismissed it, and then continued toward the rain-dampened parking lot.

He recalled the horrific moments that followed in emotional
fragments shared with the *Los Angeles Times*: "I heard what sounded
like firecrackers or cherry bombs. . . . I spun around . . . saw the
muzzle flashes . . . saw two figures firing at us. . . . I saw Marc go
down . . . I was hit simultaneously by a blast from a sawed-off shotgun . . . I started to go down, then for some silly reason I ran in the
direction of the shotgun . . . and was hit again."

Blackburn still held his keys in hand, despite two double barrels
being emptied into him. He unlocked the door of the Board of
Education building, staggered inside and collapsed. David Tom, a
printer who worked for the school system, heard the muffled shots
and ran up from the basement.

"Marc's been shot! Marc's been shot!" Blackburn, even in his own precarious state, was concerned about his boss.

Foster died before the ambulances arrived at Highland Hospital in Oakland. His body was delivered to the Alameda County Morgue. He was struck by eight pistol shots fired from a .38 and a .380 pistol with cyanide-tipped bullets, a brutal, quasi-military approach that surprised the police as much as the public.

Blackburn was rushed to Highland as well, where a team of young surgeons, led by Dr. Coyness Ennix, worked all night to keep Blackburn alive. His heart stopped three times. He lost his spleen. His kidneys, liver, and central nervous system were seriously damaged. Despite all this, Ennix and his team miraculously saved Blackburn's life. His shirt, which Blackburn retained, displayed twenty-four different entrance and exit perforations from shotgun pellets.

On November 7, 1973, Communiqué Number 1 appeared from the Symbionese Liberation Army and under that heading were the words "Western Regional Youth Unit." (The SLA did not have its core ten members at this point, let alone other units.)

The communiqué was read aloud, in a hushed, somber, incredulous voice, by news director Paul Fischer at Berkeley's KPFA-FM, shortly after it was found at 10:30 a.m. among other mail. The introduction to the killers of Marcus Foster was published, in its entirety, in the *San Francisco Chronicle* and the *Oakland Tribune*. The charges were threefold, including the use in Oakland schools of a "Political Police Force," compiling of "Bio-Dossiers through the Forced Youth Identification Program" and building of files for "the Internal Warfare Identification Computer System." In fact, by using initial capitalization, the SLA suggested there was a specific computer system for identifying students. Nothing of the kind existed. And the SLA accused the Peace Corps, for whom Blackburn once worked in East Africa, of being a CIA front.

As John Spencer's *In the Crossfire: Marcus Foster and the Troubled History of American School Reform* made clear, anyone who actually followed Oakland Unified School District activities and politics knew that Foster had taken bold steps to improve the status of non-white children, not deprive them of their privacy or other rights. Foster's discussion of security in the Oakland school district did not include weapons or police.

Foster's accomplishments were many. The Oakland Education Institute he started earlier in 1973 for excellent students and innovative teachers was one of the nation's first local education funds. During his watch, teams of parents, teachers, and students chose two-thirds of the district's ninety-one principals. The Master Plan Citizens Committee involved 2,400 people, black and white, working harmoniously together on educational issues. The central council was run by Foster, Blackburn, and a coterie of older black women.

The year before, there had been forty-two assaults on students and staff, and a female student was stabbed to death by an outsider at Oakland Technical High School. Foster responded right away with a $1 million plan for the integration of police, the juvenile court system, county probation, and parole departments, including "peace officers" and "safety coordinators" in selected schools, a truancy coordinator, and student ID card program. No one objected to it, either in the administration or in the community. It simply could not get sufficient funding. Two years before that, student ID cards were already approved for the school budget with no outcry from the public. According to Robert Blackburn, Foster eliminated that ID card program in order to save the district $17,000.

In October 1973, though, the California Council on Criminal Justice (CCCJ), about to provide $275,000 to the district, changed their previous agreement with Foster, saying in a revised draft of the new program that school security had to have a police background. Foster's staff checked the revised draft and missed the change.

Just before the October 9 school board meeting, Foster caught the oversight, very upset.

"He called me over and pointed it out," Blackburn remembered. "He said, 'Have you seen this? The most incredible thing!'"

The community objected strongly at the school board meeting, having seen public mention of the change in the agenda. Foster explained what had happened and assured a concerned audience at the meeting that he did not and would not endorse the CCCJ provision on security with police backgrounds in schools. He even agreed to back away from an ID card proposal.

The CCCJ was a conduit for the Law Enforcement Assistance Administration (LEAA). The SLA did not know much about the LEAA but were led to believe that the funder of state and local police department initiatives and programs, according to an interview with Russ Little, "was set up to provide funding for local police agencies with the intention of generating a nationally centralized police force." It wasn't at all true. But if Westbrook fed the rumor to DeFreeze, it would have been highly motivational for DeFreeze's militant and obedient cadre.

Robert Blackburn said that the October 9 meeting was not any more raucous or emotional than most. Interestingly, Willie Wolfe was sent to the meeting to report back to the SLA. Wolfe's interaction with the SLA after the school board meeting is a crucial moment in the group's history. If Wolfe had vociferously argued in front of the others that Foster was not pushing a police agenda for Oakland schools, it might have altered Foster's fate. But no one ever strongly questioned DeFreeze's mandates. And Wolfe was likely sent because he was the most malleable and least confrontational of all the SLA members.

If Wolfe privately told DeFreeze of Foster's firm resolve at the meeting, no mention of it was ever made among the other SLA members. Many in the SLA later spoke as if Foster was about to create a school system not unlike apartheid South Africa. But Wolfe was not one of them. When he was visited in Oakland by his father the month before the assassination, Willie made no mention of the SLA or politics. Willie, according to Dr. Wolfe, talked animatedly about Eva Olsson, a Swedish girl he planned to marry.

The crux of the matter was this: Foster was the first superintendent who had the respect of all parties, including the Black

Panthers. Elaine Brown of the Panthers offered to provide security in the schools for a fee. Foster politely demurred, saying added security would only create more problems.

The worst fear that Reagan, Younger, Procunier, and law enforcement had about Oakland was that a first-time black superintendent, in the hometown of the Black Panthers, was going to allow kids to become radicalized via the school system, increasing the militant influence of the Panthers and their white radical sympathizers.

Other outright lies in the SLA's Foster communiqué included the claim that Foster and Blackburn "represent the rich ruling class and big business and not the children and youth of our community." The two had been honored as innovators in the much more violent schools of Philadelphia. Foster was widely respected for bringing together everyone from archconservative *Oakland Tribune* publisher William Knowland, formerly a Red-baiting Republican senator during the Eisenhower administration, to parents of the 64 percent black Oakland students. Earlier in the year, both Foster and Blackburn had been given four-year contract extensions with pay raises, suggesting there was no strong opposition in any quarter to their continued work together.

The second page referred to the black prisoner reform movement. The prison systems were called "concentration camps," and special attention was given to Tehachapi Prison where youths as young as fifteen were incarcerated for an "indefinite" period of time. The dialectic of the SLA was all over the map, and yet no one in the media challenged its points or did fact checking.

The final full paragraph of the floridly written communiqué revealed a topic that connected to an accessible and raw issue, announcing that "the death of our manchild comrade youth, fourteen-year-old Tyrone Guyton, murdered on November 1st by three goons from the Emeryville Political Police Patrol is, NOT FORGOTTEN."

Tyrone Guyton, killed less than a week before Foster, was seen with friends attempting to break into a car on San Pablo Avenue in

WANTED BY THE FBI

BANK ROBBERY
INTERSTATE FLIGHT – POSSESSION OF HOMEMADE BOMB, ROBBERY, RECEIVING STOLEN PROPERTY, ASSAULT WITH FORCE
DONALD DAVID DE FREEZE

Photograph taken 1973   Date photographs taken unknown   FBI No. 606,723 D

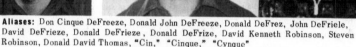

Aliases: Don Cinque DeFreeze, Donald John DeFreeze, Donald DeFrez, John DeFriele, David DeFrieze, Donald DeFrieze, Donald DeFrize, David Kenneth Robinson, Steven Robinson, Donald David Thomas, "Cin," "Cinque," "Cynque"

DESCRIPTION

Age: 30, born November 16, 1943, Cleveland, Ohio

Height:	5'9" to 5'11"	**Eyes:**	Brown
Weight:	150 to 160 pounds	**Complexion:**	Medium brown
Build:	Medium	**Race:**	Negro
Hair:	Black	**Nationality:**	American

Occupations: Autobody shop worker, carpenter, chef, painter, restaurant manager, service station attendant, stationary engineer, typist, key punch operator

Scars and Marks: Scar on bridge of nose, scars on forehead, face, left arm and wrist, right elbow and palm of right hand, appendectomy scar

Remarks: Reportedly drinks plum wine, may be wearing tinted glasses

Social Security Number Used: 042-34-4002

Fingerprint Classification: 9 S 1 R 1OI 12

                                    S 1 U 0OI

CRIMINAL RECORD

DeFreeze has been convicted of robbery, possession of homemade bomb, possession of stolen property, assault with force, and forgery.

CAUTION

DE FREEZE, AN ESCAPEE FROM A PENAL INSTITUTION, REPORTEDLY HAS HAD NUMEROUS FIREARMS IN HIS POSSESSION AND ALLEGEDLY HAS FIRED ON LAW ENFORCEMENT OFFICERS TO AVOID ARREST. DE FREEZE, WITH ACCOMPLICES, ALLEGEDLY ROBBED A BANK USING AUTOMATIC WEAPONS. TWO INDIVIDUALS WERE KNOWN TO HAVE BEEN SERIOUSLY WOUNDED DURING SHOOTING AT THE BANK. DE FREEZE SHOULD BE CONSIDERED ARMED AND EXTREMELY DANGEROUS.

A Federal warrant was issued on February 8, 1974, at Salinas, California, charging DeFreeze with unlawful interstate flight to avoid confinement after conviction for robbery, possession of homemade bomb, receiving stolen property, and assault with force (Title 18, U. S. Code, Section 1073). Also on April 16, 1974, a Federal warrant was issued at San Francisco, California, charging DeFreeze with bank robbery (Title 18, U. S. Code, Sections 2113(a), (d)).

IF YOU HAVE ANY INFORMATION CONCERNING THIS PERSON, PLEASE NOTIFY ME OR CONTACT YOUR LOCAL FBI OFFICE. TELEPHONE NUMBERS AND ADDRESSES OF ALL FBI OFFICES LISTED ON BACK.

C. m. Kelley

DIRECTOR
FEDERAL BUREAU OF INVESTIGATION
UNITED STATES DEPARTMENT OF JUSTICE
WASHINGTON, D. C. 20535
TELEPHONE, NATIONAL 8-7117

Entered NCIC
Wanted Flyer 473
April 17, 1974

Wanted poster of Donald DeFreeze, a.k.a., "Cinque"
FBI

Patty Hearst in handcuffs, inmate entrance of Criminal Courts Building,
Los Angeles, 1976
*Los Angeles Times Photographic Archive, UCLA Library, Copyright Regents
of the University of California, UCLA Library*

2135 Parker Street, Berkeley, where Donald DeFreeze lived with Patricia
Soltysik after he left Soledad Prison
David Newman

Donald DeFreeze and Patty Hearst during SLA robbery of Hibernia Bank, San Francisco, April 15, 1974
FBI

2603 Benvenue Avenue, Berkeley, where Patty Hearst lived with Steven Weed when she was kidnapped
David Newman

1827 Golden Gate Avenue, San Francisco, an SLA hideout walking distance from the FBI field office
David Newman

Mel's Sporting Goods, Inglewood, where Patty Hearst fired weapons to free Bill and Emily Harris after shoplifting incident
Los Angeles Times Photographic Archive, UCLA Library, Copyright Regents of the University of California, UCLA Library

California Governor Ronald Reagan (center) and Attorney General Evelle Younger (to his right)
Los Angeles Times Photographic Archive, UCLA Library, Copyright Regents of the University of California, UCLA Library

Ron Karenga, head of Black Nationalist group United Slaves, outside courtoom
Los Angeles Times Photographic Archive, Department of Special Collections, Charles E. Young Research Library, UCLA

Bill and Emily Hearst of the SLA, outside Hall of Justice jail, Los Angeles, 1976
Los Angeles Times Photographic Archive, Department of Special Collections, Charles E. Young Research Library, UCLA

Onlookers among remnants of 1466 E. 54th Street, South Central Los Angeles, the next day after LAPD shoot-out/fire involving SLA, May 18, 1974
John Hayes

Patty Hearst wearing a "Pardon Me" shirt with bodyguard and future husband Bernard Shaw after being pardoned by President Jimmy Carter, Hillsborough, CA

Los Angeles Times Photographic Archive, UCLA Library, Copyright Regents of the University of California, UCLA Library

Emeryville, about a mile from his home in West Oakland. Guyton, spotted by two undercover policemen, drove off and got into a high-speed chase. The policemen recklessly rammed the car Guyton stole into a house, immobilizing it a block from Guyton's own home. As the boy broke from the car and ran on foot, the two plainclothes officers were joined by an Emeryville officer and all three opened fire. One bullet knocked Guyton to the ground. Face down, he was shot in the back and killed. Officers claimed they thought he had a gun. None was found.

Because the policemen involved took the Fifth Amendment numerous times in court and were never punished, a furious, galvanized East Bay community organized to bring the officers to justice, though to no effect. Much like the white police–black citizen violence of 2014–2015, the Guyton case created conditions for more violent confrontation.

Nothing about the murder of Marcus Foster made sense. Blackburn summed up the incongruity of blaming Foster for any school police presence. "In Oakland, we'd had one student killing. But in Philadelphia, there are two or three dozen every year. He had managed schools far worse than any in Oakland and without police. He just didn't think it was effective. He didn't think it was a problem that could be attacked with paramilitary force."

The editors in *Ramparts* put into print what many radicals were privately saying to each other about the assassination, namely, "the act itself was so brutal, so morally unjustifiable, and so politically incomprehensible that most Bay Area radicals assumed the SLA to be a cover for some right-wing or police group."

While members of the SLA might have secretly objected to DeFreeze's order to kill Foster, the only one who spoke publicly about it was Russ Little. "I remember saying to DeFreeze, 'Why, why would you kill a black guy? Jesus Christ, man, it's like, there's black people being killed all over the place, man. You know, if you're going to kill somebody, why in the world would it be him?' And as far as DeFreeze was concerned, Foster was the front man for some horrendous police apparatus that was set up."

Little was right to suspect DeFreeze's motives but wrong to assume the plans originated with him. Despite its speculative nature, the assertion that DeFreeze was ordered to kill Marcus Foster is the only logical conclusion based on known facts.

Colston Westbrook had condemned Marcus Foster back when DeFreeze was attending the BCA in Vacaville. Westbrook even called him "a fascist," a completely nonsensical charge, ignoring the white racism Foster diplomatically battled within the school district.

As DeFreeze was given more of a role within the BCA by Westbrook, including delivering speeches to other inmates and visitors at the meetings, he mimicked the fiery and baseless rhetoric of Westbrook against Foster. Clifford Jefferson referred to Westbrook's verbal assaults on Foster as "murder-mouthing," whipping some inmates into an emotional frenzy.

The *Pacific News Service* reported "according to Bay Area journalists with connections on the left, and according to a group of activists who split from the SLA last fall, Foster had been marked for assassination by the SLA 'last summer.'" The mission to eliminate Foster was initiated well before any discussion about security in Oakland schools.

It must be remembered that Donald DeFreeze spent nearly three years in Vacaville, when the average stay before reassignment to a penitentiary was sixty to ninety days. As a prisoner, he was neither aggressive nor political, and yet he was administered Prolixin and then rewarded with the right to deal marijuana and with highly irregular sexual visitations with followers Hearst, Soltysik, and Perry. Colston Westbrook chose him, not because of any polished political rhetoric or commitment to ideology. DeFreeze was seduced to serve the state because he had already been a snitch for the LAPD, and in the dangerous world of prisons, that role is a rare one.

Donald DeFreeze was not a wild-eyed prison revolutionary, suddenly committed to killing Marcus Foster, a man he knew nothing about until he met Westbrook. As KQED and the *San Francisco Chronicle* reported, his first actions after an engineered escape were to offer his services as a hitman to radicals and then reverse course and try to enlist radicals to kill an unnamed target. Those he encountered instantly suspected him of being an agent provocateur.

The most fascinating psychological question is not whether DeFreeze was manipulated but at what point he knew he was expected to personally kill Foster. This moment came after his failure to enlist members of the radical left in the Bay Area. His vitriolic naming of Colston Westbrook as a CIA asset in the April 3, 1974, communiqué can only be explained as an act of furious, if ineffective retribution: DeFreeze's condemnation of his former friend, Westbrook, was that of an informant who felt betrayed and was likely threatened into a criminal act and then abandoned. It was the kind of scenario Robert Hyde, Fred Braswell, and Damyon Tomita all anticipated when they refused to be involved with the SLA outside of prison walls.

If the intent with the Foster–Blackburn attack was to prompt reprisals from white radicals and the Black Panther Party, there would few more emotionally potent times than six days after the murder of Tyrone Guyton and on election day. The execution of Foster was intended to create a politically charged war in the Bay Area, one that police and the FBI would be given free reign to violently quell, finally pacifying that tumultuous political landscape.

THOSE ON THE left who briefly aligned with the SLA rescinded their support after Foster's death. "Ex-Symbionese Send Letter to the People" was published in the February 22–28 *Berkeley Barb*. "We are ex-members of the Symbionese Federation. We resigned collectively from the Federation immediately after the assassination of Dr. Marcus Foster. . . . By resorting to abstract violence, the SLA not only separated itself from the rest of the revolutionary movement but became the example to avoid, the stereotype of the 'mad terrorist' so indispensable to our oppressors to put us down even more with new laws and restrictions."

Knowing the SLA was prone to violence, these former Federation members admitted they were in hiding to avoid reprisals. Echoing what other radicals said to KQED and the *San Francisco Chronicle* when DeFreeze was looking to hire or be a hit man, the letter went on to report the estrangement they felt when they first agreed to be involved with the SLA.

> Serious conflict developed over the subordination of the support units, as of all non-military activities of the organization, to the combat units: that is, the "Army" came to be seen as the chief agent of the revolution. We began to suspect that the War-Council was manipulated either by some local right-wing organization or the CIA itself. The secret decision to kill Marcus Foster, and its execution, confirmed our suspicions.

Oakland Mayor John Reading and other Republicans, as well as local writer Ishmael Reed and Democratic Congressman Ron Dellums, who later helped protect SLA prison organizer Robert Hyde, all came to the same conclusion: Foster was killed for daring to compete in white mainstream society. But despite general suspicions about the CIA, FBI, or unnamed right-wing organizations, no one investigated the origin of the SLA, Vacaville, and the BCA.

And the murder of Foster led to more tragedy—the conviction of two SLA members who did not fire any weapons.

New Times magazine interviewed Bill and Emily Harris and Russ Little and Joe Remiro in 1976 and cowriters Robert Scheer and Susan Lyne were told categorically that Little and Remiro did not fire upon Foster and Blackburn.

"I found out much later," admitted Bill Harris, "that Nancy (Ling Perry) and Mizmoon (Soltysik) and Cin (DeFreeze) were the ones who carried out the action."

Little went on the record, as a prisoner, stating, "Who actually pulled the trigger that killed Foster was Mizmoon. Nancy was supposed to shoot Blackburn. She kind of botched that and DeFreeze ended up shooting him with a shotgun."

Patty Hearst, at her trial, testified that she was told by the Harrises that Little and Remiro were in a backup car, in case they were needed. And yet, according to the rules of an army that never exceeded ten, Remiro and Little were sacrificed, soon to be jailed as murderers, rather than, at most, accessories.

Bill Harris denied they were at the scene, saying in an interview, "Hearst has testified that it was Mizmoon, Nancy, and Cin who shot Foster and Blackburn, which supports Russ and Joe's innocence. But then she lied and said that Russ and Joe were in a car outside as backup."

After the shooting of Foster and Blackburn, Willie Wolfe approached the Harrises, Little, Remiro, and Angela Atwood and asked them if they wanted to be a part of the SLA. They agreed and Perry drove them in a van to the safe house in Clayton in the East Bay, where DeFreeze and Soltysik awaited them. Asked if they wanted to be in an above-ground support unit or combat unit, they all chose the latter. The last time all ten of the original members were together was on New Year's Eve 1973, when Camilla Hall finally joined the group. They planned to have the Harrises, Atwood, Little, and Remiro move to the San Jose area, financially supported by a "people's garage," to be run by Remiro, a mechanic. It was another idea overruled by DeFreeze and it was one that might have saved the lives of six people.

NANCY LING PERRY, using the pseudonym Nancy Devoto, rented a three-bedroom house in Clayton, near the East Bay city of Concord. The $31,000 house was in the center of a cul-de-sac, at 1560 Sutherland Court. Neighbors who were questioned for the study on the SLA prepared by the Committee on Internal Security, House of Representatives, in February 1974, reported a strange event shortly after the attack on Foster and Blackburn.

On November 11, three months after the house was first rented, a boy of about sixteen knocked on the door, confronted Perry, and asked if her husband was home. When she replied in the negative, he pulled out a .22 pistol. Perry quickly reacted, shoving and kicking him. The boy fired one errant shot and fled. He was later apprehended. With a history of raping women at gunpoint, he had chosen a female revolutionary not afraid to kill.

Neighbors called the police, and Perry, not at all interested in having them inside to see SLA weapons, explosives, plans, propaganda, and research on terrorism, told them outside on the lawn what happened. There was a photo taken of Perry in front of Sutherland Court that became well known. Perry's dark hair was tousled and her defiant eyes furiously stared into the camera lens. But the SLA headquarters went undiscovered for the moment.

Russ Little looked back at the location on Sutherland Court as an error in judgment. "The SLA should never have had a safe house in Concord (Clayton), because we didn't fit into that middle-class suburban community."

The SLA was driven out of Sutherland Court due to circumstance and bad planning, in keeping with the lack of discipline often shown by the ragtag group.

On January 10, 1974, Russ Little and Joe Remiro drove around, looking for 1560 Sutherland Court, unfamiliar with that area. For some reason, they were without a map. Their orange-red Chevrolet van was highly conspicuous in the quiet suburban neighborhood. At 1:23 a.m., Officer Dave Duge, in his unmarked Dodge Polara, spotted Little at the wheel of the van, driving ten miles an hour. When Duge circled back and flashed his side-mounted spotlight and honked once, the van pulled over.

Duge was told by Little that he was looking for a friend named "Devoto" on Sutherland Court. Little handed the officer his driver's license, which had the pseudonym Robert James Scalise on it. Remiro also provided his license, which had his actual name. Duge learned that neither name was connected to outstanding warrants, but he had also radioed in the last name of Devoto, the false name Perry used. There was no directory listing for that name for either Sutherland Court or nearby Sutherland Drive.

Duge suspected the two tense men who did not seem relieved to get directions in the middle of the night. He asked Remiro to step out of the car, and when he did, Duge asked if he had any guns or knives on him. Not getting an answer, Duge told Remiro, "I'm going to frisk you."

Remiro took a step back. Duge testified he saw Remiro go for a gun on his right hip. Remiro testified that Duge moved quickly behind him and that Remiro thought the officer was going for his own gun.

Remiro leaped in front of the van, firing two quick shots.

Duge took refuge behind his own car. "I drew my pistol and returned fire, two shots," Duge later stated. "I fired at the muzzle blast. It's very similar to flashbulbs going off in your face." Duge moved to the left rear. Again, Remiro fired twice and Duge returned fire twice. Little was still in the van.

Remiro squeezed off one more shot as he ran off down the street in fear and Little squealed away in the van. Duge called in the incident. Two cars responded immediately. The van had to make a U-turn and came straight at them. The officers blocked the street, pulled out shotguns, and demanded Little's surrender. One of Duge's shots had penetrated the van, gone through Little's right shoulder and out the windshield. Little surrendered, his wound bleeding profusely.

The .38 used in the Foster killing was recovered, along with a nine-millimeter rifle and a paper bag filled with SLA leaflets, printed in brown ink on a yellow background. They had been reproduced at a Gemco department store. The paper bag was emblazoned with the name of the store and the words "America's Finest."

Officers began a manhunt for Remiro. He was caught between two houses on Sutherland Drive at 5:31 a.m. and surrendered. He had the Walther PP .380 on him, used in the shooting of Foster. Neither man had bothered to get rid of the murder weapons.

Either Joe Remiro wandered around for four hours, trying to find the Sutherland Court safe house, literally about a block away, or he did in fact find it and reported to DeFreeze and others what had happened. Rather than giving up their location or all of them surrendering, DeFreeze probably sent Remiro back out, as a good soldier, to surrender. The police never bothered to track down the so-called Devoto residence and neither Little nor Remiro gave up their cohorts.

Frantically, the SLA prepared to leave Clayton. Bill and Emily Harris were notified and did not report for their jobs that morning, going underground.

At 6:15 p.m., a white 1967 Oldsmobile belonging to Willie Wolfe, who was visiting his father in Pennsylvania, backed out of the driveway of 1560 Sutherland Court. A six-inch fuse burned, between the attached garage and house. Perry had scattered gun powder and splashed gasoline from a five gallon can on the floors and walls. At 6:21 p.m., the Concord fire department was called by neighbors who saw billowing black smoke emanating from the residence. The windows were closed, and due to the lack of oxygen, the fire did not consume the house. It was put out by one hose from the first fire truck to arrive.

Perry later explained that the attempt to burn down the house was an effort to "melt fingerprints" tied to the SLA. Instead, the Concord Fire Department preserved a huge cache of evidence, including the plan for the Foster killing, boxes of bullets, cyanide, maps, bombs, (including six Molotov cocktails made from DeFreeze's Akadama plum wine bottles) and over a hundred clippings from newspapers and magazines of the exploits of revolutionaries around the world.

Perry, in her introductory letter to media outlets on behalf of the SLA, explained their historical perspective. She tapped into the despair many felt after the assassination of President John F.

Kennedy, claiming it had been a military coup "that blatantly destroyed the constitution that some of us still believed in." As with future communiqués, Perry cited shameful American historical events, but rather than suggesting specific remedies, the SLA abandoned the idea of working within the system for any kind of significant change.

The local police did not cordon off the house immediately. As a result, when KQED's Marilyn Baker arrived at Sutherland Court, she and other curious onlookers helped themselves to SLA souvenirs. "As kids and neighbors paraded by, clutching their Symbionese trophies, I kept pulling more papers from under the bed."

The walls sported slogans here and there, all signed "Cin," and on one particular bedroom door, a strange note by DeFreeze, which attempted to portray him as humane, simply came across as jumbled and unbalanced. Scorch marks obscured many of the words, but one could readily see that this verbiage was nothing like the SLA communiqués.

"I say myself," the slogan concluded, "in this room because it has become the only one that comes without being asked, because it understands that it is sexist that a man must ask before a woman will come to see or talk with him so if I don't ask, don't you either, just come on in and find out who lives in here and that he's 90% human, the other 10% we are working on. Cin."

The core of the SLA miraculously escaped. But among the evidence was a long list of targets for assassination or kidnapping. None were contacted by the police to warn them of their status. Most were older, white males connected to such entities as the Bank of America, Wells Fargo Bank, Standard Oil of California, Kaiser Industries, Del Monte Corporation, Safeway Stores, and others.

Three names on the target list, near the bottom, represented a past that still haunted DeFreeze:

"Raymond Procunier, fifty-one, director of the California Department of Corrections."

Below it was listed "Marcus Foster, schools superintendent of Oakland—executed."

And underneath Foster, the man whose death so many people did not understand, was written, "Patricia Campbell Hearst, nineteen years old; daughter of Randolph and Catherine Hearst—arrest warrant issued."

8 ✦ PEOPLE IN NEED

THE MOST FAMOUS KIDNAPPING IN the history of the United States occurred during an extraordinarily chaotic time. Before 1973 ended, President Richard Nixon offered as evidence of his Watergate innocence a group of subpoenaed audio tapes, one of which had a gap of eighteen and a half minutes. Chief of Staff Alexander Haig claimed one possible explanation for the erasure was "some sinister force."

That might well have been sufficient to explain a series of murders in San Francisco, the Zebra Killings, which began in October 1973. Named for the "Z" radio band police used to communicate about the murders, the Zebra killings involved black suspects randomly killing whites. There was no pattern, and the murders occurred in various San Francisco neighborhoods. Most were shot with handguns, but an early female victim was hacked to pieces with a machete.

In this atmosphere of terror, Donald DeFreeze's SLA was alienated from any support on the left. Willie Wolfe, confused by the Foster-Blackburn action, was still at his father's home in Pennsylvania, again talking about marriage to Eva Olsson. Little and Remiro, before their arrests, both tried to reach Willie on the phone, and Little finally did, urging him to return to the Bay Area.

Wolfe did not immediately do so. Whether he was sincere about getting married or not, Wolfe was going through a psychological crisis about his participation in the SLA.

But on January 10, Wolfe received a long distance phone call at his father's house from Bill Harris, informing him of the arrest of Little and Remiro for the alleged killing of Foster. Willie evasively told Dr. Wolfe that he had a sick friend on the West Coast and had to leave immediately. Willie canceled a visit with his father on January 11 and got his sister Roxie to drive him to a bus station. He gave her his most prized possession, a duffel bag that had previously belonged to his father. Neither his father, his sister, nor anyone else in his family ever saw him again. The last contact Willie had with his family was the Valentine he sent to his mother.

If Little and Remiro had not been arrested, Wolfe might have left the SLA and lived a full life. While none of the white members of the SLA defied the dictates of their black convict leader, Wolfe, unlike his fellow white revolutionaries in the group, knew Foster was not the enemy he was portrayed to be. The trip to see his father served as time to get some distance from and perspective on his SLA involvement.

Wolfe had lived with Joe Remiro in a small cottage on Bond Street in Oakland. He knew Remiro and Little were innocent of the Foster killing, and he had to grapple with the strong possibility that they were going to be in prison for life.

But while Wolfe returned to California out of loyalty to his compatriots, what he didn't realize was the SLA was about to execute its second mission, one that would bring it notoriety around the world. It would allow the state of California and the federal government to not only further demonize the SLA but also link its activities, without proof, to other leftist groups.

Donald DeFreeze's plan to kidnap Patty Hearst was not only logistically easier than the taking of three Hearst sisters, as the prison SLA had planned, it also was different in two very significant ways: there was no traditional financial ransom, and DeFreeze had actually become a revolutionary, answerable to no one.

The repulsion felt by the left in the Bay Area regarding the Foster assassination was so deep and so strong that it was still being expressed days before the Hearst kidnapping. The *Berkeley Barb*, a major voice in underground politics, asked if the murder was perpetrated by a "CIA dirty tricks team . . . or is the SLA a bunch of sincere people long on revolutionary theory but short on tactics and common sense."

The unanimity of loathing that came from killing Foster alienated DeFreeze from Colston Westbrook and the California Department of Corrections and led DeFreeze to a crystalline realization: he would rather die alongside those white radicals who totally believed in him than serve one more minute as police agent, infiltrator, spy, snitch.

The DeFreeze that worked for Lt. Nelson of the CDC and Westbrook wanted a money ransom for Hearst and her sisters. The DeFreeze that now truly believed he was General Field Marshal Cinque wanted revenge for Hearst's rejection of him, but he also desired to seriously effect social change. And after Hearst was kidnapped, he made a demand unparalleled in the history of US criminology, one that dramatically and astonishingly altered the revulsion many people felt for SLA tactics.

STEVEN WEED, PATTY Hearst's fiancé, had radicals as friends when he attended Princeton University. But he and Hearst led a very quiet domestic life in Berkeley when they began living together at 2603 Benvenue in the fall of 1972. Weed left the Crystal Springs School for Girls, where their relationship had started, and he pursued work as a graduate student in philosophy and as a teaching assistant.

Patty Hearst had always been as rebellious as she was intelligent. She was thrown out of the private Santa Catalina Boarding School in Monterey for smoking marijuana. Her mother wanted her to go to a Catholic school, but Randolph Hearst sent his precocious daughter to Crystal Springs, about a mile up the hill from them in Hillsborough.

She was a sophomore art history major at Berkeley, and despite her secretive life visiting the prisons, Hearst planned to wed Weed on June 29, the last Saturday of the month. The wild side of her life was receding. She was even getting along better with her mother.

On February 4, just before 9 p.m., Peter Benenson, a mathematician who worked at the Lawrence Radiation Lab, unloaded bags of groceries from his blue 1963 Chevrolet convertible at 1304 Josephine Street, a mile and a half from the Benvenue address of Patricia Hearst and Steven Weed.

Suddenly, Benenson was mashed against the car, food flying across the sidewalk. DeFreeze, Bill Harris, and Soltysik, armed and menacing, tied his hands and shoved him onto the floor, behind the front seats. They threatened to shoot him if he did not stay out of sight. The three SLA members jumped in and stole the car.

At 9:10, Benenson's car was outside Benvenue, joined by a white Chevrolet station wagon, with Nancy Ling Perry behind the wheel, backed up by a third car, a blue Volkswagen Beetle owned by Camilla Hall. Soltysik led DeFreeze and Harris into the patio of the brown-shingled townhouse and knocked on the glass sliding door that was the main entrance.

Inside, Hearst and Weed had finished watching *Mission: Impossible* and *The Magician* on television. The latter starred Bill Bixby as an illusionist and escape artist who helped people in trouble. Wearing nothing but white nylon panties and a powder blue I. Magnin designer robe, Hearst quizzically looked at Weed when they both heard a knock. As Weed cautiously slid open the door, Soltysik mumbled words to the effect that she had just had an accident and needed to use their phone.

Without waiting for a reply, DeFreeze and Harris burst in behind her. Hearst was smacked in the face with a rifle butt. Weed was slammed to the floor. A wine bottle was smashed into the back of his head, rendering him nearly unconscious. Weed was told to stay face down or die. Bleeding, his face buried in the carpet, he heard Hearst shout, "No, please. *Not me*. Let me go!" Her robe flew open as she continued to struggle.

Weed heard Soltysik say, "He's seen us. We have to kill him," followed by the distinct clicking of a gun. Weed screamed as loud as he could and knocked over furniture as he bolted out the back door, leaping three fences and getting a half block away before he realized he was not being pursued.

Hearing the shouting and fisticuffs, the next door neighbor, Steven Suenaga, twenty-two, bravely tried to intercede but was pummeled to the ground by the men.

Hearst, barely conscious, was dragged down the stairs of the building and hurled into the trunk of Benenson's convertible. The three-car convoy tore out, stopping on a quiet street, Tanglewood Drive, half a mile away. There, among the elegant homes, Hearst was transferred to the white station wagon, Benenson was ordered to stay on the floor of his car, the SLA fled into the night, and America's first political kidnapping was complete.

Indicating a lack of direction, the SLA did not get the communiqué concerning the kidnapping to KPFA in Berkeley until February 7. In it, the group confirmed it had captured Hearst and would kill her if anyone tried to rescue her. In a move atypical of most kidnapping cases, no ransom demand was made in this initial contact.

If the previous communication told too little, the one on February 13 told too much. KPFA received the exceedingly long, at times well-intentioned but meandering sixteen goals of the Symbionese Liberation Army. The last mandate, bold but a little too all-encompassing, was "to destroy all forms and institutions of Racism, Sexism, Ageism, Capitalism, Fascism, Individualism, Possessiveness, Competitiveness and all other forms of such institutions."

The leaflet that accompanied the goals was an illustration of the seven-headed cobra and the seven qualities Colston Westbrook lifted from Ron Karenga's creation of Kwanzaa. The leaflet was written in English, Spanish, Chinese, and Swahili.

DeFreeze spoke on audio for the first time, introducing himself as Cinque and condemning repressive regimes like South Africa,

Mozambique, Angola, Rhodesia (Zimbabwe), and the Philippines. He attacked the corporate holdings of Randolph Hearst and promised to take over all buildings so that no one would pay rent, and yet, in all of this, his voice seemed distant, not passionate. DeFreeze referred more than once to his revolutionary band as the Court of the People. He alluded to Randolph Hearst providing seventy dollars' worth of free food over the following four weeks to poor Californians on certain forms of welfare, as a good faith gesture.

An indication of DeFreeze's conflicted state of mind came with a personal aside. "In closing and speaking personally for myself and as a father of two children . . . I am quite willing to lose both of my children, if by that action I could save thousands of white, black, yellow, and red children from a life of suffering, exploitation, and murder."

DeFreeze often made reference in communiqués to the idea of saving the children and protecting their futures, yet the previous quotation ignored Gloria DeFreeze's three children prior to being with DeFreeze. Also, by reducing the number of their three biological children to two, DeFreeze concluded that Gloria had one of their presumed children with another man.

Patty Hearst's February 13 voice recording, which was oddly placed within the last third of DeFreeze's message, revealed a slightly shaky speaker, as she did her best to dissuade any rescue attempts and to reassure her parents she was being well treated and making the statement of her own volition.

Kidnap victims, by definition, do not make statements of their own free will, and as for her treatment, the SLA was keeping Hearst blindfolded in a dark closet at 37 Northridge Drive, Daly City, two towns south of San Francisco.

Donald DeFreeze knew how drugs, isolation, and psychological coercion in a prison could wear down the resolve of a human being. And Hearst's first attorney, Terence Hallinan, suggested that both drugs and isolation changed her to the point that she was no longer responsible for her coerced actions. "She was placed in a closet on the floor. The closet was approximately five to six feet in length and about two and a half or three feet in width. During all this time, she was in a constant state of fear and terror and expected at any moment to be murdered by her captors. After an interminable length of time, which seemed to her to be weeks, she was released from the closet and seated with the gang of captors. When the blindfold was removed, she felt as if she were on an LSD trip. Everything appeared so distorted and terrible that she believed and feared that she was losing her sanity."

According to the FBI's HEARNAP files on the SLA, their audio analysts believed, based on Hearst's voice on the first tape, that she may have been "drugged."

Adding to the surreal maelstrom of activities was the misidentification in Bay Area newspapers of Thero Wheeler as the second male kidnapper, rather than Bill Harris. Wheeler, on a bus in Houston, saw his own face along with DeFreeze's on the front page of a *Houston Chronicle*, held by a man who had just sat down next to him.

"What do you think of this stuff?" asked the man, not recognizing Wheeler.

"It's crazy, man," replied Wheeler. "Those people are crazy."

The SLA that kidnapped and converted Patty Hearst was so beyond the realm of experience for Americans that it overwhelmed the news for eighteen months, dominating TV newscasts, newspaper and magazine headlines, and cutting into the coverage of other major news stories. In February 1974, the last troops were leaving a disastrous war in Vietnam that had killed over 58,000 Americans and more than 3.2 million Southeast Asians. An oil embargo resulted in huge lines of cars at gas stations across the country. And Richard Nixon's fight for survival as president looked more and more like a slow-motion defeat.

TV viewers became accustomed to seeing partial external shots of the twenty-two-room Hearst residence on Santa Ynez Avenue in Hillsborough, an upscale, solely residential community that relied on the next town, Burlingame, for its shopping district. Randolph

Hearst delivered press conferences at a cluster of microphones in front of his black, lacquered front door, framed by Greek columns and topiaries in marble pots. Radio, TV, magazine, and newspaper reporters lived in campers in front of the mansion. The local phone company rigged up lines for media outlets that could afford it. The lines literally dangled from the surrounding trees. It was not unusual to hear someone shout, "Hey, *LA Times*, your tree is ringing."

The Hearst family, emotionally wrung out from their concerns for Patty, the constant media bombardment, and the unclear negotiating tactics of the SLA, turned to anyone they thought could help. Former mob boss Mickey Cohen, shortly after the kidnapping, was enlisted due to the respect he engendered in the black community. Cohen met with numerous contacts, both black and white, in a series of late-night meetings that involved switching cars often, but it came to nothing.

Special Agent Dan Groves of the FBI explained that the Bureau went to extraordinary efforts to find the SLA because beyond the kidnapping, the case was being treated as an act of terrorism. "The U-2 was flying sorties up over the High Sierra, looking at campsites and things like this during the initial search days. The [communiqué] tapes were sent to CIA headquarters to be listened to by blind people whose hearing is extremely acute."

The SLA kidnapping had a profound effect on the Nixon and Reagan administrations. Disinformation about the origins of the group and discussion about new, draconian laws to prevent similar actions occurred after Hearst was taken. But no such fervor existed when DeFreeze and the SLA killed Foster. DeFreeze, now operating without governmental guidance, set off a firestorm of state and national accusations.

As attorney general of the United States, William Saxbe spoke out less than a week after the kidnapping. "There are indications— but no hard evidence—that this group extends beyond the Bay Area. People familiar with this group warn that it could show up in Washington or elsewhere."

Saxbe, as the country's top law enforcement official, was ready to connect the SLA, without evidence, to the brutal Zebra slayings that haunted San Francisco. The *Los Angeles Times* reported, "Saxbe said Bay Area authorities—who will not say so for publication—believe the SLA may be responsible for eight or more apparently motiveless killings on the streets of San Francisco."

The SLA's activities created more sociopolitical polarization. The California state legislature actually debated for a time after the kidnapping whether wealthy and famous people should be afforded state-salaried bodyguards and "human shields" to protect them from radical groups.

The 1974 California Senate Subcommittee on Civil Disorder, hitting the media just in time for the Hearst kidnapping, jumped to the conclusion that the SLA was actively working with the Black Guerrilla Family, based solely on Nancy Ling Perry's early visits to black inmates affiliated with that prison group. Furthermore, the ghost of Venceremos was once again dredged up, with the pronouncement that the SLA was working with them as well. The Subcommittee did not seem to notice the 1972 dissolution of Venceremos after the arrest of a group of Venceremos leaders, including its founder, Bruce Franklin, already fired from his teaching position at Stanford University.

The 1974 report not only predicted a paradigmatic shift in the nature of kidnappings but also assumed a spate of similar actions by radical groups would follow. Legal actions, beyond existing kidnapping laws, were urged. "In light of the Patricia Hearst kidnapping and its attendant publicity, it is obvious that such incidents will increase. . . . The time for preventive measures against terrorism has arrived, and the Subcommittee will endeavor to assist in creating those measures, as well as being instrumental in their implementation, particularly should investigations deem legislation essential." There was even a recommendation in the sixty-three-page report for constant surveillance of radical groups and the use of a network of neighborhood "busybody" informants.

The Subcommittee, of course, was unaware of the prior history between DeFreeze and Hearst. Even so, they thought it "bizarre" that a group would choose feeding the poor, even for a few days, over the personal enrichment of ransom money. "Demands may take the form of wanted publicity for a cause, release of the group's members being held on other offenses, or may take the bizarre form of those recent SLA demands, requesting $70 worth of food to be distributed to every needy Californian over a one-month period."

The SLA's People in Need program, whether it was influenced by it or not, resembled the tactics of the Tupamaros rebels in Uruguay. The Tupamaros, a revolutionary group the SLA was definitely aware of, began political kidnappings in the early 1960s, distributing ransom money and stolen food to the poor in Montevideo. As the Tupamaros engaged in assassination in the early 1970s, their popular support dissolved.

There was nothing in American history to compare to the situation DeFreeze had conjured. Distribution centers for free food were first set up in Oakland, San Francisco, Richmond, and East Palo Alto. Inevitably, it expanded to twelve sites, including Southern California. The People in Need program not only put DeFreeze in control of the kidnapping narrative, but also played strongly in the media, garnered support among the underclass in America, and minimized the discussion of the murder of Marcus Foster and maiming of Robert Blackburn. Whether it was by luck or by calculation or both, DeFreeze's People in Need concept was an unpredictable and staggering reversal of fortune.

Randolph Hearst was told that if all four million poor Californians receiving welfare were given $70 in groceries just once, not the four times as requested, the bill would come to $28 million, upwards of $134.5 million in 2016 dollars. The SLA hatred of the corporate state made it hard for them to understand that Hearst's personal liquidity could only provide $2 million, and $1.5 million of that came from a charitable trust that required the approval of the Internal Revenue Service and Evelle Younger's office. And this money, according to the SLA, did not even guarantee the release of Patty Hearst.

Evelle Younger represented Reagan's law-and-order culture in Sacramento and, as such, he was furious about the People in Need program. "In the future, every crime committed in connection with the kidnapping will be prosecuted. And I'm including any persons who participated in any sort of a food distribution plan or a television set distribution plan or any other kind of a distribution plan. If it's done in response to extortion or kidnapping, we'll encourage the local district attorneys to prosecute under existing law, and if they won't, we'll do it."

Reagan himself drew headlines. He predicted few people would accept free food as part of a kidnap demand. When proven wrong, he accused the recipients of "aiding and abetting lawlessness." The first day of food distribution, February 22, turned out massive crowds. In Oakland, people climbed into the backs of the trucks. Boxes of food were hurled into the out-of-control crowd, injuring some of the mostly black participants.

There simply was not enough time or experience to properly launch People in Need, because of the timeline demanded by DeFreeze. Scores of hustlers pitched their services to Randolph Hearst at the headquarters for PIN, ironically located at the Del Monte Building on Townsend Street in San Francisco. Del Monte was a company on the SLA list of targets.

PIN director Ludlow Kramer, former Washington state secretary of state, was chosen by Randolph Hearst as director because he had established the "Neighborhoods-in-Need" program in the Seattle area in 1971 to help aerospace workers during a period of massive unemployment.

On Day 19 of the kidnapping, Kramer spoke to the press. "Four days ago we had nothing, and in four days, we've created the largest private volunteer organization in the history of the country. The SLA is correct in the sense that people need funds, that people need the additional money. We are not questioning that at all, and the four thousand volunteers that are working on this program believe the same thing. But we believe that it must be and can be an ongoing program."

Kramer opened the door to the possibility of PIN continuing after the resolution of the kidnapping. This was ignored. It was as if the SLA were mesmerized by the publicity, without considering a bigger picture. One of the most often shown television clips from the People in Need distribution is a black woman who sympathetically told a reporter, "I hate to take advantage of what could happen to the young lady (Hearst). But my children need food, just like anybody else's kids."

Among the wide variety of volunteers was Sara Jane Moore, a psychologically unbalanced woman in her early forties, fascinated with the left, who shortly after becoming a bookkeeper for PIN also offered her services to the FBI as an informant. Moore then decided she wanted to be a radical, terminated her agreement with the FBI, announced she was a former informant, and was duly labeled a snitch by the leftist United Prisoners Union. Unable to pay her rent and support herself and her nine-year-old son, Moore, in September 1975, fired a single bullet in the direction of Nixon presidential successor Gerald Ford in San Francisco, and was restrained and imprisoned.

FOR DONALD DEFREEZE, the Hearst kidnapping and the People in Need program were his own independent attempts to submerge a litany of calamities: his cruel father driving him away from home; his inability to be with Reverend Foster's daughter in Buffalo; Gloria's deceit and the children he could not support; failure at crime after crime and the LAPD's callous disregard for his services; the behavior modification at Vacaville; more humiliation at the Black Cultural Association. And his only way of remaining outside of prison was his agreement to kill a man of his own race, lionized as a great leader.

Foster was nationally eulogized, with numerous Bay Area memorials, including one at the Oakland Coliseum Arena (now Oracle Arena) which drew 4,500 people. To DeFreeze's mind, he and the SLA were unanimously vilified. Thero Wheeler had abandoned him. And DeFreeze didn't even have enough money to live.

Russ Little, of all the original SLA members, was again the only one who spoke out, in retrospect, about the glaring inconsistencies in DeFreeze's behavior. And although none of those nine radicals ever knew of DeFreeze's life as informant, Little sensed DeFreeze had ulterior motives.

"DeFreeze made mention of some psychological warfare against the police," Little noted of his own time in the SLA. "It was like trying to fake the police out. But it seemed like he totally lost track of that. Are you doing this for the police? Is the communiqué for the police or is it to try to explain to people what you're doing? I mean, who is it for? . . . Why would you even worry about the police? Who cares what they think? They hate you. They want to kill you."

Little pinpointed a crucial issue. DeFreeze, if captured alive, could indict Lt. James Nelson, Colston Westbrook and the agencies they served. As it turned out, DeFreeze, according to the government, once again outlived his usefulness, as he had done with the LAPD.

Patty Hearst gave a clear picture of the paranoia and distrust that ruled DeFreeze's life during that time. She recounted how, during SLA meetings, he made the group turn the television toward the wall, because he believed that the government could use it to spy on them.

Hearst also offered candid insight into the mind of General Field Marshal Cinque during an appearance on the *Larry King Show* on CNN. She spoke of the fear Cinque instilled in her while an SLA captive. "It was considered wrong of me to think about my family. When Cinque was around, he didn't want me thinking about rescue because he thought that brainwaves could be read, or, you know, they'd get a psychic in to find me. I was even afraid of that."

DeFreeze's record as police informant for the LAPD was known to Westbrook and the California Department of Corrections. Similarly, when he was let out of Soledad Prison looking to hire or be an assassin, DeFreeze's history was also known to the Federal Bureau of Investigation.

Proof of this comes from an FBI undercover agent, Wayne M. Lewis. Lewis filed a lawsuit against the FBI for nonpayment of salary. He also provided affidavits to Lake Headley, who was working on behalf of Dr. L. S. Wolfe, Willie's father.

Born in Canada, Lewis worked fulltime for the Bureau from June 1968 to November 1973. This was confirmed to Headley by two letters, one signed by FBI Director Clarence Kelley. Initially, Lewis was assigned to infiltrate organized crime, according to an interview he conducted with the *Berkeley Barb*. It was Lewis's contention that he met with the fugitive Donald DeFreeze in July 1973. Lewis, working for Los Angeles FBI agent Donald L. Grey, nephew of former FBI head L. Patrick Grey, was told DeFreeze had to be "removed" as an FBI informant who was no longer reliable. DeFreeze had not worked for the FBI. Lewis was told only enough about DeFreeze to motivate him to help.

Since Lewis had already served well as informant and undercover agent, and was struggling to stay financially afloat, Donald Grey allegedly offered Lewis the role as head of the SLA, after DeFreeze was taken out. Lewis agreed.

Lewis, a black man in his mid-thirties, was not the standard kind of informant in that he was not a former convict. In using his underground contacts to get a face-to-face meeting with DeFreeze, Lewis was an informant facing an informant. Both of their lives were ruled by suspicion and deceit. Lewis's job was to gain the trust of DeFreeze and, most likely, monitor his location. The significance of the involvement of Lewis is clear: even before the murder of Marcus Foster, DeFreeze was not seen as cooperative or reliable. In case he ran or refused to kill Foster or bungled the assignment—in fact, even if DeFreeze was successful—the FBI could replace him with a much more dependable asset in the guise of Lewis.

The unpredictability of Donald DeFreeze can be attributed to the fact that any informant for a government agency cannot be completely controlled, as long as human emotion enters into the performance of duties. Frank Donner's essay, "The Agent Provocateur as

Folk Hero," referred to an FBI document stolen from their Media, Pennsylvania office. In it, the FBI recounted how some collaborating informants infiltrating the New Left got so lost in the role that they actually violently attacked police during street demonstrations.

The FBI document went on to counsel control over the informant. "They should not become the person who carries the gun, throws the bomb or by some deeply violative act becomes a deeply involved participant."

Donner's most significant insight was about the psychological melding of the informant with the role.

> The control theory ignores the strange drives and hostile passions that cause people to act as spies in the first place, as well as the ways in which the atmosphere of risk in which they work is likely to intensify such feelings. As the informer becomes more involved, new and terrible energies are released in him. The need to preserve his 'cover' gives him a pretext to act out hatred and anger, washing away the cautions prescribed by his "controllers" or "handlers."

If Donner's analysis is then applied to a psychologically scarred, gun-obsessed convict who had drugs and coercive behavior modification experimentally used upon him, then Donald DeFreeze's decision to kidnap Patty Hearst, without the cooperation of the government, becomes that much more comprehensible. With his treatment of Hearst, he had revenged her rejection of him. Additionally, DeFreeze had the media, the nation, and the world obsessing about his actions.

But he also agonized over what move to expect from those who had controlled him. Colston Westbrook had psychologically molded DeFreeze. Lieutenant James Nelson had set up the logistics. But they no longer gave him orders. It was all on him. He was the leader of a movement he was in the process of inventing. He had no idea what he was going to do next. But for the first time in his life, Donald DeFreeze, despite the jeopardy of his position, felt powerful and truly free.

9 · Two Very Different Revolutionaries

DeFreeze and the SLA demanded that police be nowhere near the main warehouse for People in Need in San Francisco, nor near the distribution sites in the Bay Area. As a result, a riot in Oakland during the first week of the PIN giveaway occurred. A woman lost an eye in the melee. There were scores of thefts. One man who said he wanted to volunteer at the Del Monte building on Townsend Street was given the keys to a truck filled with at least $20,000 of hams and told to drive them to Oakland. He and the truck disappeared. The thief was not even asked for his ID before being given the keys by a supervisor. In total, nine trucks were either stolen or hijacked.

The seven SLA audio tapes furnished to KPFA for airing were the mode the SLA used to communicate with the Hearsts. In mid-February, one of those tapes defended the People in Need program. SLA member Angela Atwood, now called "General Gelina," among much bombast in her recorded message, made one of the most powerful indictments heard from the SLA, in language stripped down a single sentence of disgust and hate.

Atwood explained the purpose of People in Need. "We did this to point out how the enemy can easily afford to feed the people if it were forced to, but what the enemy cannot afford is to reveal to the people the total extent of the sum of the wealth that it has robbed from the people."

For the first time in his life, Donald DeFreeze's criminality bene-fited him. The more discordant things grew, the more his SLA acted irate and demanded a better response from Randolph Hearst and Ludlow Kramer. The Oakland PIN melee increased press coverage and Hearst was in no position to dig in his heels during negotia-tions. As the second food distribution began, on February 28, wid-ening the number of locations and improving the quality of food, DeFreeze still had not asked for a ransom deal.

Little and Remiro were in "the hole," the abandoned Death Row of San Quentin. Their bails were set and then reset to astronomi-cal amounts. Ronald Reagan, shortly after the People in Need pro-gram began, announced that under no conditions would the state of California allow the SLA to make the liberation of Russ Little and Joe Remiro part of a negotiation. DeFreeze did not explicitly ask for a trade in the prior twenty days, probably realizing the FBI and Reagan would never agree to it.

DeFreeze never set an amount of money to be paid to the SLA for the ransom of Patty Hearst. People in Need was called a gesture by DeFreeze, and after his ongoing renegotiation of the money for PIN, the final agreement was left at $2 million from Hearst and his trust, with a Hearst counteroffer of $4 million more when Patty was safely released.

The FBI and the Hearst family had no way to communicate with the SLA other than through the media. In addition to the histrionics of SLA political rants on social justice, the public was witness to a Patty Hearst who changed before the public's ears, if not eyes.

Because the media and the American public did not realize that Patty Hearst, while taken violently and against her will, was in fact a closet radical, her later conversion to SLA doctrine stunned every-one. It gave the perception that DeFreeze had an almost Svengali-like power. This swift change even fomented false rumors that she engineered her own kidnapping. Patty Hearst, from the start, already agreed with much of the SLA's political ideology about racism, pov-erty, and corporate totalitarianism before she was torn away from her life on Benvenue Avenue in Berkeley. The difference between them was primarily tactics and soon, even that distinction disappeared.

DeFreeze not only utilized some of the behavior modification techniques on Hearst that had been subjected upon him in prison, but also he had Hearst talk, albeit briefly, about the need for prison reform in one of the communiqués in the first month.

"In the last few days," Hearst stated, "members of the Federation have spoken with me. They have given me some newspaper reports to read about the current practices of psychosurgery and the use, daily, of drugs and tranquilizers in prisons throughout the country."

Doctor Rona Fields, at the time a social psychologist and researcher for Amnesty International, equated Hearst's change of personality with the studies Fields had done of the British military and their use of behavior modification on Irish Republican Army prisoners in Northern Ireland.

She reported that 60 percent of the two hundred subjects she interviewed, who were prisoners of the British, manifested signs of permanent brain damage. They had all been put in isolation and "during that time, they would lose track of time, place and their own identity." She disagreed with those who felt that the "brainwashing" of Hearst would have to be done by an expert in the field. "It's quite possible to have this simply happen as a product of an environment that provides prolonged stress and a questioning of values."

The testimony of Hearst regarding her sexual experience with the SLA included DeFreeze touching her breasts and pubic area four days after her kidnapping and then, approximately a month later, a sexual encounter with Willie Wolfe, followed by one with DeFreeze. She said at trial these acts were accepted passively, as molestation and rape. Her reaction to the death of Willie Wolfe a few months later, to be discussed, showed a different view of her relationship with him.

Hearst's transition from Patty to Tania was a success on both a personal and political level for DeFreeze. Hearst claimed he announced to the group that the revelation of Tania to the world would be "a great propaganda coup if the prisoner wants to stay." He gave her the name Tania, based on Tania Bunke who fought alongside Bolivian revolutionary Ernesto "Che" Guevara during the insurgency of 1966–1967. This was an oversight, as "Tania" had previously been given to Robyn Steiner. Both DeFreeze, as Cinque, and Hearst were given previously used pseudonyms, indicating, if not callousness, a lack of attention to detail. The Harrises objected to Hearst being called Tania, to no avail. DeFreeze gifted Hearst with the book *Tania: The Unforgettable Guerrilla.*

Patty Hearst's history with Donald DeFreeze when he was in prison had created a bond, one he could not leave behind. DeFreeze's past with Colston Westbrook could not be forgotten either, although it would have been better for DeFreeze if he could have done so.

Westbrook wrote an open letter to "Brother Cinque," published in a March *Berkeley Barb*, hoping to reestablish contact. In his bombastic, street language style, he urged, "I just want to talk to you, man-to-man, brother-to-brother, n—to-n—. Can I help and if so, how?"

But this open letter taunted DeFreeze more than it offered aid. In one paragraph, Westbrook made a veiled reference to Patty Hearst not being aware of DeFreeze's preferential treatment as informant, as well as the fact that certain BCA members were:

Did you tell her (Hearst) about the UNISIGHT thing. Yes, do you remember the night when you asked me if you could have some time on my program so that you could do your UNISIGHT thing? I gave it to you. The brothers didn't want to give you the time, but I did.

The letter ended with a clear indication that Westbrook was insulting DeFreeze and had no intention of helping him. "P.S. . . . Say Cin, I dig your Field Marshall [*sic*] rank; too bad you couldn't be a Messiah."

In a March 4 press conference, Westbrook, always ready to talk with brashness and confidence, inadvertently raised questions about what he knew about DeFreeze in Vacaville.

Regarding the denigration of Marcus Foster at BCA meetings, Westbrook said an unspecified woman "along with Wolfe made an impassioned speech at Vacaville in September 1973, urging the inmates to do something to prevent Foster from implementing student identification and police patrol programs in Oakland public schools." Westbrook, who used the good-natured Wolfe to help widen the circle of radicals going to the BCA, not only made fun of Wolfe's naïveté privately but now blamed the least militant male in the SLA for the plans to kill Marcus Foster, based on one alleged speech by an anonymous woman.

Westbrook also admitted at the press conference that he "gave the FBI pictures of the BCA meetings at Vacaville." He did not say if they were subpoenaed or given of his own free will, nor did he say how many times he had dealt with the FBI.

Finally, in another slip of the tongue, Westbrook shed light on the complex relationship he developed with DeFreeze at Vacaville. Asked about the history of behavior modification at Vacaville as it related to the SLA and the Patty Hearst kidnapping, Westbrook said, "At least, the top leadership of the SLA has been trained in this process." The top leadership of the Symbionese Liberation Army was Donald DeFreeze. And Westbrook did not say DeFreeze was subjected to the process. He said DeFreeze was "trained" in it.

Hand-typed notes belonging to Lake Headley revealed that one member of the press quoted Clifford "Death Row Jeff" Jefferson at the press conference. Jefferson not only claimed the prisoners wanted to get rid of Westbrook and did, but also that the outside coordinator for the BCA "was always murder mouthing about stopping Foster, screaming about his putting cops on campuses and giving identity cards to students. He should have known better. He knew how easy it was to get cons riled. Of course, maybe he wanted that."

On March 5, Colston Westbrook was quoted in the *New York Times* as saying he doubted DeFreeze was in charge of the SLA, that Westbrook didn't know who was and that white radicals had taken over the Black Cultural Association, a charge he continued to levy, despite attendees requiring his permission to enter Vacaville Medical Facility. Tellingly, for all his outspoken bravado, Colston Westbrook never said anything in the press about the tragedy of Marcus Foster's murder.

In the FBI's HEARNAP files on the SLA, there is a heavily redacted interview dated early March that is obviously conducted with Westbrook, talking about the structure of the BCA and when it was formed. With a lawyer present, Westbrook, advised by the FBI that he was not a person of interest in the case, felt free to spin a web of deceit. He claimed he did not know DeFreeze's political beliefs. Asked who else lived at Chabot Road in addition to Wolfe and Little, Westbrook declined to answer. Even though he had befriended Wolfe, Westbrook told the FBI he did not know where he lived. When the FBI agent interviewing him inquired if Westbrook had ever heard DeFreeze using the name "Cinque," Westbrook again avoided answering. When he was asked to try and identify any voices on the SLA communiqué audio tapes, Westbrook refused.

The war of words in the press continued, moving to the state capital. On March 6, after a festive Republican fund-raising luncheon, Governor Reagan, asked for his opinion about the SLA's People in Need program, declared, "It's just too bad we can't have an epidemic of botulism." His comment was roundly criticized in the media, a rare miscalculation from the politician who would be known as the Great Communicator, and the governor eventually had to apologize to quell the reaction.

By the middle of March, DeFreeze moved his entire group to a three-room apartment at 1827 Golden Gate Avenue #6, on the northwest edge of San Francisco's Western Addition, the district where Thero Wheeler and Nancy Ling Perry had lived. It was a risky move, about a mile and a half away from the twenty-five-story black marble and glass tower of the Federal Building, where Special Agent in Charge Charles Bates and his associates at the FBI were pursuing leads from all over the country.

Despite the overcrowding, DeFreeze's small army ran around the apartment, doing military-style drills, presumably without the approval of the person who lived downstairs. There was support for the group in their own neighborhood, as well as the Haight-Ashbury, where spray-painted slogans like "SLA LIVES" and "SLA FEEDS THE POOR" were seen.

There were reports that members of the SLA were seen in local grocery stores, like the New Laguna market. They seemed unafraid of discovery and felt protected by those fellow San Franciscans who shared their revolutionary fervor and their support of the underclass via People in Need.

Emily Harris admitted, "Members of the SLA stood in the food lines to find out the reaction and effects of the program." It is not inconceivable that members of the SLA, in disguise, walked down to the nearby PIN food giveaway on Divisadero Street and observed with pleasure that they had effected some social good, even on a small scale.

People in Need concluded on March 25, with approximately $30,000 of food, better in quality than during the first distribution, at sites in both Northern and Southern California.

By the time PIN had its final disbursement, it had cost Randolph Hearst about $2.3 million. The people of the state of California had a law enforcement bill exceeding $10 million. And 100,000 struggling citizens received free food. Among the confused rhetoric and the violence, the bizarre accusations by DeFreeze, the intended and unintended demonization of the left in California, it was the one charitable act that redeemed, to some degree, his life.

On the heels of People in Need, in a three-day hearing, the Alameda County grand jury indicted Russ Little and Joe Remiro on March 28, after forty-seven persons were called to offer testimony.

The very next day, the last American fighting troops left Vietnam. The war and its attendant draft, with its disproportionate number of black and Hispanic soldiers, had once mobilized the left into action. But over those years, as the Vietnam War wound down, numerous revolutionary groups and factions appeared and dissolved, many of them infiltrated. Donald DeFreeze, in the guise of Cinque, decided to leave behind his life as informant and provocateur. But he was about to make a huge miscalculation by publicly indicting the man who he most resented.

THE INFAMOUS APRIL 3 communiqué from the Symbionese Liberation Army featured Patty Hearst announcing she was now to be known as "Tania." The transformation of Patty into Tania was startling. She attacked her parents, twice calling her father a "liar," protested the treatment of Little and Remiro at San Quentin, and made famous a simple statement: "I have decided to stay and fight."

Included with the tape that aired on KSAN-FM in San Francisco was a photograph of Hearst, its colors smeared. She posed in front of a red flag with the seven-headed cobra and the letters "SLA." Wearing a brown jumpsuit and a beret, she held what looked like an assault rifle with scope. Marilyn Baker of KQED's *Newsroom* did a little investigating and learned it was a standard M-1 carbine with a three-battery flashlight taped to the top of the gun, to make it appear more menacing.

Hearst's absorption as a revolutionary garnered more attention than DeFreeze's citing three enemies of the SLA who should "be shot on sight by any of the people's forces."

Robyn Steiner, Russ Little's girlfriend, had mixed with the group at Chabot Road and attended the BCA at Vacaville. She admitted to the *San Francisco Chronicle* that she kept the SLA financially solvent, at one point bringing in up to $2,000 a week via stealing, forging, and shoplifting. But when DeFreeze started talking about killing "pigs," Steiner was done with her involvement. After DeFreeze personally informed Steiner that he and two others had shot Foster and Blackburn, she ended her relationship with Little and returned to Florida.

Around the middle of January 1974, an Oakland police detective flew to Florida to interview Steiner about the SLA. DeFreeze, hypersensitive to any colleagues talking to law enforcement and intolerant of SLA members leaving the fold, considered her a traitor.

Steiner's flight from the Bay Area likely had to do with fear about her admission that she stole the cyanide that was used in the bullets that killed Foster. She planned to have her family financially help her attend medical school in Florida. But DeFreeze contacted her through her parents, four days before the kidnapping of Hearst, trying to entice her to return by touting "the biggest action since Foster." Finally, when a friend called and informed Steiner that she was on an SLA list of those marked for death, she moved to England under an assumed name.

Chris Thompson, for much the same reason, was the second name on DeFreeze's hit list. He was labeled in the communiqué "a government agent, a paid informant for the FBI."

When the Alameda County grand jury assembled for the case of Russ Little and Joe Remiro, one of those subpoenaed was Thompson, who had registered the Rossi .38 eventually used in the slaying of Foster. DeFreeze automatically assumed that Thompson, who helped DeFreeze find refuge with Patricia Soltysik, had given up crucial, actionable information to the grand jury.

Marilyn Baker met with Thompson a few times, with the hope of interviewing him for the KQED newscast. She was with him at the station the moment it was learned that he was on the SLA list of enemies marked for death.

Baker was quoted as saying Thompson "did not appear to be afraid. He was cool. . . . He said they, meaning the SLA, made another mistake, just as they made when they murdered Foster."

Like many on the periphery of the SLA, Chris Thompson's story shifted often. After mentioning other dates, he finally admitted to Baker that the last time he saw his ex-girlfriend Nancy Ling Perry was the previous Christmas, when she was hiding in the Clayton safe house. Like Steiner, he may well have withdrawn from association with the group after hearing about the Foster assassination. If Steiner and Thompson knew about the planned killing beforehand, it would have fueled DeFreeze's suspicions even more about their informing on him. Also, it likely infuriated DeFreeze to know that Thompson was promised a $10,000 reward from the *Oakland Tribune* for information regarding the Foster hit. It was madness: DeFreeze, a former informant, wanted to kill his former friend, suspected of being an informant.

But by far the most significant name on the list of SLA targets was that of Colston Westbrook. DeFreeze stated categorically that Westbrook was "a government agent, worked for the CIA in Vietnam as interrogator and torturer in Phoenix [Program] operation . . . now working for military intelligence while giving cross assistance to the FBI."

Like so much of the SLA rhetoric, this accusation both touched upon and obscured the truth. DeFreeze knew from newspaper coverage that Westbrook provided the FBI photos of those attending the BCA. DeFreeze may have been told directly by Westbrook of his CIA past or learned it from another source.

But DeFreeze and the Symbionese Liberation Army could have struck a blow against the California Department of Corrections, discussing in a written communiqué or tape recording the specific cruelties he and other prisoners endured. He did not and it raises the question of how much DeFreeze was governed by fear of revelations that he was an informant. The respect and allegiance of his fellow revolutionaries was all he had left in life. But even in a mind as feverish and suspicious as Donald DeFreeze's, certain facts were incontrovertible. Westbrook was protecting his own identity and directed all blame upon DeFreeze and his followers, and it infuriated DeFreeze. Westbrook had befriended him and advocated for him. The full force of being used and abandoned led DeFreeze to his homicidal condemnation on the tape.

The likelihood of his impending death was also the impetus for DeFreeze to become emotional and personal in his audio message. He honored Little and Remiro, maintaining that they were innocent and that he deeply regretted their capture. There were no other details on the Foster-Blackburn attack. A wellspring of compassion came out of the Field Marshal as he said to Little and Remiro on tape, "I send you my love and the love of all your comrades and courage in your determination to carry on the struggle even from that side of the wall, as we will NEVER relent from this end. In this way we do expect to meet again." The last sentence seemed more a reference to the afterlife than prison.

While DeFreeze claimed to have two children in an earlier message, he concluded his April 3 communiqué with a tribute to all six of his children:

> I would like to take this opportunity to speak to my six lovely, black babies. Victor, Damon, Sherry, Sherlyne, Dawn and DeDe. I want you to know that just to say your names again fills my heart with joy. . . . I want you to understand that I have not forgotten my promise to you, that whenever you needed me I would be there by your side, and so am I now, even when you may not see me. I am there, because no matter where I am, I am fighting for your freedom, your future, your life. Daddy wants you to understand that I can't come home because you are not free, and as long as the enemy exists, I can find no rest nor any hope for you or our people as a whole.

The section about his children continued, the longest passage of his on the tape. In conclusion, his voice, clenched with the sorrow of his abandonment of those children, introduced the "national anthem" of the Symbionese Liberation Army. In the background was an instrumental song by the jazz group The Crusaders. It had the feel of a melancholy march, with an elegiac sax line cutting through. Its title must have had multiple meanings for DeFreeze: "Way Back Home."

Questioned by the press, after the announcement of his name on the April 3 hit list, Westbrook revealed that he had been interviewed by the FBI regarding the SLA "at least four times."

Westbrook acknowledged that he was concerned about the death threat but also displayed arrogance about his control over the SLA. "In general, I have a lot of information about them, both material and mental. I know many of them, know how they think, and how they react. They know I can analyze the things they do."

Westbrook's next statement seemed intent on taunting Donald DeFreeze. "I'm also a threat to his ego. I'm stealing his thunder."

Ignoring the fact that what the known SLA members had in common was the Black Cultural Association he ran, Westbrook made another outrageous claim. "They have been recruiting in the Bay Area for a while, and one of their ways is to get members to commit a revolutionary act, and right now, that is wiping me out."

On April 4, KPFA received an audio tape from Little and Remiro, asking the "War Council" of the SLA, namely DeFreeze, to rescind the death warrant for Robyn Steiner. On the tape was the Remiro statement that "she has in fact several times refused to talk to the FBI. We think further investigation into the matter is necessary." Little and Remiro were willing to keep their mouths closed about the actual perpetrators of the Foster-Blackburn attack. But they now felt that DeFreeze's paranoia was overtaking his common sense.

Patty Hearst recalled when DeFreeze was told by an SLA member that Little would be very upset by the death warrant for Steiner. She said DeFreeze's reply was "that both Osi [Little] and Bo [Remiro] deserved to have death warrants issued against them. They had violated the 'Codes of War' by allowing themselves to be captured." Hearst also wrote that Atwood and Perry tried to convince DeFreeze to rescind these pronouncements, with no success.

Concerned for his own safety, Westbrook returned to his hometown of Chambersburg, Pennsylvania, to visit his mother for Easter. The sardonic home phone message in his absence included him saying, "I am not dead yet but I still am high on the SLA hit list. If the caller is a terrorist, please include your affiliation so the credit for my demise can be properly awarded."

Even while in Chambersburg, he could not bear to be out of the limelight. In talking with the *Hagerstown* (Maryland) *Daily Mail*, Westbrook continued his narrative that whites had taken over the BCA and were running the SLA, with DeFreeze as mere figurehead. "I think the honkies are calling the shots in the SLA and they're letting Cinque take the glory, but he's not running it. When I say this, he gets even madder."

Inevitably, Westbrook returned to California, to file his taxes by April 15 and continue his verbal war. One new outgoing phone message baited DeFreeze more aggressively than any other. "Are your SLA punks afraid of dying and why do you send kids to do your work? Are you a man or a boy? The tide is turning."

The next Westbrook phone machine message returned to the comically confrontational tone of the others, noted by the *San Mateo Times*. "*Jambo* [Swahili greeting]. This is Colston Westbrook. I have returned to the Bay Area to prepare my income tax returns and hope that SLA agents give me a death warning extension. If granted, I will kiss Cinque's feet in Union Square in San Francisco and give him an hour to draw a crowd."

Westbrook admitted to providing information to not only the FBI, as he'd stated before, but also to the Oakland police. And ever the showman, Westbrook told the *San Francisco Examiner* he would "take a lie detector test on TV concerning my past. Let the public put me on trial."

In his book *My Search for Patty Hearst*, Steven Weed recounted a very revelatory meeting with Colston Westbrook after he was pronounced a target.

Westbrook had the following recording when Weed called to set up a meeting: "I am not dead yet. But I am fully dressed [armed] and looking forward to a reunion with my old brother, the General Field Marshal."

Weed found Westbrook living in University Village in Albany, near the Berkeley border. It was an area of similar-looking apartments adapted as university housing, formerly known as Veterans'

Village during World War II when a new Navy training base had been built. Inside, the apartment was littered with papers and books as well as toys for his infant son. Westbrook's life had become as chaotic as his dwelling. He checked under his car during the visit, telling Weed, "I got to check for bombs every time I go anywhere."

Westbrook had become nearly as obsessive as DeFreeze about his own potential death, but he still maintained the same outlandish personality. There was a callousness, too, about the other white SLA members, with whom he had been friends.

Willie Wolfe, whom Westbrook had kindly driven to Vacaville and cheerfully introduced to DeFreeze, became the object of his glib scorn, described as "wide-eyed and grossly naïve."

Westbrook even cruelly imitated Wolfe in front of Weed, to emphasize his point about Wolfe's lack of political acumen. "Goddamn, look at this shit," said Westbrook, mimicking Wolfe. "Blacks and revolution in prison."

When Weed asked Westbrook about the reports of white radical women having sex with black prisoners at Vacaville, Westbrook never brought up the favoritism toward DeFreeze, allowed to use a trustee trailer for his assignations. Instead, Westbrook claimed that a couple of the white women had sex under the stage set up for meetings. It was not only absurd to think of it—sex allowed in front of up to one hundred other BCA attendees—but also never addressed Westbrook's responsibilities within the prison.

Weed questioned Westbrook about DeFreeze's accusation that Westbrook was connected to the CIA and provided information to the FBI. Weed's evaluation of Westbrook's reaction was powerful. "He laughed at the idea of his alleged CIA/FBI connections but did not deny them. Westbrook was a colorful character and I got the feeling that he enjoyed being something of a man of mystery in the case."

Before their meeting was over, Westbrook cracked a final joke, something far from humorous. "Not even my old lady," Westbrook announced with a laugh, referring to his wife, "knows everything about my background."

In an interview with *Encore* magazine, Westbrook returned to the story that white Maoists had taken over the BCA and, without details, he claimed to have tried to alter the group and failed.

When he was asked how the Patty Hearst kidnapping came about, he replied, "I understand Cinque has a three-point plan. One was to knock off a black educator. Another was to kidnap someone of importance. And three was to blow up something."

When Westbrook was asked, in a rare follow-up question, how this alleged program was created, he struggled for words, a rarity for him. "I really don't know. A lot of things happened on the inside, and people on the outside were getting together for a long time and planning things."

Steven Weed grew desperate to find a respected radical to communicate with the SLA and negotiate Hearst's release. He flew to Mexico City to speak with Régis Debray, the French Marxist intellectual. Debray wrote *Revolution in the Revolution?* on socialist militancy in Latin America, which radicals read—including the burgeoning SLA. Debray offered to write an open letter to the SLA, urging them to let Hearst freely state that she willingly joined the SLA. Debray had his doubts about the upstart revolutionaries and the American left in general.

"Usually they do nothing," Debray sniffed, "and when they finally do something, it comes out like this."

Debray's April 12 letter in Randolph Hearst's *San Francisco Examiner* referred to Tania Bunke, Che's fellow revolutionary, whom Debray had known. Debray subtly criticized Patty Hearst and the SLA, saying the original Tania had spent "years among the workers" and studied "the theory of scientific socialism and the reality of the actual world. . . . You will understand that we must be cautious to protect the moral integrity and international purity of her commitment."

But Patty Hearst was not in charge, and Donald DeFreeze was now beyond the control of anyone on the left or the right.

APRIL 15, TAX Day, also coincided in 1974 with a press conference held by Evelle Younger in San Francisco. He ridiculed the People in Need program and challenged the assembled reporters, "We need to ask ourselves whether the food reached the people in the greatest need. Should we allow a small band of extortionists to dictate our welfare policies?"

Younger, to no one's surprise, was not about to sensitively comment on the need in a legal manner to help the state's poor. He did, however, make many reporters ruminate on a more ethically ambiguous question regarding the media itself. "It is a fair question to ask whether a free press can responsibly comply with extortionist demands that it publish political rhetoric designed to influence public opinion in favor of the kidnappers."

It was a worthy and complex argument, as the media had fully published or aired the SLA's written and recorded communiqués, knowing they would grip the public. Younger obliquely suggested that his office disapproved of the FBI's measured approach, attacking "the timidity of the police response." He also gave the impression that Patty Hearst did not warrant different treatment from the other SLA members, now that she had verbally lacerated her parents and American society.

"We cannot," Younger declared, "place the safety of one citizen above all of the others." The Attorney General of California was not about to afford her special treatment in a raid or shoot-out.

At the end of Younger's press conference, as reporters posed private follow-up questions, one of the most famous bank robberies in American history was about to take place.

In a closed gas station parking lot, across the street from the Hibernia Bank at 22nd Street and Noriega Avenue in San Francisco's Sunset district, a rented red AMC Hornet Sportabout sat. Its passengers, Willie Wolfe, Angela Atwood, and Bill and Emily Harris, watched the front of the bank tensely.

Camilla Hall drove a green Ford LTD station wagon. Her former lover, Patricia Soltysik, sat beside her. In the back seat, Donald DeFreeze and Nancy Ling Perry each held an automatic rifle. Patty Hearst cradled a sawed off M-1 carbine under her coat. Hall, about to park, suddenly spotted a police car and she circled the block a few times, making sure the path was clear. Then, Hall parked in a bus zone. They weren't going to be gone long.

At 9:50 a.m., Zig Berzins, owner of a nearby stereo store, entered the Hibernia Bank and pushed the door closed behind him. In the process, he heard a thud and clinking noises.

"Christ," he later admitted thinking, "I've slammed the door on a little old lady and everything's spilled out of her purse."

He had knocked to the ground clips of ammunition and some bullets belonging to Patricia Hearst. A parade of other women, carrying guns, entered, backed up by DeFreeze, wearing a short leather coat and floppy hat. He shouted, gun at the ready, to the eighteen employees and six customers to get on the floor or be shot.

Eden Shea, sixty-six, a security guard, was the only one who did not comply. His hands went up in the air as he stood by the door. Soltysik pulled out a pistol and with a canvas bag in the other hand, she leaped gracefully over the four-foot-high counter to collect money.

One teller did not move fast enough, so DeFreeze dragged her through a swinging gate to the main floor of the bank. It was then that DeFreeze and Shea locked eyes. Shea had a .38 revolver, which he had never fired, in a holster on his hip. DeFreeze quickly grabbed it and motioned for Shea to hit the floor, which he did.

Berzins and others heard a woman, about to become the most well-known female bank robber since Bonnie Parker, announce, in a phrase that suggested an identity crisis, "This is Tania Hearst." Behind her, on the other side of the counter, Soltysik and Hall furiously emptied cash drawers with both hands.

None of the SLA members bothered to search upstairs, where manager Jim Smith, sixty-two, was reading the *San Francisco*

Chronicle, not expecting his bank would be written about on the front page of the nation's newspapers the next day. He heard shouts, peered out of a small window down at the main floor, and, jolted by the robbery in progress, hit the silent alarm. Two high-speed cameras with wide-angle lenses shot the now historic black-and-white images, while a "211" via a dedicated phone line was signaled to the police. It was 9:51 a.m., and the bank had never notified the SFPD that they had new hours, opening at 9:30. The police assumed it was a malfunction. One pair of officers later admitted they drove to that Hibernia Bank at a leisurely pace, until the radio reported that shots had been fired. Then, they flipped on the red lights and siren and drove at top speed.

The SLA was on the way out the door. But Perry proved to be a less-than-competent robber. Pete Markoff, fifty-nine, silver-haired, small in stature like Perry, entered the bank with the weekend receipts from his store, Noriega Liquors. Accompanying him was Gene Brennan, seventy, a pensioner and friend.

They were greeted at the door by a panicked Perry, who began firing. A .30 caliber bullet ripped through Markoff's right buttock, exiting his right leg and putting a hole in the glass door. Two other slugs missed him but the fourth tore through Brennan's right hand.

Ken Outland, sixty-two, a pharmacist, was having a rather early Bloody Mary down the street at Greg's Cocktail Lounge, chatting with Greg Higuera at the bar, when they both heard piercing, cracking sounds. They exited the bar, no more than twenty feet from Donald DeFreeze, who swung around, spotted them, and opened fire.

Higuera dove into an alley. Outland, unprotected, instinctively flattened himself against a building wall. A bullet whizzed by, sizzling the air. It missed him by inches. Both cars screeched away, west, toward the ocean. The police arrived barely more than a minute later. The two abandoned getaway cars were soon found at an elementary school ten blocks away. Despite injuring two unarmed citizens and their oversight of the bank manager, the SLA had miraculously escaped with $10,692.51.

The explosiveness of Hearst's participation in the bank robbery so captivated the nation that Attorney General Saxbe could not contain his anger, calling her a "common criminal," which created a storm of protest in the media. The attorney general had presumed her guilt without even mentioning the possibility of her coercion as a kidnap victim. The FBI's Clarence Kelley ameliorated the anger toward Saxbe, declaring the Bureau was operating on the assumption that "Patricia is the victim of pressure or coercion." Saxbe disappeared from public view for a few weeks, and when he reemerged, he spoke more diplomatically in public.

Randolph Hearst was staggered by his daughter's act, even more than when she had referred to him as a "pig" and "liar." His consultant, Dr. Frederick Hacker, in a confidential memorandum obtained by authors Vin McLellan and Paul Avery, explained pointedly why Patty had to be included in the Hibernia Bank robbery. "One of the frequent rites of revolutionaries such as the SLA is initiation. You involve the hostage in an act of violence. The guilt is thus shared and it greatly increases the difficulty for the hostage to return to the outside community. It is a participation and a bond sealed by blood."

An often overlooked fact that raises the possibility of Hearst's help in planning the Hibernia Bank holdup is that the president of the bank happened to be the father of her best friend, Trish Tobin.

United States Attorney James Browning, who eventually prosecuted the case against Hearst, said after the Hibernia Bank heist, "I think this is the first time in the annals of legal history that a kidnap victim has shown up in the middle of a bank robbery."

Some argued that DeFreeze had his gun trained on Hearst during the robbery, to make sure of her acquiescence. But FBI Agent Dan Groves learned that Hearst was, at least verbally, an enthusiastic participant. "I took the tape of Patricia Hearst in the bank robbery over to the Berkeley School for the Deaf. And they read her lips as to what she was saying in the bank. 'I'm Tania. Up, up, up against the wall.' And then everybody giggled because they couldn't say it. And I said, 'M.F.' And they said, 'Yeah, that's it.'"

During the period that immediately followed, some San Francisco comedians utilized two SLA quotes in their routines. One was the slogan, "Death to the fascist insect that preys upon the life of the people." The other was Patty Hearst bank robbery order: "Up against the wall, motherfucker."

YET ANOTHER COMMUNIQUÉ from the SLA hit the media on April 24. Hearst declared the robbery had "expropriated" $10,660.02, a different amount than the bank reported. DeFreeze tried to explain the shootings were due to one man being uncooperative and another posing a threat. DeFreeze then weighed in on the ongoing horror of the Zebra murders and the racial profiling that Mayor Joseph Alioto had approved to try and find the killers.

The San Francisco Police Department's mid-April search for the Zebra killers utilized the profiling of black men and included the issuance of "Zebra Check" cards, issued by the SFPD in case the cleared suspect was stopped again. After more than five hundred black men were detained in a week, US District Judge Alfonso Zirpoli declared the emergency profiling unconstitutional the following Tuesday. Operation Zebra was condemned by DeFreeze as a "planned enemy offensive against the people to commit a race war."

DeFreeze remarkably reconfigured the murderous SLA into radical Robin Hoods, to some observers, providing food to some of California's poor and instantly dominating the covers of *Newsweek* and *Time* after the haphazard but successful Hibernia Bank robbery. But DeFreeze knew he was living on borrowed time, metaphorically looking back over his shoulder. He both feared for his life and the lives of his SLA brothers and sisters.

Lawrence Ferlinghetti, San Francisco's beloved Beat generation poet, three years before the Patty Hearst kidnapping, wrote a piece called "Las Vegas Tilt," in which he used the structure of newspaper headlines. In part, it read, "Hearst's Daughter Castigates Hearst's America/Attacks Absolute Spiritual Bankruptcy."

Ferlinghetti's predictive poetry had come to fruition. And Donald DeFreeze, alcoholic, secretive, overcome with a hypervigilant view of his underground existence, made the disastrous decision to leave the Bay Area and return to that place where his world as an informant had begun.

10 · IGNORING THE EVIDENCE

AFTER THE OPERATION ZEBRA PROTESTS and the Hibernia Bank robbery, the Symbionese Liberation Army debated whether they could remain undetected in San Francisco, despite estimates that up to a thousand FBI agents nationwide were engaged in the search for the group and Patty Hearst, whom the Bureau had cautiously labeled a "material witness."

DeFreeze and the SLA befriended four Black Muslim neighbors on Golden Gate Avenue, who helped buy them food and other necessities. About a week after the bank holdup, DeFreeze gave them cash to purchase three vehicles for an exodus from the Bay Area.

At about the same time, the original head of the first Symbionese Liberation Army, in the prison system, Robert Hyde, was in jeopardy. Late in 1973, Hyde contacted the FBI a second time and was visited at Soledad by two agents. As Hyde wrote to Superior Court Judge Elliot Daum, then a San Jose attorney, "The day after I talked to agents Pat Beatie and Carl Gosting, I was sent to segregation [O-wing, "the hole"]. . . . It has been decided I know too much and must be silenced."

Part of the effort to intimidate Hyde was an incident in which eyedrops he was using turned out to be acid and blinded him in one eye. He continued writing to Daum and the political researcher Mae Brussell about threats to him and they in turn reached out to others.

Daum said he was denied access to Hyde at first. "They were absolutely adamant I could not see him." When Daum insisted, as Hyde's lawyer, a correctional officer informed him that Hyde, a mild-mannered, well-spoken jailhouse lawyer, was in a highly volatile and dangerous unit. Daum was surprised when he saw the silver-haired black convict. "He was in chains from head to toe. He had a black patch over one eye."

On April 24, while DeFreeze and the SLA planned a move to Southern California, Robert Hyde was transferred to Vacaville. He wrote again to Daum, in fear for his life. "I am scheduled for psychosurgery, brain section removal. All my papers and property have been taken from me." Representative Ron Dellums, whose embrace of left-wing politics had endeared him to the East Bay, made an inquiry, and with the additional scrutiny, the CDC decided to send Hyde back to "the hole" in Soledad. The attention from Dellums saved Hyde from psychosurgery.

On April 29, another Bay Area politician, Representative Leo Ryan, along with Democratic Senator Harold Hughes of Iowa, introduced the Hughes-Ryan Act, mandating that the president notify congressional committees of all covert Central Intelligence Agency activities. Ryan, as a member of the House of Representatives International Relations Committee, was the foremost critic of the CIA in Washington. He cagily decided to challenge the Agency just as impeachment proceedings were beginning in the House Judiciary Committee for the removal of Richard Nixon from the office of president.

Unlike the president, whose offer of 1,200 pages of edited transcripts of his White House tapes was rejected by the House, DeFreeze's decision to move the SLA, like his other dictates, went unchallenged.

Bill Harris praised him for behavior others might consider strange. "Cin was really self-reliant. At first, it wasn't possible for him to go out to the shooting range or out to the country to practice with a gun. So he'd stand in front of a mirror for hours, just aiming at his image."

Harris's wife Emily confirmed that DeFreeze did not have the stature of a typical revolutionary leader. "And he certainly wasn't dominant in political discussions. The only time he got excited was when he thought someone hadn't really internalized some aspect of racism. He usually talked less than anyone else."

Far from being loquacious, DeFreeze was also not concerned with physical organization in the crowded, third-floor apartment at 1827 Golden Gate Avenue. Clothes were strewn about the floor. Dishes jammed the sink, bags of garbage accumulated, and the space had an ongoing problem with cockroaches that did not seem to bother anyone.

Members of the SLA felt so safe in their hovel on Golden Gate that they took turns shopping at the New Laguna grocery store. "Practically all of them were in and out of here but I didn't know who they were," admitted the owner, Mrs. E. G. Jamerson. "The girl I thought was Patty was thin and pretty, beautiful. Once I asked her, 'Are you Patty?' But she just smiled and said, 'A lot of folks think that.'" Jamerson insisted all the SLA members she inadvertently met were pleasant and she even remembered DeFreeze coming in to ask, without success, for plum wine.

Retimah X was a young, single, Black Muslim mother who provided help to the SLA, including the purchase of groceries and vehicles. She was quoted as saying she thought "all white people were devils," echoing a term used by Malcolm X. But when she visited Golden Gate Avenue, seeing the mix of black and white people and, according to her, many sympathizers who dropped by, it changed her viewpoint.

"All these white people came from good homes," she recognized. "They didn't have to become revolutionaries, but they chose it themselves. Fahizah [Nancy Ling Perry] talked a lot about how important it was that blacks and whites get together, and every time I came up to Golden Gate she embraced me. They all did. I had never embraced a white before, but the SLA changed my thinking about the race question."

While minorities generally forgave the SLA for its excesses after People in Need, not all radicals did. Bruce Franklin, now stripped of his professorship at Stanford University, the Venceremos Organization he had founded defunct, lashed out at the Army, calling them "counterrevolutionary." Like many on the far left who either met DeFreeze or heard of his early plans after fleeing Soledad, Franklin also felt that DeFreeze might be a provocateur for a police agency. He also said that the SLA did "a great deal of damage to the revolutionary movement and played into the hands of the most reactionary forces in the United States today."

Franklin and radicals like him, despite the willingness to bomb buildings that represented the failed system they lived in, did not advocate murder, kidnapping, and bank robberies. Nor did they expect a vanguard force of less than a dozen using militaristic rhetoric to lead the way to revolution.

It is an irony above and beyond the many ironies associated with the SLA that their Golden Gate hideout was revealed by a blind woman. The elderly Lolabelle Evans was sightless but had acute hearing. "They was up to all hours of the night, making all kinds of noise, funny kinds of noise. One time it sounded like they was dragging something like machines across the floor. Another time it was like they was drilling through the floor." One night, shortly before the tiny army left the premises, Evans heard their voices upstairs. "It sounded like they was counting money."

It was Evans's complaint about a swarm of roaches in her own apartment that led the manager to force his way into number six, which then had a total of six locks on the door. What he saw prompted an immediate call to the police.

The SLA escaped a gun battle with San Francisco police at the Hibernia Bank by one or two minutes. The police and FBI arrived at the Golden Gate hideout just about one week late. Donald DeFreeze was cursed with the worst kind of luck during his pre-prison criminal career. But somehow with the SLA, he always seemed to be blessed with close calls that went his way.

On May 2, the FBI began a detailed forensic examination of the Golden Gate Avenue apartment. They found piles of clothes, wigs, women's underwear, empty gallon bottles of wine, and a bicycle, but no actionable documents like those the group had left at Sutherland Court.

A huge, black, seven-headed cobra was spray-painted on one bathroom wall. Near the door to the hallway, written in pencil, was "Freedom is the will of life. Cinque." On another wall was "*Patria o Muerte, Venceremos*. Tania."

It defies the imagination how the entire group lived in the $125-a-month apartment. There was a double bed that lowered from the wall. Furnishings include three metal folding chairs and a lawn chair, its webbing sagging.

The SLA believed in "death to the fascist insect," but they encouraged the cockroaches at 1827 Golden Gate. The stove and kitchen walls were covered with grease, and bits of food and grime were everywhere. The refrigerator had a foul odor from decayed groceries that had not been thrown out.

Documents and half a dozen keys had been dumped into the bathtub, with various caustic chemicals poured in to dissolve them. The makeshift army taunted everyone who came to mind in the opening line of a diatribe written in felt-tip pen on the wall behind the toilet. It began: "WARNING TO THE FBI, CIA, DIA, NSA, NSC AND CBS." It was written that there were "juicy" clues scattered around the apartment, that potassium cyanide had been added to the "home brew" of chemicals, and finally, in an obvious reference to San Francisco FBI Special Agent in Charge Charles Bates, they painted the words, "Happy Hunting, Charles."

The move to 1808 Oakdale Street in the primarily black Bayview–Hunters Point section of San Francisco was a stopgap measure, intended to buy the SLA more time before the trip to the Los Angeles area. The faded brown stucco apartment building was in a neighborhood generally avoided, stuck among dreary industrial yards in the southeastern corner of the city. Possibly affecting the decision to move to that location was the fact that the two-bedroom apartment on Oakdale was one block from the Bayview distribution point for People in Need.

Jamellea Muntaz, a twenty-one-year-old Black Muslim woman, was among the four who helped the SLA when they hid in the Western Addition. Muntaz is thought to be the one given $375 by DeFreeze to rent the Oakdale hideout, using the name "M. Jackson." Neighbors said they saw three black men in army jackets entering the house. The SLA clearly had some trustworthy friends. But DeFreeze, ruminating about his past in those waning days of his life on the run, must have assumed that he could find support in certain underprivileged neighborhoods in Los Angeles. He was both right and completely, gravely wrong.

THE BEGINNING OF the end for DeFreeze and the SLA was the decision to leave the Bay Area, and the first sign that it was a tactical error came on May 1. With a $30,000 reward for information leading to the arrest of the Zebra killers, a young man named Anthony Harris, whose face was depicted in an artist's sketch in Bay Area newspapers, came forward to San Francisco police. He admitted seeing slain bodies where most of the men worked, Black Self Help Moving and Storage, but swore he didn't participate in the murders.

To protect himself, Harris became an informant. Seven men were arrested after a massive raid that numbered around one hundred officers in three locations. Two of the convicted lived in an apartment complex at 844 Grove Street. It was, astoundingly, only nine blocks from the Golden Gate apartment that housed the most wanted criminals in America. Another convicted killer was arrested at 339 Fillmore Street, eleven blocks from the SLA hideout. Four of the so-called Death Angels were eventually given sentences of life in prison with the possibility of parole, which has never been granted. One has since died behind bars.

The Zebra case headed for closure, totaling fourteen known homicides, although *Zebra* author Clark Howard found similar black-on-white cases nationally and could not discount other Death Angel murders that might have numbered up to fifty. In the Bay Area, there were seven injuries, including future San Francisco mayor Art Agnos, who survived two bullets in his back.

DeFreeze, who unwisely exposed the Golden Gate hideout to numerous local residents with his pleas for help, fled just as the extraordinary police presence in San Francisco for the Zebra killings abated.

He created friction in the group by replacing Perry as second-in-command with Bill Harris. There was no explanation. Contributing factors may have included the fact that Perry fired at Foster instead of Blackburn, failed to burn down Sutherland Court, and argued against the death warrant for Robyn Steiner. Perhaps DeFreeze wanted more male militancy in the discussions and Wolfe was not, in his mind, appropriate for the role. The decision to reconfigure the SLA into three three-person units, move to Los Angeles, and engage in home invasions and ambushes on police signaled yet another change in DeFreeze's thinking. There was no dissuading him, and a kind of fatalism, according to Hearst, seeped into the atmosphere of the SLA.

His answer to SLA member objections about change of locale was to study Los Angeles area street maps. DeFreeze and the group again narrowly escaped detection when, around the beginning of May, he took his revolutionaries down to Los Angeles from Oakdale Street.

The stark contrast between the FBI and the Justice Department's attitudes about the SLA continued. Attorney General Saxbe, frustrated like all those trying to apprehend the group, said that a continued increase in crime in general in the United States might lead to the establishment of a national police force. FBI Director Kelley said he would fight any effort to create such a force. It was clearly perceived as an affront to the Bureau. Kelley urged more cooperation between different levels of law enforcement to reduce crime.

Echoing the current ongoing discussion about the National Security Agency spying on American citizens to detect potential acts of domestic terrorism, Kelley did address the need, in his opinion, for the right to wiretap American citizens in domestic security cases. He made this extralegal argument in connection with the numerous escapes of the Symbionese Liberation Army.

"For example, in the SLA," he told reporters in Seattle, "we cannot put a wiretap on them because they are a domestic security matter." He mentioned the success of certain domestic cases where wiretaps were secured and said he wanted to see legislation authorizing the use of wiretaps to apprehend "revolutionaries."

On the same day as Kelley's press conference, Private Investigator Lake Headley, working with Donald Freed and Rusty Rhodes at the Citizens Research and Investigation Committee, got LAPD Sergeant R. G. Farwell on the phone and both tape recorded and transcribed the conversation.

Toward the end of the discussion, Headley talked about DeFreeze's 1970 letter of fourteen pages to Judge Ritzi, especially DeFreeze's reliance on religious dogma.

"Well, that is why I cut him loose," Farwell admitted. "He was getting into that and I knew that he was . . . as far as psychological things are concerned."

Headley and Farwell discussed the possibility of talking again, possibly face-to-face, but Farwell knew that the FBI was in charge of the SLA investigation and that he could not say much more. But in closing, he did state that DeFreeze's informant background would very probably be his undoing. "Okay, right now, I am going to stand where I am. I don't mind talking to you, but the guy [DeFreeze] is in trouble, and if word gets out that he did anything at all for the police, he is dead."

Headley had a different view, namely, that making the public aware of DeFreeze's LAPD informant background would make the capture of the SLA, rather than its possible annihilation, more likely.

But Farwell's concerns had occurred to others as well. Jeanne Davies, one of Headley's investigators, learned on May 7 that numerous files previously accessed regarding Donald DeFreeze were "lost" at the Los Angeles County Clerk's offices. These included probation reports, letters from DeFreeze to Judge Ritzi, and letters from Gloria DeFreeze to Judge Barrett.

Fighting his own public relations war, on May 7, Colston Westbrook was in Toronto, taping radio and television programs, and providing the press with new, absurd contentions about the SLA, goaded by the addition of his name to their hit list. He still battled the questions about his background and his cooperation.

"I'm not an informer but I am an informant," he began with a highly provocative choice of words in the present tense. "I collect information from a lot of people and sift it and pass it on. I've given it both to the FBI and the SLA."

With more false bravado than he had previously exhibited, Westbrook bragged that there were California prisoners "loyal to me" who would kill ten SLA supporters if he were killed.

Following up on the astounding interview Headley had with Farwell at the LAPD, the CRIC held a press conference at the San Francisco law office of Charles Garry. Major West Coast papers, including the *San Francisco Chronicle*, *Los Angeles Times*, *San Mateo Times,* and other media outlets, heard a presentation by Headley, taken from more than four hundred pages of documents.

Headley concluded the press conference, referring to the inevitability of DeFreeze's demise, predicting to the media gathered, "He'll be killed, probably in a shootout."

In its coverage, the *Chronicle* stressed the fact that DeFreeze had been a "highly protected and valued" informant for the LAPD from 1967 to 1969 and that he continued to be a snitch in Vacaville and Soledad. The newspaper contacted Farwell, who only said that his superiors ordered him to say nothing more about the subject to anyone.

Los Angeles police chief Ed Davis admitted that DeFreeze had once turned in a partner to police, referring obliquely to Ronald

Coleman and the two-hundred–gun heist in Torrance. But Davis then suggested the LAPD had a longer history with him, saying DeFreeze "proved himself to be a cheap, undependable, turnover punk." Evelle Younger denied knowing anything about DeFreeze, saying, "At no time during my tenure has Donald DeFreeze been an informant for the attorney general's office." It was a carefully worded evasion. No one had suggested DeFreeze worked directly for Younger's office.

On May 14, one of the few people who could prove DeFreeze did not "escape" from Soledad Prison, James Mayfield, had a surprising visit from the FBI at his Oakland apartment.

After all that had happened, it was not that remarkable that the Bureau asked Mayfield, who had been involved with the Black Cultural Association, to help them find Donald DeFreeze and the SLA. What was memorable was the fact that a briefcase with $20 and $50 bills was shown to Mayfield, totaling $250,000. But despite an offer in excess of $1.2 million in 2016 US dollars, Mayfield claimed he had no knowledge. There was no other publicized offer of this kind to any other informant regarding finding the SLA.

Concerned that he might be labeled as a snitch, Mayfield went public about the generous offer. Charles Bates tersely commented, "The FBI handles its own business. I'm not going into any details." Bates deflected criticism by mentioning the $50,000 Randolph Hearst offered for the safe return of his daughter. "The FBI," he added, "does its own job."

RATHER LESS IN value than $1.2 million, it was the theft of an item worth less than five dollars that began the demolition of the Symbionese Liberation Army in Southern California.

After the group exodus from San Francisco, the SLA set up a refuge at 835 West 84th Street, in the volatile South Central ghetto. Bill and Emily Harris were shopping in Mel's Sporting Goods at 11425 S. Crenshaw Boulevard in Inglewood on May 16, a bit after 4 p.m. Patty Hearst was in a Volkswagen bus parked outside, as she was much more recognizable than the married couple. Tony Shepard, a twenty-year-old security guard, happened to look up just as Bill Harris stuffed a cloth bandolier up his sleeve.

Emily purchased a sweater, sweat pants, several pairs of sweat socks, and a knitted cap. As the couple moved toward the front door, Shepard grabbed his pistol and a pair of handcuffs and gave a hand signal to his boss, Bill Huett, to follow him to capture the shoplifters.

The Harrises began to jaywalk across Crenshaw Boulevard when Shepard confronted Bill Harris, who denied stealing and continued walking away.

"You're under arrest!" shouted Shepard, and he and Harris began to grapple, as Emily Harris cursed and kicked ferociously at Shepard. Bill fell to the asphalt, Shepard landed on top of him, and Huett and two other employees yanked the hysterically violent Emily off the young security guard.

Bill Harris pulled out a snub-nosed pistol but Shepard ripped it from his grasp, jammed the gun into one of his own pockets and clamped a handcuff on Harris's left wrist.

The screaming, kicking, and punching came to a sudden halt as .30 caliber bullets, twenty-seven of them, shattered the glass storefront of Mel's. Three slugs entered adjoining buildings.

From a window of the VW, Patty Hearst fired a semiautomatic rifle, across the busy street traffic and above and around those fighting in front of the store. One of the slugs ricocheted and hit one of the clerks in the chest, bending a ball-point pen in the man's pocket. Remarkably, he was uninjured. Huett's wife was cut on the head from a flying shard of glass.

"Let us go!" shouted Bill Harris. "Let us go or you're going to be killed!" With the handcuff still dangling from his left wrist, Harris and his wife dashed through traffic on Crenshaw as Hearst fired one more volley. Shepard shot twice at the fleeing van, missing.

It was pure chance that no one was killed from the two M-1s Hearst fired. Years later, she tried to tell Larry King on CNN that her coming to the aid of the Harrises with gunfire was a reflex, although she used a word that meant the opposite.

> I thought I was kind of fooling them for a while, and the point I knew I was completely gone, I'm quite convinced, was at Mel's Sporting Goods store when I reflectively [*sic*] did exactly what I'd been trained to do that day, instead of what any sensible person would have done or person still in control of their senses and their responses, which would be, the minute the Harrises left the van, to have just run off and called the police.

Showing rather remarkable devotion to his job, Shepard leaped into his own car and pursued the red and white Volkswagen around Inglewood, until it zoomed up residential Ruthelen Street, a half mile away, pulling alongside a black and yellow Pontiac that had just parked. Bill Harris and Hearst, holding their weapons in the faces of a man and woman, had no trouble commandeering the vehicle, and Emily transferred the rest of their weapons inside of it.

It was then that Bill Harris noticed Shepard a few car lengths away, watching them from his vehicle. Harris, ready to engage in gunfire, began walking toward Shepard, pointing his weapon at the young security guard. Shepard, faced with three people possessing semiautomatics, threw his car into reverse and screeched backwards down the street, getting away before any shots were fired in his direction.

But typical of the SLA's quickly receding fortunes, the stolen Pontiac stalled blocks away at 115th and Cimarron, just inside the border of Hawthorne. They stole a blue Chevrolet Nova station wagon from a father and son, again transferred their weapons to a new vehicle, and fled quickly.

By seven o'clock that evening, Emily Harris approached the front door of a house at 10871 Elm Street in suburban Lynwood, asking blonde, lanky eighteen-year-old Tom Mathews about the Ford van parked outside with a "For Sale" sign in its window. Emily stopped the car to let in her husband and Hearst. But Mathews seemed more fascinated than afraid by the three kidnappers. The "test drive" lasted hours.

At the same time, the VW abandoned on Ruthelen Street was inspected by police. The .38 wrestled from Harris proved to have a registration in Sacramento in the name of Emily Montague Harris. An even bigger blunder, and what essentially was the beginning of the end for DeFreeze and five others, was the presence of a parking ticket for the van, from three days before, left in a shirt pocket of Bill Harris, listing 835 W. 84th Street as the site of the infraction. Officers were sent to the area instantly.

The third store that the Harrises and Hearst stopped at had a hacksaw. Harris was furious when a news radio station recounted the robbery and shoot-out, erroneously reporting that he had shoplifted a forty-nine-cent pair of sweat socks.

They had planned a rendezvous with the rest of the SLA, hunkered down in South Central at the Century Drive-In in Inglewood at midnight. Of all films, they were showing the adaptation of crime novelist Joseph Wambaugh's *The New Centurions*, an action film about the Los Angeles Police Department. Making the meeting even more unconventional was the large, upside-down paper cup on top of the speaker stand next to their car, a signal as to their location, in one of two outdoor theaters with a capacity of 918 cars.

The obliging Mathews cut the handcuff off Bill Harris's wrist, while they waited. But DeFreeze and the rest of the Army never showed up. The news of Patty Hearst blasting bullets into the front of Mel's Sporting Goods in order to free the Harrises must have dissuaded DeFreeze from taking a chance on going to the drive-in to meet. There was no alternate way to contact each other and there were no accomplices in Los Angeles when they arrived.

DeFreeze, Perry, Soltysik, Wolfe, Hall, and Atwood, rather than going to the drive-in, returned to the bungalow they had arranged to stay in on 84th Street, around midnight. They frantically gathered their weapons and other possessions. They knew there would be a massive operation to find them and they had no idea where to go.

The Harrises and Hearst drove Tom Mathews's car north from Inglewood into the Hollywood Hills. Emily parked on a quiet stretch of the ironically named Outpost Drive, above the Hollywood Bowl, lights twinkling in the distance, so they could rest and rejuvenate their crisis-riddled minds. Mathews, concerned less with his own well-being than a baseball championship game he had in a few hours, even with the excitement of the evening, drifted off to sleep in the back of the car.

When he awoke, Hearst and Emily Harris decided to pretend to hitchhike, and sure enough, fifteen minutes later, they had a one-year-old Lincoln Continental and another hostage, building contractor Frank Sutter. Mathews was offered gas money by Bill Harris, refused and parted warmly from his captors, driving sleepily home. When his parents, strained with worry, demanded to know where he had been, Mathews admitted he was kidnapped, but, impressed like so many by close proximity to a celebrity, he mentioned two people and identified a picture of Emily Harris. But the name Patty Hearst was never uttered.

At 4:30 a.m., FBI agents and police stopped a South Central Los Angeles resident who said that a Caucasian man and woman who owned vans fitting previous police descriptions had rented a bungalow at 835 W. 84th Street.

DeFreeze assumed that the SLA would be supported in Los Angeles the same way it was in San Francisco. The Western Addition was predominantly black in composition, but nevertheless, the neighborhood had an ethnic mix. In addition, the Bay Area was more highly politicized by the SLA activities than Los Angeles.

In San Francisco, DeFreeze and his followers had numerous sympathizers to help them, people who embraced the message of a multicultural revolution and never reported the SLA's presence. In South Central on the Compton border, black residents were separated from other ethnic neighborhoods by freeways and long boulevards. The rare presence of blacks and whites together instantly aroused attention.

The safe house chosen for the relocated SLA was found by Soltysik and Perry. Their choice represented the worst conditions they had experienced. The 84th Street safe house was an unpainted, dilapidated, two-bedroom wooden shack. It had no electricity, gas, or phone. It did have running water.

Kyle "Prophet" Jones, the property manager who rented the cottage to DeFreeze and his group, stated honestly that "whites were not tolerated and even police came into the area at their own peril." DeFreeze apparently heard only the second part of Jones's warning.

It was yet another irony that the nickname of the property manager was Prophet, because with his increasing insularity and expectation of death, Donald DeFreeze began to revert to his previous religiosity. But now, he was not trying to manipulate a judge or probation officer. He was lapsing into a world that was both part of and separate from his white soldiers. Hearst remembered that while drinking plum wine, he told the assembly, "I am really a prophet. I am here on Earth to lead the people." He further announced that he was going to write a book about his life and wisdom. DeFreeze was living in one of the most dangerous areas of Los Angeles with no phone contact with the outside world. And yet he said his book would replace George Jackson's *Blood in My Eye* because "George had lost touch with people in the street."

By seven in the morning on Friday, May 17, there were about 125 policemen, FBI agents, and Specials Weapons and Tactics team members surrounding the house on 84th Street. Marksmen were poised on roofs with sniper rifles.

Increasing the urgency of this tactical response was a major article that had come out that very morning in the *New York Times* about Donald DeFreeze. John Kifner wrote in-depth on "Cinque: A Dropout Who Has Been in Constant Trouble." The piece summarized many of the crimes for which DeFreeze had suspiciously been given probation, over and over. It pointed out DeFreeze's connection to the Criminal Conspiracy Section of the Los Angeles Police Department. It included the assertion of Sergeant Farwell, before he was muzzled by his superiors, that DeFreeze was out of control and would likely be killed rather than captured.

When the CRIC press conference on May 10 in San Francisco was covered by West Coast papers, all reported DeFreeze as a police informant. Not one detailed the research on Patty Hearst's relationship with DeFreeze while he was in prison, the prison origins of the SLA, or the CIA background of Colston Westbrook. Whether this was due to a case of self-censorship, reticence about relying on prisoners as sources, an inability to accept the outrageousness of the facts, a concern about legal liability for those facts, or any combination of these factors, no major paper recounted the full story.

If the SLA had evaded law enforcement for a while longer, it is possible major new media might have followed up on the revelations of the Citizens Research Investigation Committee. That increased examination, especially if it had come from the *New York Times* or *Washington Post* (which had no comparable coverage to the *Times*) could have enlightened the public to the behavior of the CIA and California Department of Corrections. That knowledge could have put pressure on law enforcement to take a much more cautious approach to the inevitable capture of the Symbionese Liberation Army.

Instead, DeFreeze and five of his followers were about to be on live television, nationally, in a brutal, relentless, and disproportionate display of military and police force.

IT WAS 8:50 IN THE morning, and there was absolutely no way the Symbionese Liberation Army was going to escape scores of FBI agents and LAPD officers plus sheriff's department deputies and California highway patrolmen, armed and aiming their weapons at the rundown house on 84th Street.

An LAPD sergeant used a bullhorn to demand that everyone inside come out with hands raised in the air. Five minutes passed with no activity inside the house. The FBI's officer in charge ordered the use of tear gas, and seven canisters were fired into the residence. Police and FBI agents burst in the back door, guns at the ready. But it was too late. The Symbionese Liberation Army had once again, barely, escaped.

Five hours earlier, at about 4:00 a.m., DeFreeze and his group found a house at 1466 East 54th Street that had all its lights on. DeFreeze knocked on the door and Christine Johnson, thirty-five, and her cousin Minnie Lewis, thirty-two, answered. They had been involved in a game of dominoes while drinking wine, followed by listening to the radio in the wee hours of the morning. DeFreeze identified himself and his army and offered them $100 if they would house the most wanted criminals in America. They agreed but must have had second thoughts when it took twenty full minutes to unload all nineteen rifles, shotguns, and pistols; more than 4,000 rounds of ammunition; and explosive devices from the two vans and bring them into the house. Four M-1s had been converted to be fully automatic. DeFreeze personally carried a .38, a Smith and Wesson snub-nosed Chief's Special.

Johnson and Lewis were not alone. Freddie Freeman, a neighbor, offered to help DeFreeze ditch the vans at a nearby spot where nonfunctioning cars were often abandoned, 1451 East 53rd Street. He and DeFreeze went off in the vans, leaving the SLA with no transportation. What Freeman neglected to tell DeFreeze was that the spot was known for the abandonment of stolen vehicles and the LAPD regularly patrolled it. No attempt was made to change the appearance of the vehicles or remove their license plates or vehicle identification numbers.

Very early in the morning, as two of Lewis's children woke up for school, Brenda Daniels, seventeen, another neighbor and friend of the household, was entrusted with twenty dollars to get bread, lunch meat, beer, and wine for the SLA, plus cigarettes for DeFreeze. Three other children belonging to Lewis lived in the home of Mary Carr, their grandmother, who was within walking distance of them.

Freeman left briefly around 9:30 to call friends from a pay phone and see if he could secure the use of a car, for which the SLA would pay up to forty dollars a day. He returned to 1466 unsuccessful. By late morning, a number of people had dropped in on the Johnson and Lewis household, only to discover the well-armed, primarily white Symbionese Liberation Army jammed into the house.

DeFreeze showed no hesitation about identifying himself to anyone who entered Lewis and Johnson's home. His options for escape were diminishing, and yet on he talked about his noble crusade to lead the people, presuming the black population of South Central Los Angeles would instantly embrace him and help him.

Two LAPD officers went by 1451 East 53rd Street at 12:20, to see if any new stolen-and-stripped vehicles had been deposited there. The two vans DeFreeze and Freeman left there caught the officers' attention immediately, especially the light blue van with the dented front, which fit a previously reported police description.

Thirty minutes later, Hearst and the Harrises, at around one in the afternoon, secured new transportation yet again. They purchased a used car they found listed in a newspaper, using the $250 they had "expropriated" from the previously kidnapped Frank Sutter. They gave him back his keys and told him where they had parked his car and he left them, unharmed.

As for young Tom Mathews, who later admitted Patty Hearst was one of his abductors, that afternoon his Lynwood High baseball team, with him at first base, won a local area championship over Bassett High, 2-0.

At the same time the separated unit of the SLA bought its latest car, Freeman left the house in South Central, after he was given $500 by DeFreeze to secure a new vehicle for the group. He never returned.

Daryl Gates, later to become police chief, was in charge of LAPD operations on May 17. His meeting at the Newton Street police station with other LAPD and FBI officials was meant to coordinate efforts. Gates, in 1965, had approved Officer John Nelson's concept for SWAT. Chief Ed Davis was told by Gates that it stood for "Special Weapons Attack Team." Davis knew the aggressive LAPD would be wise to avoid the use of the word "attack," so "Special Weapons and Tactics" was born.

William A. Sullivan, assistant director of the FBI field office in Los Angeles, in the hours before the assault on 54th Street, insisted that the FBI, currently coordinating a national search for the SLA, lead the operation. Gates, according to the LAPD Draft Report on the event, flatly refused. The FBI was reliant on the LAPD to cordon off the area and provide logistical support with the fire department, ambulances, and other services. So the LAPD directed the operation, surrounding the area of Compton Avenue, East 53rd and East 54th streets, a four-block staging area.

As police presence grew on the street, Lewis and Daniels left the house, fearful of what was about to transpire. They tried to wake up Johnson, who was unconscious due to her ingesting a mixture of alcohol and pills. Lewis and Daniels were told by SLA members, "Leave her alone. Let her sleep."

After he came home from school, Johnson's son Timmy, eleven, was alarmed to see the house filled with one black man and a group of white men and women who possessed many guns. His mother was in bed, unresponsive. The boy immediately reported this to his grandmother. Mary Carr quickly walked to her daughter's house, only to be told despite her demands that the SLA was not leaving. Carr claimed one woman from the SLA smiled at her and patted the pistol she wore. DeFreeze mumbled something to Carr about "black people needing to stick together." She took her two grandchildren and stormed out. At approximately five o'clock in the afternoon, Mary Carr notified the police.

At 5:30, Emily and Bill Harris and Patty Hearst paid for a hotel room in Anaheim, in Orange County. Emily had spent a summer in college working at Disneyland. So the three SLA members, cut off from communication with the rest, entered the quiet of their hotel room, exhausted, hoping to finally rest and figure out how to reconnect with their comrades. The TV was turned on, and to their complete shock, a live news story, using technology recently developed, was being broadcast. The report stated that the SLA had been found and at a minimum, 425 officers and FBI agents now surrounded 1466 East 54th Street.

The first bullhorn notice from the LAPD came at 5:44, stating the house was surrounded and the occupants needed to come out with their hands raised. Tony, Minnie Lewis's eight-year-old son, came outside and froze in terror, looking at the multitude of armed men. He was picked up by an officer. Clarence Ross, twenty-three, another friend who had dropped by, gingerly stepped outside and surrendered.

The first official LAPD report mentioned "at least 18 separate surrender announcements were made," between the nine minutes of the first bullhorn demand and the firing of the first tear gas projectiles. It was also reported that during the shoot-out that followed, eleven separate surrender announcements were made.

The next day, the *Los Angeles Times* front page said there were two announcements. A SWAT officer was ordered to fire "two 509 CS Flite-Rite tear gas projectiles through the top of the west window of the SLA residence." After the second tear gas projectile entered the house, the report stated that members of the SLA opened fire.

The police report said that by 5:53, automatic weapons fire from the house was being fully met with semiautomatic weapon fire and more tear gas. During the firefight, about one dozen residents within the cordoned area refused to leave their homes. At 6:41, black smoke billowed out of the house, and then flames were seen. Another bullhorn announcement again asked for surrender.

Then, Christine Johnson, just awakened from a surfeit of alcohol and pills, stumbled out of the house, hysterically shouting, "They held me. They held me." She was cuffed and dragged away by police. She had a superficial wound from a shotgun pellet. Johnson was arrested as an accomplice and treated, but eventually charges were dropped.

At 6:47, the last message over the bullhorn was, "Come out. You will not be harmed. The house is on fire. It's all over." Gunfire continued to come from the house and the crawl space under the floorboards. The Los Angeles Fire Department allegedly refused to send its men in to fight the flames, due to firing of weapons.

Nancy Ling Perry, according to officers nearby, emerged from the southwest corner of the house, via the crawl space. She cautiously moved about ten feet from the house. Camilla Hall soon followed. Weapons fire continued from the house, and Hall began to fire at SWAT team members, who returned fire, killing both women. By 6:59, all gunfire had ceased from inside the burning house.

Perry, Hall, and Soltysik expired from gunshot wounds. Atwood and Wolfe died due to smoke inhalation and burns. Coroner Thomas Noguchi ruled DeFreeze died of a self-inflicted gunshot wound to the head.

Two policemen were injured, neither from SLA gunfire. One fell from a roof and broke his leg. The other was struck in the stomach by a piece of concrete thrown by an unseen onlooker.

The LAPD report concluded, "The cause of the fire was undetermined." In the ruins of 1466 54th Street, a two-gallon gas can was found with perforations in it. Nearby were two pipe bombs, two blasting caps, and other homemade explosive devices.

THE SHOOT-OUT AND fire in South Central Los Angeles changed certain aspects of American society. But it was by no means the first time a SWAT team had been used. It was not even the first time SWAT had been employed against radical activists.

The idea for SWAT originated after the LAPD did not know how to respond to the 1965 Watts race riot, which took place just about three miles from 1466 East 54th Street.

On December 4, 1969, Fred Hampton, deputy chairman of the Black Panther Party, and fellow Panther Mark Clark were infamously shot dead in their sleep during a supposed drug raid by Chicago police. Despite the international furor that came from that event, five days later, a three-location raid by 350 LAPD officers occurred, and SWAT led the attack on Black Panther headquarters in Los Angeles, with search warrants for illegal guns in tow.

A phenomenal four-hour gun battle ensued, resulting in four Panthers and four SWAT team members being wounded. Recognizing that ten men could not outlast hundreds of militarily trained and armed officers, the Panthers surrendered. After SWAT's initial success, other police departments asked LAPD's SWAT officers to train their units. The growth was instantaneous and exponential.

May 17, 1974, became burned into the consciousness of Americans who watched that day, not only because of the introduction of SWAT to a national audience but also because the coverage became the first major, live, national television news event using a new "minicam" technology.

In Los Angeles, CBS-TV affiliate KNXT called its evening rush hour broadcast "Big News," and it proved to be just that. They were first on the scene at 54th Street and had semi-experimental portable cameras that used videotape instead of film. KNXT's Rey Hernandez and Rich Brito got closer to the SLA hideout than any other news team. Reporters Bill Deiz and Bob Simmons joined them, but so did KNBC, the NBC affiliate, with a large studio truck. The KNBC truck transmitter was flipped on, sending their signal from South Central to a relay tower on Mount Wilson in the San Gabriel Mountains. But KNXT used a tower on Mount Wilson as well, and the surge knocked them off the air.

Back at KNXT, according to the *American Journalism Review*, editor-news writer Bob Long quickly contacted KNBC, telling them that if they stayed out of the CBS crew's way, KNXT was willing to pool the coverage. Suddenly, the largest gun battle in US history was live on the broadcast networks, nationally.

Ray Beindorf, head of the CBS station group, who trademarked the name "minicam," learned about the live coverage and rushed back to his office in Manhattan. "I was in trouble," Bob Long mused, "until Beindorf could watch [KNXT news anchor] Jerry Dunphy on five channels in New York City."

The live feed of the May 17 shoot-out and fire changed the nature of television news. Electronic news gathering (ENG), via mobile cameras, went from five stations in 1973 to 550 in 1979, 86 percent of television news broadcasts nationwide. The age of covering crimes and catastrophes live was born and has yet to fade.

But viewers had a selective view of the event. There were major discrepancies between what the police reported and what was learned by some members of the media and by Lake Headley.

Headley, hired by Dr. L. S. Wolfe to investigate the shoot-out and fire that took his son's life, plus five others, created a document entitled "Investigation Report: An Inquiry into May 17, 1974 and Surrounding Events." With the help of his coinvestigators Elizabeth

Schmidt and Jeanne Davies, Headley cited some startling contradictions to the official narrative.

There was a functioning telephone at 1466 East 54th Street, listed in the Pacific Telephone directory under the name of Minnie Lewis, and yet no attempt was made to negotiate a surrender. Doctor Frederick Hacker, whom Randolph Hearst hired as consultant, was on the scene and had the ideal experience to negotiate with the SLA but was refused by FBI agents onsite. This failure of communication particularly haunted Dr. Wolfe because the FBI field office in Philadelphia assured him that there was no felony arrest warrant for Willie Wolfe.

Also, the FBI in Philadelphia told Dr. Wolfe that they possessed information suggesting Willie had left the "violent" faction of the SLA for a nonviolent one, prior to the shooting of Marcus Foster. They suggested this endangered Willie and urged Dr. Wolfe and his wife Sharon to go into hiding, which they did for a while.

The Philadelphia FBI field office also promised Dr. Wolfe numerous times that they would immediately contact him if Willie was located, in order for Dr. Wolfe to negotiate a surrender of his son.

Captain Marvin King of the LAPD, the operational commander, explained why the phone was not called inside 1466 East 54th Street. He said he learned about the phone only at the last minute, and by then, according to him, it was too late. Other policemen said they feared the SLA would use the "classical" urban guerrilla tactic of tunneling out of the house, a tactic that was, in the United States, neither classical nor one used by revolutionaries.

The news media covering the biggest shoot-out in US history was also deceived. There was a decoy house on East 53rd Street, where journalists were told that the SLA members were suspected to be hiding. After a long period of inactivity and lack of communication between the police and the press, one of the most darkly comical moments in the sad history of the Symbionese Liberation Army occurred.

Reporter Christine Lund, the blonde Swedish native who eventually became an anchor for KABC-TV in Los Angeles, got tired of waiting for something to transpire and regally marched up to the front door of the alleged hideout and knocked, with the expectation she'd be granted an interview with armed revolutionaries. No one answered, and police quickly admonished her and moved her away from the decoy location.

The Los Angeles Police Department not only deceived some of the media but also wrested control of the crime scene away from the Feds, despite the fact that Police Chief Ed Davis was out of town on May 17. The jurisdictional chasm between the LAPD and the FBI widened as the day went on. There were fifty FBI agents present at the fruitless raid on 84th Street, early in the morning. By the time the SLA hideout was surrounded, there were only seven FBI agents present, since the Bureau had ceded authority to the LAPD.

As for the initiation of the gun battle, Headley quoted Richard West and John Mosqueda in the *Los Angeles Times* of the next day. "He [a police officer] dropped to one knee almost directly in front of the yellow stucco bungalow at 1466 and fired a tear gas round through the front window. Then he scrambled to his feet and ran for his life. As soon as he was out of the way, scores of policemen and FBI agents started pouring bullets into the house."

Los Angeles Police Commission President Samuel Williams told the press that the reason no effort was made to negotiate with the SLA was that those inside the house opened fire before the police could do so.

Researcher Rusty Rhodes learned that SWAT teams were told that the SLA was responsible for the murder of police officer Michael Lee Edwards a week before in order to encourage them to fire without discrimination. Rhodes's sources were listed as John Babcock, assignment editor at KABC-TV; Suzanne Yanok, NBC researcher; and newsman Clete Roberts, in a KNXT-TV minicam report.

Florence Lishey was the owner of the house Johnson and Lewis rented on 54th Street. She lived across an alley and two doors down from the SLA hideout and swore to Rhodes that when the firing began, she dropped to the floor. She was evacuated only after police shot the lock off her front door, entered, and used her house as a firing position.

A house and an apartment building on either side of 1466 were also completely gutted by the fire. They belonged to Lishey as well. After the SLA hideout was reduced to rubble, LAPD officers were spotted removing their bullets from adjoining buildings, to avoid any inquiry about errant gunfire. Rhodes identified the bullets as .223 caliber, not among the ammunition the SLA carried.

Nancy Ling Perry's body was found about ten feet away from the back of the house. She was shot in the back and no weapon was found, suggesting she tried to surrender and attempted to reenter the house after being fired upon.

Rhodes found that around five thousand rounds had been fired into the house and estimated that no more than one hundred rounds were fired by the SLA, disputing the LAPD estimate of one thousand rounds by each side.

Bob Simmons of KNXT told Headley in an interview that he saw and the station possessed film of fire trucks arriving at the area of 53rd and Compton, only to be stopped by LAPD officers and prevented from putting out the fire. Other journalists reported to Headley that a fire captain demanded to cross LAPD lines to fight the fire and was told by a police officer that if he attempted to do so, he would be arrested.

Further support for the assertion that the LAPD did not want the SLA to survive the fire was the testimony of Mrs. Arlelle Bryan, who lived at 1456 East 54th Street. She informed Rusty Rhodes that she heard LAPD officers with bullhorns shout to fire units, "Stop! Don't come in here! Let it burn!" In fact, there is a law enforcement term for this, a "let-burn" situation in which there is no incentive to enter a burning building, whether uninhabited or occupied by criminal suspects.

In July, a 128-page police report pinpointed the moment the house caught on fire at 6:41, after a SWAT team member tossed two tear gas canisters through a broken window on the east side of the house. One minute later, the house was ablaze.

According to Narda Trout and Jerry Belcher, writing for the *Los Angeles Times*, the police fired about seventy-five canisters of Flite-Rite tear gas canisters into 1466 E. 54th Street. Eight were manually thrown inside, including two Federal 555 canisters. Press coverage did not make the distinction between the use of tear gas canisters and the fact the Federal 555 is a pyrotechnic grenade. Previously unstated anywhere in the press, those grenades likely started the fire. The oddly surnamed Don Peace of Federal Laboratories, the manufacturer, said, "It is established that you don't use a pyrotechnic grenade like the 555 in a building where there's a possibility of a fire." The 555, like any other pyrotechnic grenade, is intended for outdoor riot control, not for rooftops, crawl spaces, or indoor use.

Two local 54th and Compton businessmen, Samuel Thomas Green and Al Sham, told Headley and his investigators that just before the fire started, they heard three deep explosions from inside the house. Both men said the sound resembled a hand grenade. They both have served in the military, and Sham is a former Los Angeles deputy sheriff. The Federal 555 grenades likely ignited the gasoline and/or other explosives in the house.

According to Dr. Wolfe's testimony to Lake Headley, Philadelphia FBI SAC Richard J. Baker told him that the LAPD used incendiary devices to ignite the house on 54th Street. The LAPD denied this.

One week after the shoot-out and fire, Thomas Noguchi claimed DeFreeze shot himself. One year after the event, a Coroner's Office staffer and a consultant raised a major and undeniable forensic question about DeFreeze's death.

Doctor Ronald Taylor, director of the forensic labs at the Los Angeles Coroner's Office, and scientific consultant Dr. Vincent Guinn, a chemistry professor at UC Irvine, both spoke at a meeting of the Association of California Criminalists at the Los Angeles Sheraton Airport Hotel. They both concluded that DeFreeze was shot by someone outside the house, based on the ballistics.

The bullet was not from the .38 under DeFreeze's body, as officially reported, but was a nonregulation steel-jacketed projectile, of World War II type, not copper-jacketed as the LAPD used. After examining thirteen different samples from the era, the closest match was from a Czechoslovakian manufacturer. Asked for the source of their information, Taylor and Guinn's answer was that it came "from within the police department." There were only three journalists in attendance when this was revealed.

BECAUSE THE HOME of Johnson and Lewis had about a dozen visitors stop by during the presence of the Symbionese Liberation Army, there is a record of some of the final moments of those six lives extinguished.

A report from the Board of Police Commissioners to Mayor Tom Bradley, two months later, called "The Symbionese Liberation Army in Los Angeles," detailed some touching moments in the thirteen hours they hid in the house, especially within a section of the report called "Inside 1466 East 54th Street."

A female visitor who was at 54th Street around 2:30, when police patrols were increasing in the area, was identified by the *Los Angeles Times* as Stephanie Reed, eighteen, a friend of Johnson's who lived across the street. She heard DeFreeze say, "Trish, we've got to get out of here. It's getting too hot." What is most telling about the quotation is that DeFreeze had to be talking to Patricia Soltysik. He did not call her Zoya, her *nom de guerre*. He did not call her Mizmoon, her adoptive name. It was just Trish, the woman who took him in despite his convict status, supported him, and lived with him in relative peace for a short while in a yellow cottage on Parker Street in Berkeley.

Reed, who heard from her brother that the SLA was in the house, made two trips to the jammed and anxiety-filled residence. Quiet, intelligent, observant, Reed spoke little but was welcomed by the SLA members. The white revolutionary women tried to recruit her. "They asked me to stay, you know, to join them, because they needed more black people for their revolution and all. I just said, 'Yeah, I understand,' and that's all."

Reed watched as the group loaded backpacks and ammunition. Some of the women had pockets sewn into their pants to hold knives.

DeFreeze was holding a knife. Reed calmly asked him, "Will you use that?"

"I will," he answered, but quickly added, "I won't use it on black people. But I will on the pigs."

When Reed continued to observe but not speak, DeFreeze, curious, asked, "You don't talk, do you?"

"No" was her simple reply.

DeFreeze, still waiting for a getaway van he had paid Freeman to secure, grew more animated, pacing, saying more than once, "We got to split. The pigs are getting hot."

After another request for Reed to join them, the girl politely declined and walked back to her house. But there was more on her mind. She returned an hour later to 1466, "out of curiosity," as she told the police.

DeFreeze asked Reed if she "talked," and this time, he meant if she had informed on the SLA. She assured him she had not. DeFreeze peeked through the front window again. He asked her if the number of police in the South Central neighborhood that day was out of the ordinary.

"It's not unusual," she assured him.

Reed recalled DeFreeze insisting "that he was here to fight for the rights of needy people and to help them exist in the world."

DeFreeze went on to acknowledge that he knew law enforcement was massing in the area and escape was not likely, but "that he and his children would fight to the death."

In his last hours of life, DeFreeze, who had never revealed to his followers his life as informant and agent provocateur, now saw them as his children, bravely, inexorably walking in his footsteps toward revolutionary death.

DeFreeze, drinking from a bottle of Boone's Farm plum wine, as the local market did not stock Akadama, was in that state of clarity and calm that some experience when they sense the end has come. "I know I am going to die and all my people know that they will also," he said straightforwardly, "but we are going to take a lot of motherfucking pigs with us."

Even though he had been drinking for a while, Reed felt "he appeared sober and in full control of his faculties."

Reed reported to the press that shortly before she left for the second and final time, "Finally, Cinque said that one of the reasons he came to Los Angeles was to search for his wife and six children."

DeFreeze was guilt-stricken about his estrangement from his own children. He talked of saving the children of future generations in his communiqués. But it was a child who revealed the secret hideout of the group to his grandmother, Mary Carr. An irate, black grandmother led police to 54th Street, resulting in the bullet-riddled and incendiary holocaust that destroyed the majority of the Symbionese Liberation Army.

But the SLA was still alive, in the form of Bill and Emily Harris and Patty Hearst. Lake Headley, Donald Freed, and Rusty Rhodes failed to stop the death of Donald DeFreeze, predicted by Ronald Farwell of the LAPD, but this triumvirate was intent on revealing the true story of the creation of the SLA and its conflicted, cursed leader.

12 ✦ No Peace, Even in Death

Just two days after the devastation in South Central Los Angeles, an NBC film crew visited the home of the DeFreeze family in Cleveland. Apparently, the wrong thing was said, because freelance cameraman Cliff Feldman was knocked down after a heated exchange. He was treated for facial injuries and lacerations and did not press charges.

The next day, Delano DeFreeze held a press conference in his home. He angrily revealed that after he asked an agent from the Los Angeles FBI on the phone why the body of his brother had not been sent back to the family, the reply was, "Donald DeFreeze didn't have a family."

He asked the reporters in his home, confrontationally, "Why don't the newspapers investigate why they held my brother's body so long?"

The day before Donald DeFreeze's funeral, his former friend and nemesis, Colston Westbrook, appeared on NBC's *Tomorrow* show, with Wes Davis, a researcher in mind control. Both men claimed Hearst was brainwashed by a Maoist regimen and that what happened in South Central Los Angeles was suicide, pure and simple. Westbrook, inflating the actual size and power of the three remaining active members of the SLA, said there were probably ten to fifteen members who had not yet been identified.

On the same day, there was a memorial service for Camilla Hall at the church where her father, the Reverend George F. Hall, presided, St. John's Lutheran Church in Lincolnwood, Illinois. Camilla's name was never mentioned, but Reverend Hall had already sent out a church bulletin. In part, it read, "We thank you one and all for the power coming from communing together. We sense just as strongly the abiding love and relationship with Camilla, her brothers Terry and Peter, and her sister, Nan." The Halls showed remarkable dignity despite the terrible fate of losing all four of their children.

In the case of Angela Atwood's father, the horror of losing a child was exacerbated by other woes. He had recently had a heart attack and was already overwhelmed with legal issues as a Teamsters Union official in Paterson, New Jersey.

On May 23, the body of Donald David DeFreeze was paraded, to the beat of African drums, through a crowd of approximately five hundred attendees inside a chapel at the House of Willis funeral home, in the primarily black and poor lower east side of Cleveland. White-robed Sunni Muslims wearing headdresses carried the casket. Outside, 1,500 onlookers waited for a glimpse of a procession.

There were threats to the funeral home, requiring some members of the police to be present. One caller was quoted as saying, "If you don't get that body out of there and take it down to the trash dump where it belongs, we'll blow up your place." Donald DeFreeze's death, as well as his life, was rife with tension.

In the balcony of the chapel before the service, an argument began between some attendees after a woman accused the Symbionese Liberation Army of "ripping off" the black community.

Members of a group called Black Unity House, wearing khaki uniforms and black berets, stood guard around the chapel, and two of them flanked the coffin during the services. A Baptist and a Muslim minister spoke during the half-hour ceremony.

All but one of DeFreeze's eight brothers and sisters were there to pay their respects. His ex-wife, Gloria, and all six children, biological and adopted, attended, as did his mother, Mary.

Delano, a Sunni Muslim, had shown his rage days before in a press conference, saying his brother's death "represented a sacrifice for anyone who believes in revolution. Revolution is to the death. Death to the pigs." But in the chapel, he spoke quietly, not stridently, barely audible. "My fallen brother died for a nation. The nation might not exist yet, but it will. My brother's death and the funeral with all the people who came shows unity. I will take up the banner now. Here I am. I will do the best I can for the people. The people will direct me in what cause I will go after, but definitely, the SLA shall not die."

Many in the crowd responded, "Right on."

"Is Malcolm dead?" Delano asked about the murdered leader.

"No!" came the roar of reply.

"Power to the people," Delano intoned. "He tried to get something across to the people by sacrificing himself. He lived for the people. He fell for the people. Many brothers of the nation are not here today. But one day, they will be together. We must have leaders who care and who are willing to sacrifice for the whole."

Delano DeFreeze ended his eulogy with the word "Shalom." But peace was not at hand.

As the casket was taken out of the chapel, hundreds among the crowd raised their fists in the black power salute.

Outside, one man broke the silence. "You're seeing American justice! He was burned up intentionally!"

United Press International reported that two white youths in their early twenties unfurled a banner outside that read, "Patty: Revolution Through Jesus the Liberator." Another white attendee angrily tore it. When one of the men who had brought the banner held a Bible and began preaching aloud, several black visitors began to yell at him. When he was told the DeFreeze family wanted no trouble and asked him to leave, he did.

Approximately 150 people were present at Highland Park Cemetery. There was a eulogy that transitioned, in a rather unorthodox way, into a press conference. A friend of DeFreeze's, Abdul

Raheeb, spoke in addition to Delano, who had asked for revolutionary leaders from all over the country to come in support. None did.

The tan metal coffin was lowered into the ground. Small clusters of people remained, trying to understand who Donald DeFreeze was and why he suffered the fate he had.

Near the funeral home, one of the many young black boys who made up the crowd was heard to say, harshly but honestly, "Even his own family didn't know him. Hell, they hadn't heard from him in more than two years."

Los Angeles Coroner Noguchi had previously announced that DeFreeze's teeth and fingers were being retained until the case was closed. Delano DeFreeze responded to this, saying he understood that when a man was dead, a case was officially closed. "It will definitely carry my family through some strain knowing that it's a possibility that we might have to open the grave again."

In Allentown, Pennsylvania, Dr. Wolfe's shock over his son's death changed to near apoplexy. He blamed the FBI in a press conference. "I will do everything in my power to put an end to this John Wayne approach to law enforcement. I want other parents to know that I don't believe police should kill everybody in five minutes so they can go home to supper."

Curiously, Dr. Wolfe did not initially condemn the Los Angeles police. The LAPD rationale for not spending more time trying to get the SLA to surrender was the fear of night coming and the possibility that if the SLA broke out, it might cause gun battles in the neighborhood between the police and the SLA. Based on the LAPD bullet holes in adjoining buildings, complaints by some residents, and a lack of warning to others, another reason seems more likely: under cover of night, angry citizens in extremely volatile South Central Los Angeles, sympathetic to the stated cause of the SLA, might have fired upon police.

This fear was even implied by Evelle Younger when he justified the operation. "I know there were some people who said, 'Well, gee, instead of telling them to come out in five minutes, they should have given them ten minutes.' Someone else suggested they should have starved them out. You know, these may be well-meaning people, but I think they forget the setting in which the police operated."

Lake Headley's efforts to get to the truth of the creation and destruction of the SLA did not go unnoticed by those concerned about his revelations. On May 29, he and Paul Avery of the *San Francisco Chronicle* had their cars broken into and searched in the parking lot of a Holiday Inn Motor Hotel in Los Angeles. In June and July, Headley's car was tailed. Two cars were also seen in stationary surveillance of his home in Los Angeles. There was another incident when his car tires were flattened, and as he went to get them replaced, he and Elizabeth Schmidt noticed a helicopter hovering over their route.

On May 21, the former lover of Donald DeFreeze, the purported chief theoretician of the SLA, Nancy Ling Perry, had a memorial in her hometown of Santa Rosa, organized by her family. On June 1, about seventy-five people attended another funeral for her. Mostly older blacks and younger whites jammed into a tiny East Oakland chapel. Outside of the nondescript chapel, police drove by periodically before the service, and one particular policeman, from his squad car, studied all those who entered through binoculars.

Inside, Gilbert Perry, her estranged musician husband, spoke with difficulty through his tears, pacing between the rostrum and Perry's light pink coffin. He spoke of her as "Fahizah," her *nom de guerre*, meaning "One who is victorious."

During the service, the organist played funeral music that Nancy Ling Perry had written. It was called "Wreath for an Unknown Guerrilla."

Gilbert Perry admitted to those in the chapel that his wife's spirit spoke to him as, entranced and horrified, he watched the fire burn the 54th Street house on television. "She said, 'Yes, I was in the house. Wait until you see where I am, where I am going.'"

The same day, Delano DeFreeze renewed the furor over his brother's demise by telling John Bryan of *The Phoenix* newspaper in San Francisco that the body of Donald DeFreeze was delivered without its head or fingers and that Delano did not know for sure it was in fact his brother.

Even if, as the Los Angeles Coroner's Office contended, DeFreeze's fingerprints and dental records were needed for confirmation of his identity, the coroner used strips of skin from his fingers to match against his prison fingerprints. The question remains why all the remains were not sent to the family after verification. This affront to the DeFreeze family seemed to be an intended insult to the memory of a man despised by the authorities.

An even darker possibility was that those connected to Vacaville via the CIA and California Department of Corrections feared that the DeFreeze family, led by the clearly combative Delano DeFreeze, might have a lab perform forensic analysis on the skull of the late SLA leader. It is not inconceivable that the results might have revealed that DeFreeze was killed by a bullet not his own.

And, even more speculative but not beyond the realm of possibility, if DeFreeze underwent any electrode implantation or other form of psychosurgery at Vacaville, that too might have been discovered and publicized, post mortem.

Eventually, Thomas Noguchi changed his finding that DeFreeze committed suicide. However, the explanation he gave in his memoir, *Coroner*, in terms of forensics, seemed questionable. "But tests in our laboratory revealed that there were metal elements in the fatal wound which were not present in the .38 bullets in DeFreeze's own pistol. I believed, therefore, that the gunpowder burns came from exploding ammunition near DeFreeze."

After DeFreeze's death, Colston Westbrook finally ceased his attacks on the man he recruited to run the SLA. Sara Davidson conducted the last major interview with Westbrook. It appeared in her June 2 *New York Times Magazine* article, "Patty in the Land of the Cobra."

As they talked in a Japanese restaurant on San Pablo Avenue in Oakland, Westbrook, clearly savoring the process of playing games with the media, told Davidson that he believed the person truly in charge of the SLA was still at large. She asked him who he thought that was.

"You really want to get me in trouble, huh?"

She asked him if it was someone known to the public.

"Yes. At the right time, you expose your hand. There's a theory that I'm number one because I haven't been killed yet."

"I'm no good at these games," Davidson contended.

"Are you really a reporter?" Westbrook taunted her.

"I'm wondering myself."

"How would you like to join the CIA?" Westbrook teased her. "You'd be a natural."

As they prepared to leave, Westbrook suggested Davidson contact a psychic he knew. "You might break the story. Find the head of the SLA."

Davidson replied that if she did, she was not sure what she would do.

"Tell me!" declared Westbrook confidently.

"No, I wouldn't tell you."

Leaning in toward Davidson conspiratorially, Westbrook's eyes widened and he whispered, "How do you know I don't already know?"

On June 7, the final audio communiqué from the SLA was dropped off at KPFA Berkeley's sister station, KPFK in Los Angeles.

The complex relationship Patty Hearst had with Willie Wolfe came to the fore in this recording. Wolfe, who vacillated about a role outside of a combat unit or even out of the SLA altogether, after Marcus Foster was killed, had given Hearst a stone carving that represented an ancient Mexican culture, a monkey from the Olmec people. In this last communiqué, she referred to Wolfe's gentleness and the gift of the Olmec monkey on a leather thong, which she said she would always treasure. Her words about Wolfe would be used against her, successfully, by the prosecution in her trial the following year.

Hearst, trying to keep her anger and sadness in check, stated firmly, "The pigs think they can deal with a handful of revolutionaries. But they can't defeat the incredible power which the people, once united, represent. It is for this reason we get to see—live and in color—the terrorist tactics of the pigs. The pigs are saying, 'You're next.'"

Despite the harsh slang, Hearst made the point that the disproportionate response of the shoot-out and fire served notice to anyone who protested against the status quo, law-abiding or not, that they were up against unrestricted firepower and tactics from the government.

Instead of a public debate about the execution of events in South Central Los Angeles, law enforcement turned the size of their response into mythologizing how dangerous and powerful the Symbionese Liberation Army was. Regarding the People in Need program, Evelle Younger insisted, "Extortion under the guise of altruistic purpose cannot be permitted again." Because of the SLA's effective use of the media and manipulation of Randolph Hearst, Younger suggested a wave of similar crimes were coming. He said he was going to propose a package of five bills that "would eliminate the possibility of a kidnapper's obtaining the assets of large trusts and corporations for altruistic or pseudo-political goals."

As with DeFreeze's mission to kill Marcus Foster, there was criticism of the SLA from across the ideological spectrum. *The Black Panther* newspaper maintained that the Symbionese Liberation Army's actions were "an impassioned call for reckless, defeatist, last-ditch-stand terrorism and insurrection," and further, it was "devoid of any consciousness-raising program, method or process" for social change. It was a rare day when Reagan and Younger agreed on the same political point as the Black Panther Party.

Patty Hearst and Bill and Emily Harris made contact with Kathy Soliah and Mike Bortin, two future SLA members, when there was a June 2 rally in Berkeley's Ho Chi Minh Park to commemorate the fallen on 54th Street. Then, Hearst and the Harrises were driven

cross country by sports activist and radical Jack Scott, who hoped
to write a book about them. They hid at a rural Pennsylvania farm
Scott's wife had rented. Joining the group was Wendy Yoshimura,
a friend of Scott and a fugitive from Revolutionary Army bomb
factory charges.

Bill Harris was now the head of the revolutionary group,
and he further muddied the identity and agenda of the SLA by
announcing they were a unit of the New World Liberation Front.
The NWLF was soon responsible for more bombings than any
other group after the shoot-out and fire. Unwittingly, the SLA was
doing the right the favor of undermining the left even more with
their behavior.

The undocumented correlation between the Symbionese
Liberation Army and other legitimate leftist groups continued. In
early summer of 1974, Robert Houghton, a spokesman for Younger,
made an arbitrary estimate of groups remaining in the New Left that
used the SLA *modus operandi*.

"There are probably six to eight groups such as the SLA,"
Houghton approximated, "and they represent the dedicated terrorist who believes in the destruction of the present governmental system. They range anywhere from eight to fifteen members. They are
kind of a product of evolution or distillation from the '60s, and they
are very well known to each other. Some are Vietnam veterans."

Los Angeles Police Commission President Samuel Williams, in
the official police report on the fiery devastation in South Central,
discussed how aberrant the SLA was.

> The six deceased seem to have been individuals who were, for
> the most part, well capable of making positive contributions. But
> they turned instead, as a matter of tactics, to terror. They were
> alienated and by personal choice became outlaws. They commit-
> ted themselves to violence and to provoking an official institu-
> tional counter-violence which would and did crush them. They
> involved us all in their bizarre fantasy.

But in June and July 1974, Lake Headley and Rusty Rhodes each made discoveries involving the FBI and the California Department of Corrections that are among the most mind-boggling in the entire flow of SLA history, both inside the prisons and out.

On June 20, according to an affidavit from Headley, he met with FBI agent Wayne Lewis in a Santa Monica restaurant. Lewis had an agreement with his "partner," Los Angeles FBI agent Donald Grey, to take over the role of head of the SLA now that DeFreeze was dead. When Lewis next met with Grey, after the shoot-out and fire, Grey informed him that Grey himself had fired the fatal bullet that killed Donald DeFreeze. This theoretically accounted for the different caliber and manufacture of the bullet. Grey also informed Lewis that DeFreeze had been an informant for the Criminal Conspiracy Section of the LAPD.

Grey asked a second time if Lewis would be the new Donald DeFreeze, and Lewis agreed but mentioned that he was owed back pay, needed a new background and identity, and was undergoing a severe financial hardship. According to Lewis, the Los Angeles field office of the FBI didn't treat its informants any better than the LAPD did. Grey insisted that Lewis had to serve the Bureau in the guise of new SLA leader before he received his back pay and revised identity. The latter jeopardized Lewis's life as an informant, but in desperation he agreed.

Lewis also told Headley that he managed to get Hearst on the phone through a trusted contact of hers, trying to set up a face-to-face meeting, during which he would offer her protection, while secretly reporting back to the FBI on future SLA activities.

But a contact in the Los Angeles Sheriff's Department told Lewis that if Patty Hearst was caught by the FBI, she would be killed, along with those with her. Lewis worried that he was as expendable as DeFreeze turned out to be. Before another attempt was made to infiltrate Lewis into the SLA, Lewis's cover was blown.

Lewis filed a claim via FBI Standard Form 95 on June 10, charging that an FBI employee revealed his informant status to his landlady, Julia Gatchel. Lewis petitioned for a total of $53,800 from the Bureau, not as a punitive measure but for recovery of back pay. It is also possible that Lewis, seeking a way out of a mission that could end his life, secretly and purposefully leaked his own identity as an agent of the government. The FBI refused to pay him any back wages. Donald Grey was transferred to the FBI Academy at Quantico, Virginia, as instructor.

In May, San Jose attorney Elliot Daum received a letter smuggled out of Soledad, from an inmate who claimed he was offered money and favorable treatment to kill Robert Hyde. Hyde then received a letter from another inmate who had been offered this assignment as well. Then, in late July, investigator Rusty Rhodes obtained a "death list," including a staggering 244 names of inmates. Thirteen names had three stars next to them, denoting they had already been murdered in knifings. They had been targeted by both corrections officers and gang members.

This prompted Rhodes to begin the difficult process of getting through the protective bureaucracy of the CDC to interview inmates about the still extant prison SLA. After meeting with Hyde and Fred Braswell, DeFreeze's replacement as head of the prison SLA, Rhodes showed remarkable tenacity and bravery.

Despite hearing from inmates that guards had marked him for death, Rhodes began visiting Soledad, Folsom, and San Quentin prisons, cross checking Braswell's information with thirty different inmates.

"I was going in with the hard attitude than cons will con you," Rhodes stated in Dick Russell's groundbreaking article in *Argosy* magazine. "I still think that's the right attitude. But when you've got so many men saying the same thing—men from different wings and institutions who can't possibly talk to one another—then you've got to start giving it all some credence."

Predictably, Rhodes's investigative efforts came to a screeching halt. First, there were inexplicable delays to appointments that had been approved. Then, prisoners he met with were unable to communicate clearly, due to "medication" the prison had given them. Finally, Rhodes was physically removed from Soledad during a scheduled visit. Rhodes struggled with the guards to force their hands off of him and he insisted upon a reason for his abrupt removal.

"Perhaps," one of the guards replied, "you shouldn't talk to any more newspaper people."

Members of the prison SLA were then strategically separated from each other via numerous penal transfers. The original Symbionese Liberation Army was dissolved. In an effort to combat the black prisoner reform movement and the growing interactions between white radicals and black prisoners, Raymond Procunier successfully established a culture of increased violence, drug dealing, and suspicion.

THERO WHEELER WAS the only prison member of the Symbionese Liberation Army who seemingly got away clean. Through an old friend, he found the father who had abandoned him as a boy, in Houston, and they began a tentative relationship. Despite incorrectly being identified as one of the kidnappers of Patty Hearst, he kept his head down and maintained his new identity as Bradley Bruce. Through Blue Cross health care coverage at work, he finally had two surgeries. Half of his lower intestine was removed to stop the progression of enteritis. Wheeler obtained jobs at an electric motor company, followed by one that, of all things, manufactured burglar alarms. He married and the couple had a baby girl, in the same month Hearst was violently yanked from her life in Berkeley.

Wheeler recalled May 17, 1974, with despondency. "I saw it a couple hours later on the television news. That choked me out. It didn't seem real. All those lives wasted."

Then, in July, a freak occurrence ended his new life of freedom. Interceding in a scuffle, Wheeler was superficially wounded by shotgun pellets in his right arm. At St. Luke's Hospital, a Houston policeman, Sgt. Volie Shultea Jr., ran Wheeler's pseudonym, Bradley S.

Bruce, through a link with the National Crime Information Center computer. The FBI arrested him without incident at work. His wife had not known his real identity.

At the Resurrection Cemetery, just outside St. Peter, Minnesota, a small graveside service was held for Camilla Hall on August 4, four days before the resignation of President Richard M. Nixon, later pardoned by his successor, Gerald Ford. Despite the fact that the Hall family waited to let the attendant publicity fade, FBI agents were stationed at the cemetery, in case the Harrises or Patty Hearst appeared. Reverend Hall dug a small hole and buried the ashes of Camilla next to the three other Hall children. George and Lorena Hall never spoke out against either the SLA or law enforcement, but stoically shouldered their burden, aided by a religious community that in the following year sent them over a thousand letters of a predominantly supportive nature.

Unwilling to accept the storylines provided by law enforcement, mostly echoed by the mass media, the DeFreeze and Wolfe families decided to legally fight back. On August 27, they filed a claim for $15,502,025 (about $74.5 million in 2016 dollars). It named the Los Angeles Police Department, Fire Department, and Sheriff's Department as defendants. The suit demanded $7.5 million for each family, in addition to $2,025 to the DeFreeze family for funeral costs.

The final police report listed twenty-nine surrender offers via bullhorn on 54th Street. The lawsuit contended there was not sufficient time given for negotiation with the SLA, nor numerous bullhorn appeals for surrender, as claimed.

The lawsuit cited more than five thousand rounds fired by law enforcement, and eighty-three tear gas projectiles blasted into the structure, based on Headley's investigative work. There was little agreement between the police, the media, and investigators on the statistics regarding the SLA shoot-out and fire. There are claims of 420 law officers present, ranging up to 500 officers. The day after the shoot-out and fire, someone sprayed on the remnants of a wall in pink paint, "It Took 500 Cops . . . " A figure beyond five thousand rounds fired into the house is now generally accepted.

Satirical journalist Paul Krassner claimed with a morbid yet light touch that it wasn't so much a shoot-out "as a shoot-in." And on University Avenue in Berkeley, someone spray-painted a graffiti that managed to be simultaneously cruel, racist, and, depending on one's taste, perversely humorous: "DeFreeze Done Got Defrosted."

SLA ballistic estimates shrank over time from one thousand to less than one hundred. There was a gun found near Perry, and then, it seemed, there was no gun. Two letters were alleged to have been found on the body of Camilla Hall. Only the contents of one is known. In it, she attacked bourgeois thinking and the capitalist system, and yet there is a reasonableness to her writing that wasn't often present in the communiqués of the SLA.

Hall wrote to her parents, "You know well that I have worked for change all my conscious life. I went through many stages of development, attacking the enemy on many different fronts, only to see change co-opted into reformism. I exhausted all the possibilities before finally deciding that this was the only way to actually get the revolution going in realistic terms." Hall, like Willie Wolfe, had been reticent, the last member of the original ten to go underground. She came to believe in the necessity of violence to change America for the better. But she never would have joined the revolutionaries if not for the one true love of her brief life, Patricia Soltysik, who died with her at 1466 East 54th Street, on live television, on her twenty-fourth birthday.

In its totality, the Wolfe-DeFreeze lawsuit condemned "the excessive use of fire power," "inadequate warnings," and the LAPD who "prevented the Fire Department from extinguishing the blaze by delaying their presence at the scene."

H. Elizabeth Steele was retained by the DeFreeze family as legal counsel. The attorney of record for Dr. Wolfe was one of the most celebrated progressive political lawyers of the day, Leonard Weinglass. Weinglass successfully defended Angela Davis on murder, conspiracy, and kidnapping charges in the murder of a judge; Daniel Ellsberg of the Pentagon Papers on charges of treason; and the Chicago Seven on conspiracy to create a riot during the 1968 Democratic National Convention in Chicago.

The SLA proceedings were not as successful for Weinglass, neither in his representation of Bill and Emily Harris nor the DeFreeze-Wolfe lawsuit. As soon as it was filed, Burt Pines, the Los Angeles city attorney, said, "An initial review indicates the claims appear to be without merit. We expect that they will be denied." Pines had the power in his position to solely decide if lawsuits were recommended for review by the City Council. Like the entire city government of Los Angeles, he wanted the lawsuit to go away and it did.

Neither family had the emotional strength to pursue a civil suit. Florence Lishey, who lost three properties in the 54th Street inferno, requested $80,000 in compensation. The city of Los Angeles saw fit to pay her only $14,788.10. The black-owned *Los Angeles Sentinel* newspaper, an exception to a case of journalistic indifference, carried the story on page C7.

So much was lost in the fire. The narrative for the government, the media, and the public became the search for Patty Hearst, followed by her arrest and trial. The hunt for Hearst ended on September 18, 1975. The FBI arrested Bill and Emily Harris while the couple was jogging outside their apartment in the Bernal Heights section of San Francisco. Later that day, two San Francisco policemen joined the FBI agents who were following a lead to an apartment in the Outer Mission district, where Wendy Yoshimura and Patty Hearst were both arrested. Photographs showed Hearst in the back of a vehicle, handcuffed, smiling, holding up a fist in a power salute. When she was booked and asked her occupation, it was Tania, not Patty, who famously replied, "Urban guerrilla."

San Francisco FBI agent Des Desvernine found himself alone in a room, briefly, with Patty Hearst after her arrest. He recalled the only person she wanted to talk to was Willie, her cousin.

"Aren't you glad it's over, Patty?" Desvernine asked her.

"It's not over," she answered cryptically. "It's only beginning."

It had taken nineteen months to find her, at a federal cost of $3.5 million ($15.412 million in 2016 dollars). Ten months into the case, the *Village Voice* was told at FBI Washington, DC, headquarters by Special Agents Ellie Turner and Tony Murray that there had been more than twenty-five thousand attempts to interview sources. More than half of those contacted, despite changes in the post-COINTELPRO Bureau, refused to talk with the FBI.

The Revolution was over, even though in its death throes, the Movement would not go quietly. And as with many revolutions, after it was over, exasperatingly small changes, but changes nonetheless, were still to come.

Epilogue • Revolution's End

THOSE WHO WANTED REVOLUTION IN America in the mid-1970s did not believe in the rhetoric or the methods of the Symbionese Liberation Army, and, as noted, there were many in the Bay Area underground who questioned whether the SLA was even a legitimate leftist group when it first became known to the public.

Donald DeFreeze's conversion from snitch to fatalistic leader of a failed vanguard was comprehended by only a few, as was Patty Hearst's morphing from closet radical to coerced kidnap victim to Tania, the guerrilla and *cause célèbre*. The New Left did not engage in bank robberies or abductions of rich people as a result of the group. Rather, they continued on the path forged by the Weather Underground, targeted bombings of buildings representing the corporate state.

The *San Francisco Chronicle* calculated that between February 1974, when Hearst was kidnapped, and the following February, there was a politically motivated bombing in the Bay Area once every 16 days. The same newspaper eventually announced that between 1971 and 1977, there were more than one hundred bombings from seven different radical groups in the San Francisco environs alone. The New World Liberation Front, which Bill Harris claimed was a successor to the SLA, was responsible for sixty-four of those explosions. The Pacific Gas and Electric Company was bombed the most, twenty-three times. As with the Weather

Underground, advance warnings were given so that fatalities and injuries could be avoided.

After the SLA shoot-out and fire in South Central Los Angeles, there was a significant Congressional investigation that included experimentation on prisoners. In November 1974, the U.S. Senate Subcommittee on Constitutional Rights investigated federal funding of behavior modification programs. The subcommittee included Congressman Leo Ryan, whose persistent investigation of the CIA led him to Vacaville's behavior mod operations. During the hearings, the Law Enforcement Assistance Administration, an arm of Nixon's Justice Department, was confronted with its funding of psychosurgery and drug-induced behavior modification in hospitals and medical schools, in addition to prisons like Vacaville.

Subcommittee chair Senator Sam Ervin, already celebrated for his leadership in the Watergate hearings, obtained a verbal commitment from LEAA head Donald Santarelli to stop all activity of the kind. But according to the *Napa Sentinel* series by Harry V. Martin and David Caul, 537 different mind control programs continued, despite this promise. Some of these inhuman secret projects even involved the otherwise benevolent National Institutes of Mental Health and the Department of Health, Education and Welfare.

The Symbionese Liberation Army, run at first by the CDC and then by behavior modification victim Donald DeFreeze, was gone. But on April 21, 1975, the newest permutation of the SLA robbed the Crocker National Bank in the Sacramento suburb of Carmichael. During the robbery, forty-two-year-old Myrna Lee Opsahl, a bank customer bringing in church collection money, was shot dead by Emily Harris, who insisted it was accidental.

Including the Harrises and Hearst, the reconstituted Symbionese Liberation Army now had members Wendy Yoshimura, Kathleen and Steven Soliah, Mike Bortin, and James Kilgore. Except for Steven Soliah, they would all eventually be sentenced for charges ranging from homicide to robbery to conspiracy to commit murder. Like the other SLA members who followed Field Marshal Cinque, none of the new recruits knew anything about their prison predecessors Robert Hyde, Fred Braswell, or Damyon Tomita.

Colston Westbrook, after the shoot-out and fire in South Central, announced in his typically confrontational style that he was going to write a book about his dealings with DeFreeze. The working title was *The N—Who Came Too Close*. The disinformation he planned to put into published form never came to be. Westbrook died of cancer at an early age, fifty-one, at Kaiser Hospital in Oakland.

Dr. Coyness Ennix, who worked all night to keep Robert Blackburn alive after the shotgun attack by DeFreeze, went on to become one of the nation's pre-eminent thoracic and heart surgeons. He and Blackburn became close friends and, completing the circle of irony, Ennix is president of the Marcus Foster Educational Institute, an organization that raises money for Oakland schools.

Robert Hyde survived his prison term, despite the death threats against him. Judge Elliot Daum and Hyde became friends on the outside of the prison walls. Daum said Hyde, one of the best talkers he ever met, became a swimming pool salesman in Fremont, before he passed away. According to Daum, Hyde never spoke about his involvement in the origins of the SLA.

Lake Headley and Donald Freed made a final effort to disseminate the major points of fact behind the full identity of Donald DeFreeze and the SLA. They both made presentations at a May 22, 1975, Los Angeles City Council meeting, which included a three-man Police, Fire, and Civil Defense Committee.

They calculated that their information on the California Department of Corrections would not be well received in Sacramento circles by Reagan's, Younger's, or Procunier's staffs. But what they attempted to accomplish on May 22 was almost as herculean.

Freed told those assembled at City Hall that the Public Disorder Intelligence Division of the LAPD had blackmail dossiers on employees of the *Los Angeles Times;* Mayor Tom Bradley; Supervisors Baxter Ward and Ed Edelman; and Councilmen David Cunningham, Joel Wachs, and Arthur Snyder.

Wachs, furious, demanded to know if Freed or Headley had seen the aforementioned blackmail files. The reply was that if safeguards were put in place, such as immunity to prevent reprisals, the witnesses would testify. Snyder demanded those names and Freed and Headley asked to have the information they possessed forwarded to a grand jury.

Snyder angrily shouted that the investigators were using a public forum for unsubstantiated charges. Instead of being supported in their personally funded inquiry, Freed and Headley were threatened with arrest. Commander Joseph Gunn, City Council liaison for the police, objected on the Kafkaesque grounds that forwarding the materials to a grand jury would give credence to the allegations.

Headley had no better luck when he presented his fourteen-page report on the LAPD in connection with the shoot-out and fire on 54th Street. The details of DeFreeze's relationship to Ronald Farwell of the LAPD were included in his report. Headley had sixteen-millimeter news film footage of members of the Criminal Conspiracy Section of the LAPD directing the operation in South Central. There was also a clip of two German shepherd police dogs trained to detect the scent of Patty Hearst. They were utilized near 1466 East 54th Street before the firefight began.

Snyder's reaction was that it was beyond the purview of the City Council to create an inquiry into the matter and that furthermore, he was satisfied with the final police commission report, which the Los Angeles City Council had already praised.

On June 27, after a change of venue to Sacramento, Joe Remiro and Russ Little were sentenced to life imprisonment for the murder of Marcus Foster, plus a sentence of six months to twenty years for the serious wounding of Robert Blackburn. At one point, when former ally Chris Thompson testified, Little furiously charged the witness stand, attempting to pummel him, and was restrained.

Little addressed the court after the conviction, claiming the SLA was "alive and kicking. This conviction has done nothing but increase our forces."

Little's conviction was eventually overturned on a legal techni-cality, and he lives in Hawaii under an assumed name.

Remiro, equally unrepentant, said that law enforcement helped to "make a symbol out of us." He was right and at the same time did not understand that the SLA that DeFreeze voluntarily ran could have evolved into something more effective. Remiro is cur-rently incarcerated in California State Prison, Lancaster. According to attorney Stuart Hanlon, he is still trying to get his conviction overturned.

DeFreeze, as revolutionary, stumbled upon and manipulated the media, a far more powerful instrument for announcing political grievances than a shoot-out. But he and the SLA squandered a rare opportunity to reach Middle America with concrete suggestions for change. Little and Remiro, in their hostile final statements in court, missed their chance to offer a cogent statement about what they wanted to change in America or give a practical example of how to attempt to change it.

The revolution that Headley and Freed tried to accomplish, to dramatically change LAPD intelligence, leaving aside issues con-cerning the CIA, CDC, or FBI, had failed. But the enormity of their challenge must be put into context.

In one of the few improvements to grow out of Raymond Procunier's California Department of Corrections and the radi-cal politics of the mid-1970s, the Indeterminate Sentencing Act, which had stood for fifty-nine years in California, was replaced in 1976. California Governor Jerry Brown signed the Determinate Sentencing Law on September 20, eliminating the Adult Authority in the penal system. The ability to sentence a person ambiguously and leave it to the prison system to make changes to the length of that sentence led to an ever-increasing spiral of prisoner violence, mistreatment of inmates, and the rise of the "political prisoner," a concept that set back progressive political change and led to the creation of the Black Cultural Association at Vacaville and both ver-sions of the Symbionese Liberation Army.

Ronald Farwell went public with his story, ten years after he unwittingly gave the Public Disorder Intelligence Division of the LAPD information manipulated by Sam Yorty to condemn Tom Bradley's successful candidacy. In a November 1983 *Los Angeles Times* article, Farwell expressed his bitterness about the PDID investigating peaceful individuals and organizations after militant ones like the Black Panthers dissolved. Farwell stated that society "was saying to the intelligence community, 'Now is the time for change. Now is the time to fall back and to regroup and reorganize and to establish your priorities.' The department administrators were slow and in some cases completely negligent about hearing the social demands."

But there was a revolution, at least in terms of police intelligence in Los Angeles. The American Civil Liberties Union sued the Public Disorder Intelligence Division in 1983 for spying on nearly 150 law-abiding individuals and organizations. Ronald Farwell was one of those defendants. It was settled in January 1984, when the city agreed to pay $1.8 million in damages. The PDID was disbanded in 1983, replaced by an anti-terrorist division.

The continuation of white police–black citizen violence today is an indication of the difficulty of changing law enforcement policies. And while LAPD intelligence abuses ended in the early 1980s, the department had yet another major fiasco. The late 1990s LAPD Rampart Division scandal, involving the CRASH anti-gang unit, had over seventy accusations of unprovoked shootings and beatings, planting of evidence, bank robbery, and stealing and dealing of narcotics by police officers. A consent decree from the US Department of Justice demanded five years of oversight to clean up the LAPD. Mayor Richard Riordan and Police Chief Bernard Parks objected to it, but the Board of Supervisors voted ten to two to accept the consent decree in one of the worst cases of police department corruption in a major metropolitan area in US history.

THE TRIAL OF Patty Hearst, tragically, did not illuminate any of the malfeasance in the LAPD, CIA, FBI, or California Department of

Corrections. However, in keeping with the history of the SLA, the San Francisco prosecution of Hearst was filled with raw conflict and absurdity. US Attorney James Browning had not tried a case in court in six years, and in the beginning weeks, he seemed out of his depth. At one point, he asked Hearst about DeFreeze, "And he told you you would be held until you were released?"

Hearst gave him a quizzical, "Yes-s-s," as much a question as an answer.

As Dr. Colin Ross summarized in *The CIA Doctors*, even though there was little precedent for such a defense in American court-rooms, Patty Hearst's crimes would never have occurred without behavior modification. "Doctor [Louis Jolyon] West testified that Patty had a new identity deliberately created by Donald DeFreeze. All four expert witnesses testified that Patty Hearst had been brain-washed using classical mind control techniques."

Hearst herself, when in the San Mateo County Jail in Redwood City, signed an affidavit that she was "brainwashed" and drugged by her captors, even though Randolph Hearst ordered F. Lee Bailey and five other lawyers on the team to avoid mentioning drugs.

"My defense was involuntary intoxication," Terence Hallinan recalled of his initial plan for Patty's defense, "that she had been given drugs, with the treatment they gave her, the terrible treatment in the closet, and then let out and converted to their ideology. And that was the truth of what happened and that was a valid defense."

The trial also came just three years after a holdup in a Stockholm, Sweden bank, after which several hostages refused to testify against the robbers because they had come to know and sympathize with them, thus adding the term "Stockholm syndrome" to legal lexicon. Captive airline flight attendants had similarly shown understanding toward hijackers by the time of the trial. The idea of Hearst's under-going "persuasive coercion" and finally identifying with her captors was not so far-fetched in comparison.

The closest the public came to the psychological truth of who Patty Hearst was, just before she was kidnapped, came when an expert prosecution witness so upset her that Hearst asked him to be removed from the proceedings after one meeting, claiming he was abusive.

Doctor Harry Kozol, sixty-nine, had retired from private psychiatric practice in Boston after running a state treatment center for violent offenders, including self-confessed murderer Albert DeSalvo, a.k.a., The Boston Strangler (whom Bailey had defended). Kozol, however, also inspired incredible loyalty among some patients, including the four-time Pulitzer Prize–winning playwright Eugene O'Neill, whom Kozol saw almost daily during the waning years of O'Neill's haunted, depressive, alcoholic life.

The first of five jail interviews between Kozol and Hearst ended abruptly, about ninety minutes in, after he asked Hearst about her true feelings toward Willie Wolfe, whom she had first claimed in a communiqué to love more than anyone she had known, and later condemned on the witness stand. Kozol claimed she began to "shake and quiver" and seemed to be "sobbing inside."

"I don't know how I feel about him," Kozol claimed she answered. Then, growing even more upset, Hearst said, "I don't know why I got into this goddamned thing. Shit!" With that, she stormed out of the room, ending the interview. It was the only oblique reference that ever escaped her lips regarding her days visiting Vacaville and Soledad prisons.

Kozol not only infuriated Hearst but also damaged her case when he testified in the eighth week. Kozol told the court that Hearst said that while she was captive, DeFreeze had once grabbed her crotch and pinched one of her breasts in anger. But when Kozol asked if there were any subsequent sexual assaults, she said no, despite her previous assertions of unwilling sexual contact with DeFreeze and Wolfe when she was a prisoner.

The jury was dealing not only with an unexplored area of American law, coercion leading to the commission of a crime, but also a vacillating story about the nature of the sexual contact between Hearst, DeFreeze, and Wolfe. The defense tried to overcome jurists' doubts about how compliant or defiant Hearst was during sex with two of her captors. F. Lee Bailey and his team pursued their contention that Hearst, after kidnapping and behavior modification for weeks, was no longer legally responsible for her subsequent actions.

The impediment for Bailey was that no matter what it was called—behavior modification, thought control, mind control, coercive persuasion, or any other similar term—that psychological defense was never previously used in a federal court. In his closing argument, Bailey gave a half-hearted apology to the jury for not providing evidence regarding DeFreeze's knowledge about brainwashing. One wonders whether Randolph Hearst's lawyers had more information about the history of Donald DeFreeze and Patty Hearst but decided not to use it to save the Hearst family humiliation and more negative press. In a 2015 telephone interview with the author, Terence Hallinan stated he had no prior knowledge about the prison origins of the SLA, behavior modification at Vacaville, or Hearst's secret visits to DeFreeze while he was incarcerated.

Bailey summarized the case as being about why Hearst joined in the Hibernia Bank robbery. With powerful, direct logic, he implored the jury, "And would you have done the same thing to survive? Or was it her duty to die to avoid committing a felony?"

On March 20, 1976, Patty Hearst was found guilty of armed bank robbery. Superior Court Judge Oliver Carter, who had known the Hearst family for years and remembered Patty as a child when he visited the Hearsts in Hillsborough, had refused to recuse himself from the case. He clearly took into account the kidnapping and degradations she had suffered. Carter reduced her thirty-five year sentence to seven. She served only twenty-two months, thanks to the unsung heroism of Representative Leo Ryan of San Mateo County.

Ryan petitioned President Jimmy Carter to commute the sentence of Patty Hearst, based on what Ryan discovered about the CIA, DeFreeze, and Vacaville. President Bill Clinton eventually pardoned Hearst. She wound up marrying one of her numerous bodyguards, Bernard Shaw, with whom she had two daughters. Shaw passed away at sixty-eight. Hearst lives in Connecticut and raises show dogs.

As for Ryan, his murder on November 18, 1978, at the Port Kaituma air strip in Guyana while investigating the settlement of Reverend Jim Jones, preceded Patty Hearst's February 1, 1979 commutation. On the day Ryan and more than nine hundred others died in Jonestown, Joe Holsinger, Ryan's top aide in California, received a phone call from the White House. Les Francis, of the congressional liaison office, reported the correct number of deaths and, according to Holsinger, said it was "based on a CIA report from the scene." Francis later countered, "I think I said 'intelligence report.'"

After Ryan's murder, CBS news reporter Daniel Schorr revealed that in February 1975, when he broke the story about the CIA's illegal involvement in the war in Angola, the leak had come from Ryan, the greatest legislative adversary the Agency ever had.

Ryan's five adult children filed a lawsuit in 1980 in the United States District Court for the Northern District of California for general damages of $3 million, plus costs for Congressman Ryan's funeral and for bringing the action.

The suit charged that members of the Central Intelligence Agency and US State Department worked with the Jonestown colony as part of the CIA's MKULTRA program, that mind control drugs were found at the site, and that there was a conspiracy to murder Ryan due to his investigation of Jonestown. The suit was dismissed without explanation.

Ryan was posthumously awarded a Congressional Gold Medal for his service, and his legacy is highly present in San Mateo County. The name Leo J. Ryan graces a federal building in San Bruno, a post office in San Mateo, and a public park in Foster City.

SINCE THE CIA, FBI, LAPD and California Department of Corrections had no interest in revealing their participation in the story of Donald DeFreeze and the Symbionese Liberation Army, the onus fell upon both the political left and members of the press.

Despite the numerous radicals who suspected the origins of the SLA, nothing was ever done to investigate, publicize, or widely renounce the SLA. The political underground had no effective plans for countermeasures when they suspected infiltration.

A perfect example is the fact that there was a "search team" from the Weather Underground that tried to find and influence members of the SLA. It was led by Rick Ayers, brother of the Weather Underground cofounder, Bill Ayers.

"We really thought groups like the SLA were nuts and horrible, and yet we felt some responsibility," Rick Ayers recalled. "We could recognize that level of craziness, and that someone needed to get a hold of them and say, 'Just chill.' We just tried to find them, just drove around looking for them. We felt it was bad for everyone, and we thought, I don't know, that we could save them."

The New Left, by agreeing that the black prisoner reform movement in the Bay Area would be the vanguard in the struggle for political change, not only made their organizational efforts more difficult, they also harmed themselves in other ways; there was no wide socioeconomic coalition and white guilt led to an inability to question decisions about black leadership, including the background of Donald DeFreeze.

The Weather Underground's Paul Bradley, who worked as an auto mechanic in San Francisco during the time of the SLA, explained the ambivalence the left felt about the racial component of the group. "Of course, we all thought their rhetoric was ridiculous, and none of us paid much attention to the Marcus Foster killing, a horrible thing. Frankly, everybody was confused by the SLA. It was led by this black guy, so it was hard for us to be critical. It was hard to condemn it, too."

Even Joe Remiro, in an August 1975 letter from prison, admonished the movement for its reliance on a black prisoner vanguard. "Politically oriented white folks who visit and write prisoners usually fall into the routine of only relating to black prisoners. This had been an effective way of heightening racial contradictions and deemphasizing the class nature of the revolutionary struggle. Black prisoners are not the only prisoners with revolutionary potential, but they are the only ones being focused on by the left."

The Bay Area Research Collective (BARC), which published radical writings beginning in the spring of 1974 in reaction to the emergence of the SLA, had an uncredited editorial in their issue, "Some Thoughts on the SLA." The BARC echoed the unsubstantiated claim of the SLA that the Law Enforcement Assistance Administration was the sole backer of a South African apartheid-like police program for Oakland schools, the supposed rationale for killing Foster.

But there were some salient points from this publisher of mimeographed leftist thought about the SLA. "They seemed to begin more and more to measure struggle strictly in terms of the use of weapons. . . . However, a weapon is not the revolutionary's only effective tool, especially in the most technologically advanced country in the world."

BARC raised a valid issue at a time when such things as Wikileaks and cyber-warfare were unimaginable: other than assassination, bank robberies, and bombings, how could a revolutionary unit effect positive change?

If the SLA wanted to accurately and pointedly condemn the LEAA, they could have researched the organization's funding of behavior modification projects directed against prisoners and the mentally ill. They could have investigated the CIA's MKULTRA and similar projects. For that matter, DeFreeze, once he decided to be a true revolutionary, could have discussed in his communiqués how he and other prisoners were treated at Vacaville. There already was an infrastructure of Bay Area psychiatric doctors exposing information on that issue.

Instead, the SLA provided military terminology, unfocused rhetoric, civilian fatalities, no coalition, and no specific goal. The blaming of the LEAA, whose Burlingame offices were considered as a bombing target by the SLA, likely came from the same source who originated the false rumors about Dr. Foster: Colston Westbrook.

The BARC editorial also brought up another ideological blind spot in the SLA. The group was dominated by women, and yet, one year after the Equal Rights Amendment and two years after the Supreme Court ruling on *Roe vs. Wade,* nothing was said about feminism by the SLA. "When Cinque spoke of oppression," the BARC editorial recounted, "he spoke in the first person of the destructive effects of racism he had experienced. We did not hear a similar discussion from the women of the SLA about the effects of sexism."

Ramparts magazine, an early critic after the murder of Marcus Foster, editorialized,

> If there is a lesson to be learned from the SLA, it is that in a society as violently racist, exploitative, and aggressively heartless as America's, we cannot afford to be without an organized mass movement of the Left. For what the Left means in human terms is a moral community of hope . . . to protect against both the destructive adventurism of self-obsessed quasi-revolutionaries, and a successful government repression of leftist activity, in a broad campaign of force or legal harassment, which may one day be massed with the public's fearful consent.

And some interviewees, who weighed in on the SLA during the time, showed that there is a difference between paranoia and healthy skepticism. Richard Flacks, a UC Santa Barbara professor of Sociology, told the *Los Angeles Times,* "There was evidence that Donald DeFreeze was a police informer. We don't know all the factors. There are many historical examples of this sort of thing. The police paid people to be terrorists in Czarist Russia so they could crack down on other elements of the underground they really wanted to get to."

DeFreeze's motivations were, *sub rosa*, entirely different from the generally well-educated, upper and middle class men and women who followed him. And they lived in a time that people born after that era cannot comprehend. Social theorist Theodore Roszak, author of *The Making of a Counterculture*, encapsulated the unique-ness of the period. "This is the first generation to have fashioned dis-sent into a way of life. Political liberation is all tied up with cultural, social, intellectual and even sexual liberation."

Roszak's explanation goes to the point of why well-bred, intelli-gent, young white people became so enmeshed with the politics of social justice for black citizens in the 1970s, both inside and out-side the walls of prisons. For white radicals, it was, in addition to being a moral decision, a matter of resolving their own identities as Americans.

Hearst was interviewed in 1982 by Lawrence Grobel in *Playboy* magazine and revealed she knew more about DeFreeze's past than anyone else in the SLA seemed to know. "I think he was a paid informant. His crimes were average crimes. They weren't anything spectacular or revolutionary. He was a two-bit crook. He got caught on an earlier charge and started informing to keep from going to jail." It is unknown how or when Hearst learned this. But if mem-bers of the Symbionese Liberation Army had known this from the beginning, likely they would not now be dead or imprisoned, because they never would have followed Donald DeFreeze.

The day Patty Hearst, at her San Francisco trial, invoked the Fifth Amendment nineteen times, on February 19, 1976 (out of forty-two times total), there was an exchange with prosecutor James Browning, who was attempting to show what was in the deepest recesses of Patty/Tania's mind and heart.

One of the most famous photographs in American history showed her in a tan jumpsuit and beret, holding a carbine. What everyone seemed to overlook until the trial was that Patty did not wear an engagement ring when she was living with Steven Weed. And yet, in the photo, a ring can be seen on her left hand, as if she were married.

Browning asked who gave her the ring. With a slight hesitation, she admitted it was "Cinque."

Browning asked, "What type of ring was it?"

"I don't even remember. It was just a band."

"And what was—" Browning began, awkwardly trying to elicit more information from her. "Was there a purpose for which he gave you that ring?"

"Just when I got out of the closet," Hearst replied, referring to her being welcomed into the Symbionese Liberation Army after her participation in the Hibernia Bank robbery.

"It was an item of jewelry that he gave you, as he would have given you some clothes?" Browning asked, overlooking the depth of that act of giving.

"Yes," she replied simply, unable to tell him or anyone else what DeFreeze and she had once meant to each other, unable herself to comprehend the layer upon layer of deceit that comprised their lives, separately and together.

APPENDIX

Communiqué dated April 4, 1974, from Nancy Ling Perry (Fahizah) of the Symbionese Liberation Army, broadcast on KSAN-FM, San Francisco:

Love to our sisters and brothers in prisons; courage & faith to our two captured soldiers; greetings to all oppressed peoples; may we connect. My name is Fahizah.

The SLA is taking these opportunities to speak with the people now, because we have been having a temporary period of inactivity while waiting for the completion of our unit's last action. We know that the people want far more than the 6 million dollars of food; & we will continue to fight for the total liberation of all oppressed peoples by the only means available, that is force of arms. The Court of the People has issued the Codes of War of the Symbionese Liberation Army and I wish to state that Cinque Mtume is the General Field Marshal of the Symbionese Guerilla [sic] Forces, as well as chairman of the United Symbionese War Council.

Cinque is a black brother who spent many years of his life in fascist Amerika's concentration camps: manchild years in prison cells & man years in prison cells. Cinque met literally thousands of black, brown, red, yellow, and white freedom fighters while he was locked down, courageous comrade George Jackson was one of them. The spirit of all the brothers Cinque knows lives in him now, and the spirit of all the sisters that Cinque never had the opportunity to meet, but knows by common bond—like Assata Shakur, Lolita Lebron & Bernadine [*sic*] Dohrn—is always in his heart.

When Cinque escaped alone on foot from Soledad prison he did so for one reason only: TO FIGHT WITH THE PEOPLE & TO LEAD THE PEOPLE IN REVOLUTION. He did not escape so that he could kick-back & hide & get high: he did not even escape so that he could satisfy a deep and longing personal ache to simply see the people, and be on the streets and re-unite with his family and be a father once again to his children. Cinque escaped so that he could actively stalk the fascist insect that preys upon the life of the people. The lives both he & the people's fighting forces lead now may be harsh and dangerous, but it is better to work with hard reality, than to play in pleasant, but unproductive, enslaving dreams.

Cinque Mtume is the name that was bestowed upon him by his imprisoned sisters & brothers. It is the name of an ancient African Chief who led the fight for his people for freedom. The name means Fifth Prophet, and Cin was many years ago given this name because of his keen instinct and senses, his spiritual consciousness and his deep love for all the people and children of this earth. This does not, however, mean that Cinque is from God or someone that is holy or that he has an extreme ego problem, but simply that he to us and to all oppressed peoples is the instilled hope and spirit of his people & all peoples, and that he is of the people and from the people. A prophet is a leader and fighter who is one of the people. Leaders are individuals who within themselves feel that it is time to lead and bring us one step closer to freedom for all peoples. A leader is one who is able to help the people understand the swiftness and fierceness with which they must move if they would survive.

Part of the revolutionary process in which we are engaged involves the constant redefining of thought, word, and action. We must deal with all the conditions outside ourselves which oppress and enslave us, and we must deal with the enemy within; we must deal with both these diseases simultaneously, and with an unrelenting commitment and understanding that in reality we are not living to die, but rather all who chose to fight to the death are dying to live. Cin's example to the people has taught us thru his actions and by his own words, that he or she who is scared and seeks to run away from death will find it, but he or she who is NOT AFRAID and who actively seeks death out will find it NOT AT THEIR DOOR.

We embrace the concepts of art and spiritual consciousness in material relevant terms based upon the common conditions of all oppressed peoples. We have begun to redefine art as the natural creative reflection of our desperate struggle to survive. Art for us is the total process of sharing and communally using what we learn in order to live and to fight. We recognize Cin as an artist for what he teaches the people, but we also realize as he himself has said, that truth has no author. Another thing which we feel is necessary to clarify the word spirit & all that which is called spiritual. The spirit is the bodies and souls of all the people, and the spiritual is the intensity of our common instincts, as reflected thruout history to fight for the freedom of all oppressed peoples, to save the earth and the children from the putrid disease of bourgeois mentality and the putrid disease of the corporate fascist military state. In a profound and spiritual sense, as our sisters and brothers in the SLA have said, resistance to this disease is the single greatest human endeavor today.

Comrades in struggle, there is a high price that we have paid and will pay for our mistakes, and there is an even higher price which we have been paying for the loss of our leaders. We are speaking to the people now, because we all know that in spite of the enemy's technology and prestige of terror we DO have a leader that loves the people, and lives and fights for the people. This example helps to make a love among comrades that gives attention, appreciation, care and protection—from each brother and sister to the other.

The oppressed peoples of this nation have and will continue to bring forth their leaders, prophets & fighters until they are free. The people brought forth Malcolm X who came to unite the people and warn the enemy of what would inevitably happen if the people were not freed. The enemy answered by murdering Malcolm. The people then did again bring forth another prophet, that prophet was Martin Luther King who with non-violence & humanity pleaded to the enemy to free the people. And just when King was ready to declare that nonviolent protest would accomplish nothing but the further enslavement and degradation of the people, the enemy murdered King. George Jackson was a prophet & leader from the streets & when the enemy imprisoned him, George received his education in the raw; he learned firsthand that there can be NO compromise with merciless pigs. George Jackson came from the prisons of Amerikkka & love-inspired he boldly fought the oppressor. When the fascist insect locked him down and murdered him, the people knew that they had suffered a great loss, but they failed to unite in immediate retaliation. Now, once again, the people have brought forth another prophet and leader.

This leader comes not to beg and plead with the enemy, he comes not to warn of violence, but is himself the bringer of the children of the wind and the SOUND OF WAR. He has ONE WORD to the children of the oppressed and the children of the oppressor: COME. We have joined together with love and unity and the understanding that those who would be free, must themselves STRIKE THE FIRST BLOW.

Excerpt of SLA communiqué dated April 4, 1974, in which Patty Hearst reveals herself to be a member of the SLA and criticizes her parents and ex-boyfriend, Steven Weed:

I would like to begin this statement by informing the public that I wrote what I am about to say. It's what I feel. I have never been forced to say anything on any tape. Nor have I been brainwashed, drugged, tortured, hypnotized or in any way confused. As George Jackson wrote, "It's me, the way I want it, the way I see it."

Mom, Dad, I would like to comment on your efforts to supposedly secure my safety. The PIN give-away was a sham. You attempted to deceive the people, the SLA and me with statements about your concern for myself and the people. You were playing games—stalling for time—time which the FBI was using in their attempts to assassinate me and the SLA elements which guarded me. You continued to report that you did everything in your power to pave the way for negotiations for my release—I hate to believe that you could have been so unimaginative as to not have even considered getting Little and Remiro released on bail. While it was repeatedly stated that my conditions would at all times correspond with those of captured soldiers, when your own lawyer went to inspect the "hole" at San Quentin, he approved the deplorable conditions there—another move which potentially jeopardized my safety. My mother's acceptance of the appointment to a second term as a U.C. regent, as you well knew, would have caused my immediate execution had the SLA been less than "together" about their political goals. Your actions have taught me a great lesson, and in a strange kind of way, I am grateful to you.

Steven, I know that you are beginning to realize that there is no such thing as neutrality in a time of war. There can be no compromise as your experiences with the FBI must have shown you. You have been harrassed by the FBI because of your supposed connections with so-called radicals, and some people have gone so far as to suggest that I arranged my own arrest. We both know what really came down that Monday night—but you don't know what's happened since then. I have changed—grown. I've become conscious and can never go back to the life we led before. What I'm saying may seem cold to you and old friends, but love doesn't mean the same thing to me anymore. My love has expanded as a result of my experiences to embrace all people. It's grown into an unselfish love for my comrades here, in prison and on the streets. A love that comes from the knowledge that "no one is free until we all are free." While I wish that you could be a comrade, I don't expect it—all I expect is that you try and understand the changes I have gone through.

I have been given the choice of 1) being released in a safe area or, 2) joining the forces of the Symbionese Liberation Army and fighting for my freedom and the freedom of all oppressed people. I have chosen to stay and fight.

BIBLIOGRAPHY

Books

Baker, Marilyn, and Sally Brompton. *Exclusive! The Inside Story of Patricia Hearst and the SLA*. New York: Macmillan, 1974.

Blanche, Tony, and Brad Schreiber. *Death in Paradise: An Illustrated History of the Los Angeles County Department of Coroner*. Philadelphia: Running Press, 2001.

Boulton, David. *The Making of Tania: The Patty Hearst Story*. London: New English Library, 1975.

Bryan, John. *This Soldier Still at War*. New York: Harcourt Brace Jovanovich, 1975.

Burrough, Brian. *Days of Rage: America's Radical Underground, The FBI and the Forgotten Age of Revolutionary Violence*. New York: Penguin Press, 2015.

California Assembly Select Committee on Corrections. *An Investigation into the Practice of Forced Drugging/Medication in California's Detention Facilities and Transcript of Hearing Held at Los Angeles, California on July 28, 1976*. Sacramento, December 1976.

California Senate. *1974 Report to the California Senate by the Subcommittee on Civil Disorder*. Sacramento, January 31, 1974.

Chorover, Stephan L. *From Genesis to Genocide: The Meaning of Human Nature and the Power of Behavior Control*. Boston: MIT Press, 1979.

Cummins, Eric. *The Rise and Fall of California's Radical Prison Movement*. Palo Alto, CA: Stanford University Press, 1994.

Debray, Regis. *Revolution in the Revolution?* New York: Grove Press, 1967.

Donner, Frank. *Protectors of Privilege*. Los Angeles: University of California Press, 1990.

Foner, Philip S., editor. *The Black Panthers Speak*. Cambridge, MA: Da Capo Press, 1975.

Glick, Brian. *War at Home: Covert Action Against U.S. Activists and What We Can Do About It.* Boston: South End Press, 1999.

Greenlee, Sam. *The Spook Who Sat by the Door.* Detroit: Wayne State University Press, 1969.

Headley, Lake and William Hoffman. *Vegas P.I.: The Life and Times of America's Greatest Detective.* New York: Thunder's Mouth Press, 1993.

Hearst, Patricia Campbell, and Alvin Moscow. *Patty Hearst: Her Own Story.* New York: Avon Books, 1988.

Howard, Clark. *Zebra: The True Account of the 179 Days of Terror in San Francisco.* New York: Richard Marek, 1979.

Jackson, George. *Blood in My Eye.* Baltimore: Black Classic Press, 1990.

Jackson, George. *Soledad Brother: The Prison Letters of George Jackson.* Chicago: Lawrence Hill Books, 1994.

Keith, Jim. *Mind Control, World Control.* Kempton, IL: Adventures Unlimited Press, 1997.

Kinney, Jean. *An American Journey: The Short Life of Willy Wolfe.* New York: Simon and Schuster, 1979.

McLellan, Vin, and Paul Avery. *The Voices of Guns: The Definitive and Dramatic Story of the Twenty-Two Month Career of the Symbionese Liberation Army—One of the Most Bizarre Chapters in the History of the American Left.* New York: G. P. Putnam's and Sons, 1977.

Meiers, Michael. *Was Jonestown a CIA Medical Experiment? A Review of the Evidence.* Lewiston, NY: Edwin Mellen Press, 1989.

Payne, Les, and Tim Findley, with Carolyn Craven. *The Life and Death of the SLA.* New York, Ballantine Books, 1976.

Ross, Dr. Colin. *The CIA Doctors.* Richardson, TX: Manitou Communications, 2006.

Soltysik, Fred. *In Search of a Sister.* New York: Bantam, 1976.

Spencer, John P. *In the Crossfire: Marcus Foster and the Troubled History of American School Reform.* Philadelphia: University of Pennsylvania Press, 2014.

Tackwood, Louis. *The Glass House Tapes.* New York: Avon Books, 1973.

Talbot, David. *Season of the Witch: Enchantment, Terror and Deliverance in the City of Love.* New York: Free Press, 2012.

United States Congress, House of Representatives, Committee on Internal Security. *The Symbionese Liberation Army.* Washington, DC, 1974.

United States Congress, Committee on Foreign Affairs. *The Assassination of Representative Leo J. Ryan and the Jonestown, Guyana Tragedy.* Washington, DC, May 15, 1979.

United States Congress. *Report to the President by the Commission on CIA Activities within the United States.* Washington, DC, June 1975.

United States Congress, US Senate. *Intelligence Activities and the Rights of Americans, Book II, Final Report of the Select Committee to Study Governmental Operations with Respect to Intelligence Activities.* Washington, DC, April 26, 1976.

Valentine, Douglas. *The Phoenix Program.* Bloomington, IN: iUniverse, 2000.

Weed, Steven, with Scott Swanton. *My Search for Patty Hearst.* New York: Crown, 1976.

Interviews

Bryant, Nick

Browning, James

Daum, Judge Elliot

Desvernine, Des

Hallinan, Terence

Hanel, Rachael

Hanlon, Stuart

Katz, Marilyn

Ross, Dr. Colin

Russell, Dick

Spencer, John P.

Valentine, Douglas

Weaver, Dr. Vesla

Magazines

Calio, Jim, and Sherry Keene. "National Affairs." *Newsweek Magazine*, March 17, 1975.

Cheever Cowley, Susan. "DeFreeze: The Jersey Connection." *New York Magazine*, June 10, 1974.

Davidson, Sara. "Patty Hearst in the Land of the Cobra." *New York Times Magazine*, June 2, 1974.

Donner, Frank. "The Agent Provocateur as Folk Hero." *Civil Liberties*, September 1971.

Farhi, Paul. "Going Live." *American Journalism Review*, November 2002.

Farrell, Barry. "A Let-Burn Situation." *Harpers*, September, 1974.

Findley, Tim. "Apocalypse for the SLA: The Revolution Was Televised." *Rolling Stone*, June 20, 1974.

Flanagan, Caitlin. "Girl Interrupted: How Patty Hearst's Kidnapping Reflected and Ravaged American Culture in the 1970s." *The Atlantic*, September 2008.

Grobel, Lawrence. "Playboy Interview: Patricia Hearst." *Playboy*, March 1982.

Harris, Brandon. "The Most Important Legacy of the Black Panthers." *The New Yorker*, September 5, 2015.

Hinton, Elizabeth. "A War within Our Own Boundaries: Lyndon Johnson's Great Society and the Rise of the Carceral State." *Journal of American History,* June 2015.

Lyne, Susan, and Robert Scheer. "The Story of the SLA: How and Why the Group Kidnapped Patty Hearst and Came to be Urban Guerillas." *New Times*, April 16, 1976.

Newsweek staff. "Patty on Trial." *Newsweek*, February 2, 1976.

People staff. "The Man Patty Hearst Loved." *People*, June 24, 1974.

Russell, Dick. "The SLA." *Argosy*, December 1975–January 1976.

Taylor, Michael. "Death to the Fascist Insect: Looking Back 40 Years, Does the SLA Make Any More Sense?" *California*, Cal Alumni Association, Berkeley, Fall, 2014.

Valentine, Douglas. "Fragging Bob: Bob Kerrey, CIA War Crimes and the Need for a War Crimes Trial." *Counterpunch*, May 17, 2001.

Weiner, Bernard. "Prison Psychiatry: The Clockwork Cure." *The Nation*, April 3, 1972.

Whittle, Thomas G., and Jan Thorpe. "Revisiting the Jonestown Tragedy." *Freedom*, August 1997.

Wilkinson, Frances. "Inside Her Head." *New York Times Magazine*, December 28, 2008.

Wofford, Taylor. "How America's Police Became an Army: The 1033 Program." *Newsweek*, August 13, 2014.

Newspapers

Allentown (PA) Morning Call
Ann Arbor Sun
Bakersfield Californian
Berkeley Barb
Billings (WY) Gazette
Charleston (WV) Sunday Gazette-Mail
Corpus Christi Times
Elyria (OH) Chronicle-Telegram
Eureka (CA) Times Standard
Franklin (PA) Herald
Fredericksburg (VA) Freelance Star
Fremont (CA) Argus
Harvard Crimson
Hutchinson (KS) News
Lodi (CA) News-Sentinel
Long Beach Press-Telegram
Los Angeles Free Press
Los Angeles Sentinel

Los Angeles Times
Lubbock Avalanche-Journal
The Mass Media (University of Massachusetts)
Napa Sentinel
Newark (OH) Advocate
New York Times
Oakland Tribune
Orange County Register
San Francisco Chronicle
San Francisco Weekly
San Mateo Times
San Rafael (CA) Daily Independent Journal
South Mississippi Sun
The Rag (Austin, TX)
Ukiah (CA) Daily Journal
Vallejo Times-Herald
Van Nuys News
Village Voice
Wall Street Journal
Washington Post

Other

Bay Area Research Collective. "Dragon Number 2: A Letter from Joe Remiro." Berkeley, September 1975.

Bay Area Research Collective. "The Last SLA Statement: An Interview with Russ, Joe, Bill and Emily." Berkeley, 1976.

Bay Area Research Collective. "Some Thoughts on the SLA." Berkeley, 1975.

Brandt, Daniel. "The 1960s and COINTELPRO: In Defense of Paranoia." NameBase.org. July–September 1995.

Cable News Network. *Larry King Live.* "Interview with Patty Hearst." Airdate: January 22, 2002.

Citizens Research Investigation Committee. Numerous affidavits, letters, interview transcripts, press conference statements, trial transcripts, court records and research notes from Donald Freed, Lake Headley, and Rusty Rhodes, on behalf of the CRIC.

Cumming, Gregory Garth. "The End of an Era: The Rise of the Symbionese Liberation Army and Fall of the New Left." University of California, Riverside PhD dissertation, 2010.

Dohrn, Bernardine. "Weather Underground communiqué." February 20, 1974.

Federal Bureau of Investigation, Freedom of Information/Privacy Acts Section. "Subject: Symbionese Liberation Army." CD.

Federal Bureau of Investigation. "HEARNAP files." FBI.gov.

Headley, Lake, Elizabeth Schmidt, and Jeanne Davies. "Investigation Report: An Inquiry into May 17, 1974 and Surrounding Events." Gustavus Adolphus College Archives, St. Peter, MN, 1974.

Headley, Lake, Elizabeth Schmidt, and Jeanne Davies. "Update on the LAPD-SLA Shootout Investigation." Gustavus Adolphus College Archives, St. Peter, MN, 1975.

Headley, Lake. "Confidential Conversation: Lake Headley and Sgt. R.G. Farwell." May 2, 1975.

Headley, Lake. "Testimony in Front of Police, Fire and Civil Defense Committee." Gustavus Adolphus College Archives, St. Peter, MN, May 22, 1975.

Lithwick, Dahlia. "The Brainwashed Defense." Slate.com, January 28, 2002.

McDermid, Nancy Gossage. "Closing Arguments in the Patricia Hearst Trial." California State University, Northridge. *Exetasis,* March 25, 1976.

National Broadcasting Company. *Dateline NBC.* "Kidnapped Heiress: The Patty Hearst Story." July 25, 2009.

Scott, Peter Dale. "The Assassinations of the 1960s as 'Deep Events.'" History-Matters.com.

Stone, Robert. *Guerrilla: The Taking of Patty Hearst.* Magnolia Pictures, DVD, 2004.

United States District Court for the Northern District of California. *United States v. Hearst* court transcripts, including "Closing Defense Argument of F. Lee Bailey," "Closing Prosecution Argument of U.S. Attorney James Browning," "Testimony of Eden Shea," "Testimony of Thomas Matthews." 1976.

Index

Aarons, Leroy, 15
Abu Ghraib prison, 44
"Agent Provocateur as Folk Hero,
    The", 130
Agnos, Art, 159
Alioto, Joseph, 151
American Civil Liberties Union
    (ACLU), 204
American Journalism Review, 175
American Nazi Party, 72, 78, 100
American Polygraph Association, 15
American Way of Death, The, 37
Amistad, La, 47
Amnesty International, 134
Anderson, Jack, 35
Argosy, 45, 193
Aryan Brotherhood, 72, 78
"Assassinations of the 1960s as Deep
    Events, The", 40
Association of California
    Criminalists, 179
Atascadero State Hospital for the
    Criminally Insane, 37
Atlantic, The, 37
Atwood, Angela, 52–53, 111, 132,
    143, 147, 165, 173, 184
Atwood, Gary, 52–53
Avery, Paul, 65, 150, 187

Ayers, Bill, 209
Ayers, Rick, 209

Babcock, John, 177
Bacalbos, Milagros, 25
Bailey, F. Lee, 205, 207
Baker, Marilyn, 49, 87, 115, 139–140
Baker, Richard J., 179
Barrett, Judge Newell, 20–21, 161
Bates, Charles, 73–74, 137, 157,
    162
Bay Area Medical Committee for
    Human Rights, 75
Bay Area Research Collective
    (BARC), 210–211
Beatie, Pat, 153
Beaty, Ronald, 67–68
Beindorf, Ray, 175
Belcher, Jerry, 179
Benenson, Peter, 120–121
Berkeley Barb, 109, 119, 130, 135
Bernstein, Carl, 63
Berzins, Zig, 148
"Big News", 175
Bingham, Stephen, 73
Blackburn, Robert, 102–107,
    111, 117, 126, 142–143, 159,
    201–202

Black Congress, 15
Black Cultural Association (BCA),
    42, 45–48, 50, 56–58, 60–66,
    68, 77, 83, 85–87, 89–90, 95,
    108, 110, 128, 135–137, 139,
    141, 143–146, 162, 203
Black Guerrilla Family, 72, 125
Black Liberation Army, 72, 78
Black Panther, The, 190
Black Panther Party (for Self
    Defense), 11, 13, 15–18, 23–24,
    26–30, 32–33, 38, 49, 64, 74,
    85, 87, 90, 97, 101, 105–106,
    109, 139, 174, 190, 204
Black Unity House, 184
Blood in My Eye, 167
Bortin, Mike, 190, 200
Bradley, Paul, 209
Bradley, Tom, 101–102, 180, 201,
    204
Braswell, Fred, 18, 22–23, 68, 78–
    86, 90–91, 95, 109, 193, 201
Brennan, Gene, 149
Brian, Dr. Earl, 38
Brito, Rich, 175
Browning, James, 205, 212–213
Brown & Root, 75
Brown, Elaine, 106
Brown, Jerry, 203
Brown, Sam, 71
Bryan, Arlelle, 178
Bryan, John, 51, 187
Brussell, Mae, 39, 153
Bugliosi, Vincent, 18
Bunke, Tania, 135, 146
Bush, George W., 75
Butterfield, Alexander, 95

Cable News Network (CNN), 129,
    163
California Department of Corrections
    (CDC), 32–33, 38, 56–57,

61, 63–65, 68, 71–73, 76–78,
    84–85–86, 90–91, 93, 95, 99,
    119, 129, 141, 154, 168, 188,
    192–193, 200–201, 204, 208
California Council on Criminal
    Justice (CCCJ), 104–105
California Senate Subcommittee on
    Civil Disorder, 125–126
California State Assembly Select
    Committee on Prison Reform, 76
California Supreme Court, 77
"Carlo Prescott Show", 61
Carlucci, Frank, 35–36
Carreras, Michael, 49, 57
Carr, Mary, 170, 172, 182
Carter, Alprentice "Bunchy", 15
Carter, Jimmy, 38, 207
Carter, Judge Oliver, 207
Caul, David, 200
Center for the Study and Reduction
    of Violence, 38
Central Intelligence Agency (CIA),
    27, 32, 34–35, 37–38, 40–42,
    46, 56, 63, 66–67, 77, 110,
    119, 124, 141, 145, 154, 157,
    168, 188–189, 200, 203–204,
    207–208, 210
Chan, Jean (Wah), 48–49
Charleston, Thomas, 57
Chavez, Cesar, 53
Chicago Seven, 197
Chino Institute for Men, 5, 19–21,
    61, 68
CIA Doctors, The, 42, 205
Cinqué, Joseph, 47
Citizens Research and Investigation
    Committee (CRIC), 18, 40,
    160–161, 168
City magazine, 98
Clanon, T. Lawrence, 36
Clark County (NV) Sheriff's
    Department, 18

Clark, Mark, 174
Cleaver, Eldridge, 16, 34, 85
Clinton, Bill, 207
Cobb, Ralph, 23–25, 28–29
Cohen, Jerry, 15
Cohen, Mickey, 124
COINTELPRO
    (Counterintelligence Program),
    12, 15, 17, 74, 198
Coker, C.T., 90
Colby, William, 41
Coleman, Ron, 8–10, 13, 27, 161
Columbia Broadcasting System
    (CBS), 157, 175, 208
Con Son Prison, 75
Coroner, 188
CRASH anti-gang unit, 204
Craven, Carolyn, 86
Criminal Investigation and
    Identification unit (CII), 19,
    22–24, 28, 32
Criminal Conspiracy Section,
    LAPD (CCS), 14–15, 17, 19,
    24, 26–27, 101, 168, 192,
    202–203
Crocker National Bank robbery,
    200
Crusaders, The, 142
Cunningham, David, 201

Daniels, Brenda, 170–172
Daum. Elliot, 153–154, 193, 201
Davidson, Sara, 59, 188–189
Davies, Jeanne, 161, 176
Davis, Angela, 196
Davis, Ed, 161–162, 177
Davis, Wes, 183
"Death Angels", 158–159
Debray, Régis, 146
Defense Intelligence Agency (DIA),
    71, 157
DeFreeze, Delano, 183, 185–188

DeFreeze, Donald (Cinque), 1–15,
    17–33, 35–37, 39, 42–47, 50,
    53, 55–66, 68–70, 72–73,
    75–83, 85–90, 92–100, 105,
    107–109, 111, 114, 117–124,
    126–139, 141–145, 147–156,
    158–162, 165, 167, 169–173,
    179–185, 187–188, 190, 192,
    199–201, 205–213
DeFreeze, Gloria Thomas, 2–3, 5,
    7–8, 19, 21–22, 26, 29, 122,
    128, 161–162
DeFreeze, Louis, 22
DeFreeze, Mary, 1, 24, 70, 184
Deiz, Bill, 175
Dellums, Ron, 110, 154
de Normanville, Amanda, 49–50, 64
DeSalvo, Albert, 206
Desvernine, Des, 197
Determinate Sentencing Law, 203
Deuel Educational Institute, Tracy, 76
Donner, Frank, 130–131
Dow, Michael, 22
Duge, Dave, 112
Dunphy, Jerry, 175
Dyer, Justin, 101

Eagles, Ron, 43
Edelman, Ed, 201
Ellsberg, Daniel, 197
Encore magazine, 146
Ennix, Dr. Coyness, 103, 201
Ervin, Sam, 200
Evans, Lolabelle, 156
Exclusive, 87

Farwell, Ronald, 9, 13–15, 19, 27,
    101–102, 160–161, 168, 182,
    202, 204
Feaster, Captain Stanley, 50
Federal Bureau of Investigation
    (FBI), 2, 12–13, 15–19, 24,

27, 32, 38, 55, 67–68, 73–74, 83, 86, 97, 109–110, 123–124, 128–131, 133, 136–137, 140–145, 147, 150, 153, 156–157, 159–162, 166, 169, 171–172, 176–177, 179, 186, 192–193, 195, 197–198, 203–204, 208
Federal Laboratories, 179
Feldman, Cliff, 183
Ferlinghetti, Lawrence, 151–152
Fields, Dr. Rona, 134
Fifth Estate, 40
Findley, Tim, 86, 93
Fine, Dr. Richard, 75–76
Fischer, Paul, 103
Flacks, Richard, 211
Flemming, Carl, 15
Floyd, John, 101
Folsom Prison, 35, 68, 76–77, 82, 193
Ford, Gerald, 128, 195
Foster, Dr. Marcus, 101–111, 114, 116–119, 124, 126, 128, 130, 136–137, 139–143, 159, 176, 189–190, 202, 209–211
Foster, Harriet, 2
Foster, Reverend William, 1, 20
Francis, Hugh, 26, 28–30
Francis, Les, 208
Franklin, Bruce, 52, 68, 125, 156
Freed, Donald, 18, 40, 45, 78, 160, 182, 201–203
Freeman, Freddie, 170–171
Friedman, Milton, 26, 28–30
Friends of the Panthers, 18

Garry, Charles, 97, 161
Gatchel, Julia, 193
Gates, Daryl, 171
Geneva Conventions, 41
Glass House Tapes, The, 14–15
Glide Memorial Church, 51, 53

Gosting, Carl, 153
Green, Samuel Thomas, 179
Grey, Donald, 130, 192–193
Grey, L. Patrick, 130
Grobel, Lawrence, 212
Groupe, Dr. Algin, 76
Groves, Dan, 124, 150
Guevera, Ernesto "Che", 135
Gugas, Chris, 15
Guinn, Dr. Vincent, 179–180
Gun Corral, 19
Gunnell, Dave, 48–49, 64, 87
Gunn, Joseph, 202
Guyton, Tyrone, 106–107, 109

Hacker, Dr. Frederick J., 19–20, 150, 176
Hagerstown Daily Mail, 144
Haig, Alexander, 117
Haley, Judge Harold, 32
Hallinan, Terence, 35, 122, 205, 207
Hall, Camilla, 54, 87–88, 111, 120, 148, 165, 173, 184, 195–196
Hall, Lorena, 195
Hall, Reverend George, 54, 184, 195
Hampton, Fred, 174
Hanlon, Stuart, 34, 203
Harkin, Tom, 75
Harris, Anthony, 158
Harris, Bill, 34, 52–53, 60, 96, 99, 110–111, 114, 118, 120, 123, 147, 154–155, 159, 162–166, 171–172, 182, 190–191, 195, 197, 200
Harris, Emily, 34, 52–53, 60, 99, 110–111, 114, 138, 147, 155, 162–166, 171–172, 182, 190, 195, 197, 200
Hastings, David, 61
Headley II, Lake, 18–19, 27, 34, 45, 59–61, 78, 80, 85–86, 130, 136,

160–161, 175, 178–179, 182, 187, 192, 195, 201–203
Hearst, Anne, 80
Hearst, Catherine, 58–59, 63–64, 116
Hearst, Patricia (Tania), 9, 17–18, 35, 37, 40, 42, 52, 58–61, 66, 68, 73, 78–81, 83–84, 95, 98–99, 108, 111, 116, 119–127, 131, 133–136, 139, 143, 146–148, 150–151, 153, 155, 162–167, 171–172, 182–183, 189–190, 192, 194–195, 197–200, 202, 204–208, 212–213
Hearst, Randolph, 59, 61, 64, 80, 116, 119, 122–124, 126–127, 133, 138, 146, 150, 162, 176, 190, 205, 207
Hearst, Vicki, 80
Hearst, Willie, 197
HEARNAP files, 55, 123, 137
Henderson, Rudy, 56
Henricks, L.J., 8
Hernandez, Rey, 175
Herrmann, William, 38–39, 42, 46
Hersh, Seymour, 34
Hibernia Bank robbery, 147–151, 153, 207, 213
Higuera, Greg, 149
Holsinger, Joe, 208
Hoover Center on Violence, 38
Houghton, Robert, 191
House of Representatives Committee on Internal Security, 111
House of Representatives International Relations Committee, 154
House of Representatives Judiciary Committee, 154
Houston Chronicle, 123
Howard, Clark, 158

Huett, Bill, 163
Huggins, John, 15
Hughes, Harold, 154
Hyde, Colonel John Frances, 71
Hyde, Robert, 70, 72–74, 78, 84–85, 90, 95, 109, 153–154, 193, 201

Indeterminate Sentencing Act, 203
In Search of a Sister, 88
In the Crossfire: Marcus Foster and the Troubled History of American School Reform, 103
Inslaw, 38
Internal Revenue Service, 126
Inua, David, 89
"Investigation Report: An Inquiry into May 17, 1974 and Surrounding Events", 175
Irish Republican Army, 134

Jackson, George, 32–34, 47, 51, 73, 167
Jackson, Jesse, 102
Jackson, Jonathan, 32
Jackson, Robert, 62–63, 66
Jamerson, E.G., 155
Jefferson, Clifford "Death Row Jeff", 35–36, 75–76, 108, 136
Johnson, Christine, 169–173, 180
Johnson, Daniel, 30
Johnson, Timmy, 172
Jones, Reverend Jim, 208
Jones, Kyle "Prophet", 167
KABC-TV, 177
Karenga, Ron (Ron Everett), 15–17, 78, 121
Kaye, Arnold, 6–7
Kelley, Clarence, 130, 150, 159–160
Kennedy, John F., 18, 114
Kennedy, Robert, 18
KGO-AM, 61

Kifner, John, 167
Kilgore, James, 200
King, Captain Marvin, 176
King, Martin Luther, Jr., 13, 16, 18, 34
Knowland, William, 106
KNBC-TV, 175
KNXT-TV, 175, 178
Korean Central Intelligence Agency (KCIA), 40
Kozol, Dr. Harry, 206
KPFA-FM, 103, 121, 132, 143, 189
KPFK-FM, 189
KQED-TV, 93–94, 109–110, 115, 139–140
Kramer, Ludlow, 127–128, 133
Krassner, Paul, 196
KSAN-FM, 139
Kwanzaa, 17, 121

Lancaster, California State Prison at, 203
Larry King Show, 129, 163
"Las Vegas Tilt", 151
Law Enforcement Assistance Administration (LEAA), 105, 200, 210
Lawler, Judge Bernard, 6–7
Leary, Timothy, 85
Lewis, Alfred, 63
Lewis, Minnie, 169–172, 176, 180
Lewis, Wayne, 130, 192–193
Lewis, Tony, 172
Life and Death of the SLA, The, 86
Lishey, Florence, 177–178, 197
Lister Unit, 75. *See also* Maximum Psychiatric Diagnostic Unit
Little, Russell, 34, 45, 50–51, 53, 56, 64–66, 87, 105, 107–108, 110–113, 118, 129, 133, 137–141, 143, 202–203
Long, Bob, 175

Long range reconnaissance patrols (LRRP), 51
Los Angeles City Council, 201–202
Los Angeles Coroner's Office, 179, 188
Los Angeles County Board of Supervisors, 204
Los Angeles County Clerk, 161
Los Angeles Fire Department, 173, 195–196
Los Angeles Free Press, 14, 72–73
Los Angeles Police Department (LAPD), 8–10, 13–14, 18, 20, 22, 24, 27–28, 32, 46, 72–73, 101, 108, 128–129, 160–161, 165, 168–172, 174, 176–179, 182, 186, 192, 195–196, 202–204, 208
Los Angeles Sentinel, 197
Los Angeles Sheriff's Department, 192, 195
Los Angeles Times, 27, 39, 102, 124–125, 161, 173, 177, 179–180, 201, 204, 211
Lund, Christine, 177
Lyne, Susan, 110

Magee, Ruchell, 47
Making of a Counterculture, The, 212
Manson, Charles, 18, 28
Marcus Foster Educational Institute, 201
Markoff, Pete, 149
Martin, Harry V., 200
Mathews, Tom, 164–166, 171
Maximum Psychiatric Diagnostic Unit (MPDU), 56–57, 75–77. *See also* Lister Unit
Mayfield, James, 67, 86–87, 162
Mel's Sporting Goods robbery, 162–165
McLellan, Vin, 65, 150

Mexican Mafia, 72, 78
Miller, Henry, 39
"Mind Control", 39
Mitford, Jessica, 37
MKSEARCH, 34, 46
MKULTRA, 34, 46, 67, 208, 210
Montgomery, Ed, 98
Moody, Cecil, 62–63, 66, 83–84
Moore, Sara Jane, 128
Morrison-Knudsen, 75
Morris, Paul J., 84
Morten, Morgan W., 11
Mosqueda, John, 177
Muntaz, Jamellea, 158
Murray, Tony, 198
My Lai massacre, 51
My Search for Patty Hearst, 144

Napa Sentinel, 39, 200
Napier, Samuel Lee, 17
National Broadcasting Company
    (NBC), 183
National Crime Information Center,
    195
National Institutes of Mental
    Health, 200
National Security Agency (NSA),
    157, 160
National Security Council (NSC), 157
Nation, The, 44
Navy SEAL teams, 41
Nelson, James D. "Red", 71–74,
    84–85, 90–91, 119, 129, 131
Nelson, John, 171
Nestel, William, 36, 72, 84
New Centurions, The, 165
Newsroom, 139
Newsweek, 83, 151
New Times magazine, 110
Newton, Huey, 13, 16–17, 33, 101
New World Liberation Front
    (NWLF), 191, 199

New York magazine, 26, 28
New York Times Magazine, 59, 188
New York Times, 13–14, 34, 41,
    136, 167–168
Nixon, Richard, 32, 34, 55, 64, 85,
    95, 117, 123–124, 128, 154,
    195, 200
Noguchi, Thomas, 173, 179, 186, 188
Nol, Lon, 40
Nuestra Familia, 72, 78
Nugent, Arthur, 44

Oakland Tribune, 103, 106, 141
Olsson, Eva, 105, 117
O'Neill, Eugene, 206
Operation CHAOS, 34, 46
Operation PUSH, 102
Opsahl, Myrna Lee, 200
Osborn (Osborne), Bart, 40–41
Outland, Ken, 149

Pacific Architects and Engineers,
    40–41, 66
Pacific Gas and Electric Company,
    199
Pacific News Service, 108
Parks, Bernard, 204
"Patty in the Land of the Cobra",
    188
Payne, Les, 86
Peace, Don, 179
Peking (Man) House, 48, 51, 64
Pentagon Papers, 197
People in Need program, 126–128,
    132–133, 137–138, 147, 156,
    158, 190
Perry, Gilbert, 55, 187
Perry, Nancy Ling, 55–56, 58. 66,
    68, 78, 80, 93, 96–97, 108,
    110–115, 120, 125, 137, 140,
    143, 148–149, 155, 159, 165,
    167, 173, 178, 187, 196

Phoenix Program, 40–41, 43, 46, 141

Phoenix, The, 187

Pines, Burt, 197

Political Reform Organization for Better Education (PROBE), 71–72, 78, 85

Pope, Lester, 74

Prinz, Rabbi Joachim, 23, 28

Procunier, Raymond, 32–33, 71, 106, 115, 194, 201, 203

Prout, Dr. Eugene, 76

Province Interrogation Centers (PICs), 41–42

Provincial Reconnaisance Unit (PRU), 41

Public Disorder Intelligence Division, LAPD (PDID), 14, 101–102, 201, 204

Raheeb, Abdul, 185

Ramparts, 107, 211

Rand Corporation, 38

Reading, John, 110

Reagan, Ronald, 16, 29–32, 34, 37–39, 42, 46, 59, 64, 68, 73, 77, 106, 124, 127, 133, 137, 190, 201

Reddin, Thomas, 16

Reed, Ishmael, 110

Reed, Stephanie, 180–182

Remiro, Joseph, 34, 45, 51–53, 56, 110–112, 114, 117–118, 133–141, 143, 202–203, 209

Revolutionary Army, 191

Revolution in the Revolution?, 146

Reyes, Daniel, 84

Rhodes, Rusty, 18, 34, 36, 45, 70, 72, 78, 80–82, 84, 160, 177–178, 182, 192–194

Richardson, Elliot, 38

Riordan, Richard, 204

Ritzi, Judge William, 2, 22, 27, 30–31, 36–37, 160–161

Roberts, Steven V., 14

Rockefeller Commission Report, 34

Roe vs. Wade, 211

"Roots of Violence in Soledad, The", 79

Ross, Clarence, 172

Ross, Dr. Colin, 42–43, 205

Roszak, Theodore, 211–212

Rundle, Frank, 79

Russell, Dick, 45–46, 193

Ryan, Leo J., 35–36, 154, 200, 207–208

Sanders, Gloria Yvonne, 7–8, 89

San Francisco Chronicle, 42–43, 74, 93–94, 96, 103, 109–110, 139, 148, 161, 187, 199

San Francisco Examiner, 97–98, 144, 146

San Francisco General Hospital, 76

San Francisco Police Department (SFPD), 149, 151, 156, 158

San Mateo County Jail, 205

San Mateo County Sheriff's Department Narcotics Division, 22, 78

San Mateo Times, 144, 161

San Quentin Prison, 33, 51, 61, 68, 70–71, 73–74, 82, 133, 139, 193

Santarelli, Donald, 200

Saxbe, William, 124–125, 150, 159

Scheer, Robert, 110

Schmidt, Elizabeth, 175, 187

Schorr, Daniel, 208

Scott, Jack, 191

Scott, Peter Dale, 40

Seale, Bobby, 13

Senate Committee on Intelligence Activities and the Rights of Americans, 12

Senate Subcommittee on
  Constitutional Rights, 200
Senate Watergate Committee, 95
Sham, Al, 179
Shaw, Bernard, 207
Shea, Eden, 148
Shepard, Tony, 163–164
Shultea Jr., Volie, 194
Siems (Siem), Mary Alice, 60–61,
  80, 92, 97–100
Sihanouk, Prince Norodom, 40
Simmons, Bob, 175, 178
Smith, Jim, 148
Smith, Tom, 61
Snyder, Arthur, 201–202
Soledad Brother, 32, 34, 68
Soledad Prison, 61, 67, 74, 77–78,
  80–81, 85–87, 91–93, 129,
  153–154, 156, 161–162, 193–
  194, 206
Soliah, Kathy, 190, 200
Soliah, Steven, 200
Soltysik, Fred, 88–89
Soltysik, Patricia (Mizmoon),
  53–56, 58–59. 66, 83, 87–90,
  93, 96–97, 100, 108, 110–111,
  120–121, 140, 165, 167, 173,
  180, 196
"Some Thoughts on the SLA", 210
Soul on Ice, 34
South Central Los Angeles shoot-
  out and fire, 172–177, 190–191,
  195, 200–202
Southern Christian Leadership
  Conference, 12, 102
South Vietnamese Police Special
  Branch, 40–42
Special Weapons and Tactics
  (SWAT) teams, 167, 171, 173–
  174, 178
Spencer, John, 103
Stanford Research Institute, 38

Steele, H. Elizabeth, 196
Steiner, Robyn, 51, 64, 135, 139–
  140, 143, 159
Stockholm syndrome, 205
Students for a Democratic Society
  (SDS), 52, 74
Stutsman, L.M., 76
Suenaga, Steven, 121
Sullivan, William A., 171
Sutter, Frank, 166, 171
"Symbionese Liberation Army in
  Los Angeles, The", 180
Symbionese Liberation Army (SLA),
  12, 17–18, 20, 23, 34, 37,
  39–40, 45–46, 49–56, 60–61,
  63, 65, 69–72, 74, 76–78, 81,
  83–85, 90–91, 93–96, 98–100,
  102–103, 105–107, 109–115,
  118–119, 121, 123–130, 132–
  133, 136–137, 139–144, 147,
  149–151, 153–156, 158–162,
  166, 168–170, 172, 174–176,
  178, 180, 182–183, 185–197,
  199–203, 205, 207–213
System Development Corporation,
  38

Tackwood, Louis, 14–15, 17, 73
Tania: The Unforgettable Guerrilla,
  135
Taylor, Dr. Ronald, 179–180
Tehachapi Prison, 106
Thompson, Chris, 49–50, 54, 87,
  140–141, 202
Thompson, Tom, 72–73
Time, 151
Tobin, Trish, 150
Tomita, Damyon, 47, 61, 68, 77,
  79, 82, 84, 91–92, 95, 109, 201
Tomorrow, 183
Tom, David, 102
Travis Air Force Base, 39

Trout, Narda, 179
Tucker, Jim, 86
Tupamaros rebels, 126
Turner, Ellie, 198
Unisight, 60, 65–66, 68. 77, 90, 135
United Farm Workers, 53
United Press International (UPI),
   43–44, 185
United Prisoners Union, 54, 128
United Slaves (US, US
   Organization, US, Inc.). 15–16
U.S. Army, 71
U.S. Department of Health,
   Education and Welfare, 200
U.S. Department of Justice, 159,
   200, 204
U.S. District Court for the
   Northern District of California,
   208
U.S. State Department, 208
U.S. Supreme Court, 12, 211
University of California, Los Angeles
   (UCLA), 16

Vacaville, California Medical Facility
   at, 27, 31–33, 35–37, 39, 42–
   48, 50, 56–62, 65–68, 74–77,
   80, 82, 85–87, 89, 108, 110,
   128, 135–137, 139, 145, 154,
   161, 188, 200, 203, 206–207,
   210
Valentine, Douglas, 41
Vegas P.I., 61, 85
Venceremos (Organization), 18, 52–
   53, 60–62, 65, 67–68, 76–77,
   86, 92, 97–98, 125, 156
Viet Cong, 41
Viet Cong Infrastructure (VCI),
   41–42
Vietnam Veterans Against the War/
   Winter Soldiers Organization,
   52, 65

Village Voice, 198
Voices of Guns, The, 65, 86, 99

Wachs, Joel, 201–202
Wall Street Journal, 16
Wambaugh, Joseph, 165
Ward, Baxter, 201
Washington Post, 15, 63–64, 168
Watts riots, 13, 15, 35
"Way Back Home", 142
Weather Underground, 94, 199,
   209
Webb, Robert, 16
Weed, Steven, 58–59, 119–121,
   144–146, 212
Weiner, Bernard, 44
Weinglass, Leonard, 196–197
Westbrook, Colston, 39–43, 45–47,
   50, 56–58, 61–62, 64–68, 75,
   77–79, 86–87, 90, 95, 105,
   108–109, 119, 121, 129, 131,
   135–137, 141–146, 161, 168,
   188–189, 201, 210
West, Dr. Louis Jolyon, 205
West, Richard, 177
Wheeler, Thero, 61–62, 68, 76–77,
   91–93, 95–100, 123, 128, 137,
   194
Whiters, Alfred, 23–26, 28–29
Wikileaks, 210
Williams, Samuel, 177, 191
Wolfe, Dr. L.S., 48, 57, 118, 130,
   175, 179, 186
Wolfe, Willie, 48–51, 53, 56–58,
   61–62, 64, 66, 99, 105, 114,
   117–118, 134, 136–137, 145,
   147, 159, 165, 173, 176, 189,
   196, 206
Woodward, Bob, 63
"Wreath for an Unknown
   Guerrilla", 187
X, Malcolm, 155, 185

X, Retimah, 155

Yanok, Suzanne, 177
Yorty, Sam, 101, 204
Yoshimura, Wendy, 191, 197, 200
Younger, Evelle, 23, 29–30, 64, 68, 71, 77, 106, 126–127, 147, 162, 186, 190–191, 201

"Zebra" Killings, 117, 125, 151, 153, 158–159
Zebra: The True Account of 179 Days of Terror in San Francisco, 158
Zirpoli, Judge Alfonso, 151